THE ROCKY POINT GRINGO GUIDE

to Puerto Peñasco, Mexico

by Mary Weil

Second Edition

THE ROCKY POINT GRINGO GUIDE
to Puerto Peñasco, Mexico

by Mary Weil

Published by:
Frontier Travel Adventures
P. O. Box 105-H1
925 W. Baseline Road
Tempe, Arizona 85283-1100
Phone: (602) 345-8659   Fax: (602) 345-8659

Copyright © 1998 by Mary Weil
First Edition 1994
Printed and bound by Affiliated Lithograph in the United States of America

Cover design by Three "C", Chandler, Arizona
Text, maps, and layout design by Producers Studio, Eugene, Oregon
Background cover photograph of Encanto Beach by the author.
Foreground cover photograph of the Marina entrance from Condominio Pinacate at Marina Peñasco by the author.
Photographs not otherwise credited were taken by the author.

Publishers Cataloging-in-Publication Data

Weil, Mary.
        The Rocky Point gringo guide to Puerto Peñasco, Mexico / by Mary Weil.

                2nd ed.
                296 p. : ill., maps ; 22 cm.
                Includes bibliographical references and index.
                0-9642264-1-3
                1. Puerto Peñasco (Mexico)——Guidebooks. 2. Puerto Peñasco (Mexico)——

        History. I. Title.

        917.217 — dc21   97-60293
                                                              CIP

U. S. $14.95
Second Edition

*To awaken quite alone in a strange town is one of
the most pleasant sensations in the world.
You are surrounded by adventure.
You have no idea of what is in store,
but you will if you are wise and know the art of travel,
let yourself go . . . and accept whatever comes in the spirit
in which the gods may offer it.*

- Freya Stark

Acknowledgments

A special thanks to all those who have helped me with the research and preparation of this book. I am eternally grateful.

Andrea Addison-Sorey, CEDO

The Arizona Book Publishing Association

P.J. Turk Boyer and Richard E. Boyer, CEDO Co. Directors

Guillermo Munro, historian, author and owner, Foto Studio 2000

Dave and Kelly Adams, Cholla Bay Sportsmen's Club

Anna Vejar, insurance, Gringo Pass

Yolanda Silva G., insurance sales and business owner

Jim and Janet Eckols, owners, La Casa Blanca

Jack Carlson, author, *Hiker's Guide to the Superstition Wilderness*

Patty Briguglio, sales and marketing

Leslie Christensen, instructor, Mesa Community College

Ward Albright, owner, *Southwest Storyteller Bookstore*

Marilyn Sutcliffe, retired

Pedro Cedillo Cruz, Sonoyta Police Department

Tempe Public Library

Sonoran Department of Tourism

Carlos J. Navarro, CEDO

Roberto Escalante

Bill Kinkel, instructor, Lane Community College

Ginny T. Weil, instructor, Thurston High School

Barbara Mead, instructor, Westridge Middle School

Craig Faanes, bird watcher

Clay Workman, Tempe Public Library

Kenn Peterson, man of the world

Introduction

When I tell people I am going to Rocky Point they say, "I wouldn't take my car down there," or "Aren't you <u>afraid</u> to drive into Mexico?" I reply, "Rocky Point hasn't been exposed to the problems which plague many of the other border towns. I feel safer driving down there than I do in parts of Phoenix." My first visit in 1989 was wonderful. I found paradise in Peñasco and set out to change a common negative attitude toward Mexico travel.

The *Rocky Point Gringo Guide* isn't another travelogue or motor atlas, it consolidates information, impressions, and advice on traveling to Puerto Peñasco from the United States. Hopefully, this guidebook will give you a feel for this area, make you aware of the diversity of Mexico and clear the way for you to enjoy your travels to the fullest. Take the time to look beyond the surface which separates us by language, religion, race, philosophy and history.

With the development of the 50 million dollar Marina Peñasco Resort and Marina, a new international airport, scheduled air service, and a new highway from the border to the beach, the small fishing village of Puerto Peñasco is developing into a tourist Mecca. Any visitor, long-term or short, will benefit from the information contained here.

Warning and Disclaimer

The author and Frontier Travel Adventures accept no responsibility for any loss, injury or inconvenience sustained by any persons using this book. Neither assumes any liability resulting from action taken based on the information included herein.

The book's purpose is to provide accurate and authoritative information on the topics covered. It is sold with the understanding that neither the author nor the publisher is rendering legal, financial or other professional services. Mention of businesses does not constitute endorsement.

Information in this guidebook has been obtained from sources believed to be reliable, but it's accuracy and completeness, and the opinions based thereon are not guaranteed. This book contains information on Puerto Peñasco only up to press time.

As every effort is made to provide accurate information in this publication, we would appreciate it if readers would call our attention to any errors that may occur.

TABLE OF CONTENTS

WHAT TO BRING - SURVIVAL CHECKLIST

✓ The *Rocky Point Gringo Guide.*

✓ American money.

✓ Drinking water, one gallon per person per day.

✓ Water for the radiator and road emergencies.

✓ Extra motor oil, tire pump, tow rope, flares, small shovel.

✓ Toolbox, battery cables, flashlight.

✓ Small first aid kit, aspirin, antacid tablets, sinus medication.

✓ Prescriptions in their original containers.

✓ Prescription glasses, contact lenses and solutions.

✓ Women's personal hygiene products, toilet paper.

✓ Snacks: fruit, chips, cookies, crackers, healthy stuff to eat.

✓ Two coolers, one for the beach, another for seafood.

✓ Soft drinks, fruit juice, dram of rum or tequila.

✓ Spill proof water bottle, plastic drinking cups.

✓ Paper towels, plastic bags for wet clothing, Kleenex.

✓ Sunscreen, sunglasses, hat with a large brim.

✓ Camera, extra film, don't forget reading material.

✓ Colored wash rag, small hand towel, small bar of soap.

✓ Sheet or blanket to spread out on the beach.

✓ Beach towel, beach umbrella and tarpaulin for shade.

✓ Lawn or lounge chair for each traveler.

✓ Snorkel gear, Frisbee, small bucket, shovels for the kids.

✓ Light weight long sleeved shirt and pants for too much sun.

✓ Water shoes or "jellies" for the beach.

✓ Light weight sleeping bag, a small pillow (optional).

CROSSING THE BORDER

DO'S

Do bring the Rocky Point Gringo Guide.

Do get Mexican Auto Insurance for your entire length of stay.

Do bring plenty of drinking water, plus extra for emergencies.

Do bring small denominations of U.S. dollars or American Express travelers checks.

Do bring prescription's in their original containers.

Do take a cooler to bring back fresh fish and shrimp.

Do bring your fishing gear.

Do what Customs Officers ask, willingly and politely.

Do bring your camera, film, sunscreen, hat and beach towel.

Do show consideration for others.

Do respect Mexican laws.

DON'TS

Don't Panic! almost one million people cross the border at Lukeville, Arizona every year.

Don't take a passport, Rocky Point is in the "free zone."

Don't take <u>firearms</u> in or out of Mexico.

Don't take <u>illegal drugs</u> in or out of Mexico.

Don't take <u>fireworks</u> in or out of Mexico.

Don't drink and drive.

Don't be alarmed if you are asked to pull over and open the trunk during busy times, this is common.

Don't take fresh fruits out of Mexico, eat 'em up!

Don't give the window washing *"muchachos"* money.

Don't forget to use common sense.

DO CONSIDER MEXICO AN ADVENTURE ! !

Crossing The Border

If you will be a traveler, have always . . .
two bags very full, one that is full of patience
and another of money.
                                        -John Florio

Getting There

From Metropolitan Phoenix - 212 miles - 4 hours:
Take I-10 west to Arizona 85, continue through Gila Bend to the Mexican border where you catch Mexico Route 8.

Take I-10 east toward Tucson; take Arizona 347 (Maricopa Road) and follow it about 33 miles to I-8. Continue west to Gila Bend, then head south on Arizona 85 to the Mexican border. Mexico Route 8 leads to Puerto Peñasco.

From Tucson - 212 miles - 4 hours:
Go west on Arizona 86 to the town of Why. Take Arizona 85 south to the Mexican border, then Mexico Route 8 to Puerto Peñasco.

From Los Angeles - 540 miles - 9fi hours:
San Diego - 439 miles - 8fi hours:
From Los Angeles, take I-5 to San Diego. Take I-8 east to Gila Bend, then head south on Arizona 85 to the Mexican border. Mexico Route 8 leads to Puerto Peñasco. A more direct route is to cross the Mexican border at Tijuana, continue east on Mexico Route 2 through Mexicali and San Luis. Route 2, on the Mexican side should be used in the day time only. In Sonoyta, take Mexico Route 8 south to Puerto Peñasco.

Entering Mexico From The United States

Crossing the border into Mexico is easy. Puerto Peñasco is located in an area considered the "free trade zone." You may travel in this area without the stringent regulations required in all other areas of the country. Since changes in immigration and customs regulations occur frequently, some of the information in this chapter may be modified or obsolete. Travelers can prepare in advance for unforeseen complications by contacting the Mexican Tourist Bureau at 602-947-7022.

If you will be visiting the "free trade zone."for less than 72 hours no documents are necessary. If you are traveling in the "free trade zone" for more than 72 hours, the only document needed to enter Mexico is an Immigration Tourist Card called an FMT. Tourist cards are available upon presentation of proof of citizenship from Mexican Government Tourism Offices or consular offices in the United States and on the Mexican side of the border. All tourist cards are free. The FMT is your "visa" to enter the country and must be carried with you at all times. A vehicle importation permit is not needed for travel in the "free zone." For travel past the "free zone" you will need an FMT and documentation stating you have posted a bond on your automobile. Make sure you bring a drivers license for identification.

The following documents are accepted by the Mexican Government to obtain a tourist card or visa for travel to Puerto Peñasco if you are visiting for more than 72 hours or if you are taking your automobile past the free trade zone:
1. Birth certificate (certified copy from the government agency that issued it).
2. Valid passport.
3. Military discharge papers, DD-214, or ID from the armed forces.
4. Notarized affidavit of citizenship.
5. Voter registration card.

Returning to the United States from Mexico after visiting for more than 72 hours, the United States recognizes:
1. Birth certificate.
2. Passport.

Note: *A driver's license and baptismal certificate are not proof of citizenship.*

United States citizens by birth born abroad visiting Puerto Peñasco for more than 72 hours must present:
1. U.S. birth certificate from the U.S. Consulate or Embassy in the country of origin, or
2. U.S. passport, or
3. U.S. birth certificate from the State Department in Washington, or
4. Certificate of citizenship from the U.S. Immigration and Naturalization Service.

Every visitor entering Mexico is subject to inspection by customs. At the border you are expected to ALTO (*stop*). Mexican border officials will ask "What is your destination?" If you are traveling south to a point other than Puerto Peñasco, an official will direct you to the immigration office to obtain an FMT tourist card and direct you to the bank to complete the paperwork to bond your car. See *Travel Beyond The Free Zone* for more information.

The border is closed between midnight and 6:00 a.m. Random car inspections are made at the border gate when crossing into Mexico. There are two types of inspection. As you cross the border you will see a light similar to a traffic light. The light will glow red (stop - *alto*) or green (go - *passé*) while you slowly proceed through the marked area. If the red light glows, don't panic, officials will direct you to the parking area. They will ask you where you are headed and possibly ask you to open your trunk for inspection. This is common and part of their procedure. Equipment and luggage should be packed to permit easy customs inspection. After poking around in your stuff they will permit you to continue on your way. If they find that you are bringing in something illegally, prepare to be detained. If the light is green, you are free to pass through without any inspection. If there is a long line of cars backed up, please be patient and the officials will show you where to park.

If you have items to declare which exceed your limits, park in the Gringo Pass parking lot on the U.S. side. Walk to the booth which sits in the center of the road and tell the clerk what items you have to declare and what their value is. An attendant will come and inspect the value of the items you are declaring. The attendant may hand you a form which you will take to the bank. You will pay one and one half times the value of what you declare. The taxes are in pesos, the bank will exchange your dollars and issue you a receipt which you will need to show when crossing the border. After this is completed you can cross subject to the red light, green light process.

If you pass through the traffic light with items that have not been declared you must pay four times the commercial value of each item.

It is advisable that you do not lend your automobile to anyone while you are in Mexico. You could be subject to a fine and your automobile could be confiscated.

Travel Beyond The Free Zone

If you are planning to take a day trip to Caborca you need to have your car "bonded," which means you have registered your automobile with the government and you are given written permission to take it past the free trade zone.

After passing through the check-point, park and go to immigration which is located on the right side of the street across from the traffic light. If you already have a FM3 card, immigration will stamp it, otherwise you will need to provide proof of citizenship and fill out a a temporary visa called a FMT. You will be directed across the street to get your permit. Before leaving home you will need to bring:

1. Original automobile title - 2 copies.
2. Drivers license - 2 copies.
3. Original birth certificate or your passport - 2 copies.
4. Visa, American Express, or Mastercard credit card. If you don't have a credit card you need to obtain a Mexican bond from a

Mexican bond broker (contact the Mexican Consulate in your area for a broker near you).

You will need two copies of your FMT, which you just filled out at immigration. You can have copies made at Finzias next to the office on your right for about .25 each.

Proceed to "Banjercito" located behind the permit office on the left side of the street, ask for directions. Here you will pay $11.00 in U.S. funds, this is where you need the credit card, they do not take cash. When all the paperwork is processed, an official will walk with you back to your automobile and put a sticker on your front windshield. They will give you the paperwork you need to cross from the free trade zone into the heart of Mexico. Be prepared to spend some time with this process. If you arrive during the week it takes about an hour, if you arrive right before a holiday weekend you could spend as long as four hours. It is advisable to have copies made at home and arrive early.

Automobile Insurance

U.S. automobile insurance must be replaced by insurance from a Mexican insurance company. Your U.S. auto insurance is of no help to you across the border. You could be delayed for days should you be involved in any kind of an accident.

Mexican automobile insurance can be purchased from one of the several large reputable companies located in gas stations and at insurance agencies in Ajo, Why and Gringo Pass, which is located on the U.S. side of the border at Lukeville. Just watch for the signs advertising Mexican Insurance that are located along the roadway in every town. Insurance can also be purchased on the Mexican side of the border after the gate of entry near the immigration office.

All Mexican insurance companies are regulated by the government and are required to charge the same rates for the same coverage. Prices range from around $12.00 a day for a fairly new car to $18.00 a day for a car and house trailer or car and a boat.

Your local insurance agent may be able to provide a policy for you. Insurance to travel in Mexico is available from AAA offices in

Phoenix 520-274-1116, Peoria 520-979-3700, Mesa 520-834-8296, Scottsdale 520-949-7993, Yuma 520-783-3339, and Tucson 520-885-0694.

Mexican automobile insurance coverage varies considerably from what is covered by your policy in the United States. It is advisable to read your policy thoroughly upon purchase for specific conditions pertaining to your vehicle. Some policy conditions that may apply to your automobile include:

1. Personal property in the car is not covered unless it is permanently attached to the vehicle.
2. There is a collision deductible on every policy. Broken glass, for example, falls under collision, and so does the deductible.
3. An entire automobile must be stolen before it is covered by Mexican insurance.
4. Vandalism and theft of car parts are not covered.

Pets

If you take your pet to Mexico, you are required to have a U.S. veterinarian's certificate (International Health Certificate for Dogs and Cats, form 77-043) stating the pet is in good health. A separate rabies inoculation permit valid within the past 6 months is required.

Inoculation certificates are also necessary to reenter the U.S. if the pet has been out of the country more than 30 days. The leaflet "Pets, Wildlife, U.S. Customs" can be obtained at your local U.S. Customs office or by writing, U.S. Customs, P.O. Box 7407, Washington, DC 20044.

It is advisable to leave dogs and other pets at home because of special inspections, health certificates, and the possible refusal of hotel operators to allow pets into their establishments. Almost all condo and home owners do not allow animals. If you are staying in a rented condo or home please get permission from the owner before bringing your pet with you.

Driver's License

Any valid U.S. driver's license is also valid in Mexico.

Car Regulations

Automobile registration forms should be carried in the vehicle at all times. No special documents are required to take your car into or out of the "free zone." If you plan to take your car past the "free zone," we recommend that you contact the Mexican Tourist Bureau, Mexican Consulate or your local AAA office for additional required documentation and current regulations. Telephone numbers are listed in the chapter on tourist information.

If you are planning to take a rental car, pull a rented trailer, or

> *Reminder: The International border gate at Lukeville, Arizona is open from 6 a.m. until midnight seven days a week. During daylight saving time, from April to October, Puerto Peñasco is one hour later than Arizona time.*

drive a rented camper or recreational vehicle to Puerto Peñasco, a notarized statement from the rental agency is needed. This form letter gives authority for you to take the vehicle into Mexico. Car rental agencies require additional insurance coverage to take the rented automobile across the border. The notarized statement will specify how much insurance you must have.

Recreational Vehicles

The regulations for automobiles also applies to recreational vehicles. Mexican automobile insurance coverage is needed on these vehicles prior to crossing the border. There is no Mexican government fee for persons taking campers, motor homes, boats, or ATV's across the border.

Money

There is no restriction on the amount of U.S. currency and travelers checks that can be taken into Mexico. Dollars in small denominations are accepted everywhere. We recommend bringing lots of cash in small bills as some of the most quaint and best of local fair rely on currency, not charge cards or travelers checks. Major credit cards are accepted at some of the larger tourist hotels and restaurants, however, most places will not take personal checks. ATM machines are available at BankOne in Ajo, Arizona, the Chevron station in Why, Arizona, and at the Serfín, Bancomer, and Banamex banks in Puerto Peñasco. See Chapter 8, Business Services for locations. You may obtain a cash advance on your credit card at any of the banks located in town. A picture identification is required.

Personal Property

Visitors are allowed one camera and twelve rolls of film per person. If you are planning to take camera equipment above this allowance for personal or business use, it is advisable to consult the nearest Mexican Consulate or Mexican Tourism Department for permits, restrictions, and additional information.

You are allowed to take into Mexico a portable television, a radio, a tape recorder and 20 tapes, one photographic, video or motion picture camera and up to 12 rolls of film, camping and sports equipment, clothing, food, non alcoholic beverages, two cartons of cigarettes, 100 cigars, and 3 quarts of alcohol intended for personal use and medicine for personal use only.

If you are traveling by camper you may also bring in a VCR, a bicycle without a motor, household linens, kitchen utensils, living room and bedroom furniture.

Entering The United States From Mexico

If you are coming from Puerto Peñasco no documents are needed to enter the U.S. For re-entry to the U.S. from other southern destinations in Mexico, the U.S. Government recognizes as proof of citizenship: a valid U.S. Passport or Birth Certificate (certified by the government agency that issued it) or a voter-registration card. A military discharge is also recognized.

When you are coming from Puerto Peñasco entering the United States, Customs officials ask "What country are you a citizen of?" They may also ask you "Where have you been?" "How long have you been in Mexico?" and "What are you bringing back?" Be prepared to honestly answer these questions. You may want to make a list of purchases prior to reaching the border so you will remember everything you bought while you were away.

Automobiles, boats, planes or other vehicles taken abroad for non commercial use may be returned duty free by proving to the Customs officer that you took them out of the U.S. This proof may be the state registration card for an automobile, the Federal Aviation Administration certificate for an aircraft, a yacht license or motorboat identification certificate for a pleasure boat or a custom's certificate of registration obtained before departure.

What U.S. Residents May Bring Back

Each visitor may bring back duty free, articles not exceeding $400 in retail value. Duty must be paid on all items in excess of $400. This exemption is allowed only once within a 30-day period. The $400 exemption applies only to articles or souvenirs that are for you or your families personal use. The souvenirs must accompany you on your return to the U.S. The $400 exemption may include no more than 1 liter of spirits and no more than 200 cigarettes and 100 cigars. You must declare dollar amounts totaling over $10,000.

Cuban cigars are prohibited. Border Customs officials will confiscate cigars which are being smuggled into the United States and the perpetrators will be fined and or jailed.

Restricted or Prohibited Articles

Customs information for returning U.S. residents is contained in the U.S. Customs Service booklet "Know Before You Go," available from your local customs office or by writing U.S. Customs, P.O. Box 7407, Washington, DC 20044.

To prevent the introduction of plant and animal pests and diseases into the U.S., the agricultural quarantine bans the importation of certain fruits, vegetables, plants, livestock, poultry, and meats. You must declare all food products brought into the U.S. If you attempt to conceal agricultural items, you can be fined $25 - $50 by U.S. Customs. For additional information regarding restricted items, write for the free booklet "Travelers Tips," available from the U.S. Department of Agriculture, Washington, DC 20250.

The U.S. Department of Agriculture prohibits the importation of any kind of pet obtained in Mexico.

Goods purchased in Mexico but originating in North Korea, Vietnam, Cambodia or Cuba, Libya and Nicaragua are not admissible. Lottery tickets are also prohibited.

Some perfumes are limited to one bottle, some are prohibited altogether. If you intend to purchase perfume, be sure to inquire about trademark restrictions beforehand.

Endangered wildlife species or products made of any part of these species are prohibited. Including products made from sea turtles, black coral jewelry, fur from endangered cat species, crocodile leather or stuffed birds.

Though widely available on the market in Mexico, live birds such as parrots, parakeets or birds of prey cannot be brought into the U.S. If you are thinking of returning to the U.S. with any purchased articles made of ivory, fur, any animal skin other than leather, or any product manufactured wholly or in part of any type of wildlife, write to the Wildlife Permit Office, U.S. Department of the Interior, Washington, DC 20240 for more information.

Duty Free Alcohol

Two sets of laws govern the importation of alcoholic beverages: Federal and State. When regulations conflict, state laws supersede. For this reason it is important to know the import limits of your state of residence as well as the state of entry, which from Puerto Peñasco, is Arizona.

The Federal Government permits each resident who is 21 years of age or older to bring into the U.S. one liter of alcohol duty-free once very 30 days. Since liquor laws can be quite complex, it is wise to confirm the laws at the border before entering Mexico.

Duty Free Gifts

Gifts accompanying you across the U.S./Mexico border are considered to be for personal use included in the $400 exemption.

Gifts in packages whose total retail value does not exceed $50 may be sent to friends or relatives in the United States. Undeclared and free of U.S. Customs duty or tax, provided that only one such package is received by the same person in one day. Gifts may be sent to more than one person in the same package if they are individually wrapped and labeled with the name of the recipient.

Perfumes valued at more than $5 retail, tobacco products, and alcoholic beverages may not be included in gift packages.

The name of the donor and the retail value of the contents must be clearly marked on the outside and labeled "Unsolicited Gift." Consolidated gift parcels should have listed on the outside the names of the recipients and the value of each gift. However, the safe arrival of gifts sent through the mail cannot be guaranteed.

It is also possible to ship gifts through a broker. If you choose to do so, always obtain the name of the customs broker at the border who will handle the shipment. Make sure you understand the shipping arrangements and fees involved before signing the contract.

Paying Duty

A flat rate duty of 10% will be applied to the first $1,000 worth (fair retail value) of merchandise in excess of your maximum customs exemption. The sales slip is proof of value. Family members residing in one household and traveling together must group articles for application of the flat-duty rate. Articles must accompany you to

---

the U.S. border. The flat-duty rate may be taken only once every 30 days.

Articles over the initial $1,000 flat-duty limit are dutiable at the rate applicable to the articles. Since Mexico is considered a developing country, the United States offers preferential status to many Mexican imports and these items must be listed on the customs declaration. The final authority on duty-free items and duty rates for other items is the U.S. customs official at the border.

The old airport and landing strip were built by the railroad in Puerto Peñasco, just north of the Jim Bur Shopping Center where the tracks meet Blvd. Kino. The airport was operational until 1955. The original building is now private property. Photo courtesy of Guillermo Munro.

Information For Gringos

In doing, we learn.

-George Herbert

People in Puerto Peñasco are honest, friendly and interested in making new friends just as much as you are — don't alienate yourself from these experiences. The Mexican people will treat you with friendly consideration if given the opportunity. Puerto Peñasco must be appreciated on its own terms, to take in too much without savoring the atmosphere and watching the passing scene is to avoid what is most enchanting about this town.

Airline Travel

The international airport is located about four miles north of downtown. This new airport has opened the door to increased tourism. Puerto Peñasco officials established immigration, customs, and health agencies at the airport for inspection of passengers and cargo.

In September 1994, Arizona Airways, flying the route round trip from Tucson, was the first commercial flight to land and take off from Puerto Peñasco. The airport is now serviced by Great Lakes Airlines from Phoenix. Mexican airlines are contemplating starting service in the near future. The Mexican Army provides 24 hour a day security for the airport. The state assigned Alonso Dominguez, a young pilot, as the airport manager. Mr Dominguez speaks excellent English. Currently there is no fueling service (AV gas or jet fuel), but this service will be provided within the year. The airport is fully operational and equipped with a VOR (PPE-112.10) and runway lights are operated upon request or by the pilot through aircraft radio requests. Other frequency's are 122.2 and 126.7.

Firearms

Illegally importing a gun, on purpose or by mistake, is extremely stupid. The illegal possession of a firearm is like a reserved ticket for a prison cell, for a very long time. Firearms laws are very strict.

If you are serious about hunting in Mexico write to the Wildlife Advisory Services, P.O. Box 76132, Los Angeles, California 90076, phone 213-385-9311, Fax 213-385-0782. They will explain the regulations and help you do the paperwork.

Illegal Drugs

Next to transporting illegal firearms, using drugs in Mexico is probably the most hazardous thing a traveler can do. My advice is to stay clear of all drugs while visiting Puerto Peñasco and avoid anyone else who is using them. If the local police are in doubt, they arrest everyone.

Drug abuse and drug trafficking are now considered a crisis of worldwide proportions. Permissiveness is being replaced by tougher anti-drug laws and "zero tolerance" enforcement. Drug laws are now being vigorously enforced in Mexico. Ironically, penalties for possession and trafficking are harsher in Mexico, especially if you are a United States Citizen.

You may come across a highway search of your vehicle by armed army forces or *federales*. Be polite and cooperative. Never make derogatory or sarcastic remarks. These men expect to be taken very seriously. They may speak English, but pretend not to. If you relax they will too.

Mexicans planting illegal drugs on tourists to set them up is rare. On the other hand, "sting" operations do happen sometimes. The classic sting is to have a former busted informant or undercover cop sell drugs to a tourist then move in and arrest the tourist. Such ploys are obviously only a hazard to the person and their companions foolish enough to look for drugs in the first place.

If you are busted, don't panic. The new breed of *federali* will not accept gratuities. The usual protocol is to pay the fine to the officer in charge at the police station. Ask to pay the fine when you are brought before the judge. This usually happens within three days. They can hold you for 24 hours then they must turn you over to the *federales* who can hold you indefinitely. If you are innocent but suspected of something more, they can keep you around longer. Pretrial procedures can take several months. Transporting and dealing can cost you 3 to 12 years, smuggling drugs across the border sentences are 6 to 15 years, and fines go along with jail terms. Serious charges can cost a lot of money and take months to negotiate. Some cases are settled by allowing the accused out on bond with the assumption they will leave and never return.

Each situation is different. The line between possession, dealing and smuggling is determined by the judge. In cases of minor possession you will immediately be escorted to the border.

Who Is A Gringo?

The Mexican dictionary gives the definition of *Gringo:* "Foreigner, especially the English and Greek. In Mexico and Central America, "North American;" in Argentina and Uruguay, 'Italian'." *Gringo* refers to those of us who will be traveling across the border for a holiday in the sun to enjoy good food and drink. The locals will call us *gringos* without the slightest intent of insult.

Weather

Winter here is ideal and tends to be the "peak season" for travelers. Low average monthly rainfall enables this area to enjoy sunny weather almost year round. There is an increase of rainfall in July and August while the driest months are May and June. The winter months provide a larger share of the total annual rainfall than the summer months in the Sonoran Desert.

If you are going to Puerto Peñasco for the weekend, expect to find the temperatures cooler than you would in Phoenix. If you are staying right on the beach, however, the temperature tends to be a bit cooler than inland because of the sea breezes. If you want to find detailed information on rainfall, monsoons, water temperature, and the environment in this area, head to CEDO, (Intercultural Center for the study of Deserts and Oceans. CEDO is known by this Spanish language acronym), in Las Conchas.

Temperatures And Rainfall In Rocky Point

Month	Rainfall	Air Temp.	Sea Temp.
January	.35	53 F	57 F
February	.16	55 F	59 F
March	.21	58 F	62 F
April	.05	64 F	65 F
May	.004	70 F	72 F
June	.01	77 F	77 F
July	.13	84 F	84 F
August	.32	86 F	85 F
September	.47	82 F	83 F
October	.46	74 F	75 F
November	.24	62 F	67 F
December	.50	55 F	61 F

Don't Leave Your Brains At The Border

"I'll have a couple more *Corona* beers and another plate of *nachos*, then we can go someplace for dinner, I've always wanted to try *calamares* and *pulpos* (squid and octopus)." Since most trips to Puerto Peñasco will be fairly short, wise decisions can make the difference between a great weekend or the worst weekend of your life. It is smart, both for your health and pleasure, to know when to stop and what to avoid.

Water: Puerto Peñasco has eight operating water purification plants for residents and businesses. Water can be used from the tap. It is pure enough for brushing your teeth, and can be consumed when it is served to you in a restaurant. You may choose to bring your own or purchase a jug at the *supermercado* (supermarket), *tienda* (shop), or liquor store.

Stress and tension: Plan ahead so packing and preparation is completed the day before your departure. It's easy to forget your prescription, extra money or even your purse when you are worn into a frazzle putting things together at the last minute.

Sunburn: Always use sunscreen even if the day's activities won't include relaxing on the beach. The best time to apply sunscreen is <u>before</u> you get dressed in the morning. Even in winter the sun can be very intense. As soon as you look like you are getting pink, cover yourself. The sun still reflects harmful rays through your clothing even on cloudy days. Wear white, lightweight cotton clothing for protection from the sun during the summer months.

Bare feet: Do as the Mexicans do, at least wear sandals. It's not worth the hazard of sunburn, broken glass, infections from feces and rusty metal.

Food and drink: Weekenders spend their time on the beach trying to put the beer and Tequila vendors out of business. When combined with eating, driving, and dancing, too much of a good thing can leave you uncomfortable, exhausted, and give you a case of diarrhea, or worse. The "revenge" could be too much of everything, not necessarily an under cooked street taco. Use your head and don't push it.

Common Sense Is Not Paranoia

Puerto Peñasco is safe but common sense while traveling is something you need to take with you. Keep valuables in your car trunk. Make sure your car is locked at all times. Do not leave things in the back of your truck or camper. Hotels have 24-hour security guards, but it is best to be safe than sorry. Keep your valuables on your person at all times. Make sure your hotel room is locked while you are "in" or "out."

Foreign women with blond or red hair are fair targets for unwanted attention from the *macho* Mexican man. Women traveling alone are seldom in any physical danger. Sometimes women are assaulted with looks, often with language, sometimes complimentary, sometimes obscene, all of which are best ignored. Expressions of anger usually enhances a challenge. The rule of thumb is to appear oblivious, avoid all eye contact, and respond to direct proposals with an unconditional "No," without explanation. *Machismo* is arrogance carried to the extreme, but in fact it is a mask that enables the male to conceal his insecurity. The Mexican *macho* does not want to risk being hurt.

A word of caution, however. Other lodgers or desk clerks may be looking for casual romance. When approached with this type of attention, politely and firmly refuse any invitation.

Beggars And Con Artists

Your first encounter after stopping across the border can be a band of *"muchachos"* (little boys) armed with squeegee's and dirty old rags. Before you get a chance to stop them they are all over your car, frantically scrubbing away at your windows. They expect to be compensated for their efforts when they finish. If you ignore them and walk away, they magically appear when you put the key back in the lock. I do not like these little *bandidos*, they annoy me especially when I do not request their services.

I commissioned the advice of a Puerto Peñasco friend on how to handle these awkward encounters. His advice, "Give these little *muchachos* school books, pencils or paper. Do not give money or food." Granted, Mexico is full of poverty but giving money encourages soliciting, and at times begging from the *turistas*. Instead, Mexican children should be encouraged to stay in school, get an education, and become productive citizens earning a living at something worthwhile. The best thing we can give them is the desire to work for something which can provide a stable income for themselves and their families.

Most of the beggars you will see are in bad shape and they need a handout to eat or a place to sleep. The most transparently phony beggars are small children trying to make a few *pesos* for a Coke and some candy. My reply is "Don't give money." There are organizations in Puerto Peñasco who distribute food and clothing to the needy. If you feel guilty, make a donation to one of these organizations.

Currency

U.S. currency is accepted everywhere. *Pesos* and *centavos* are similar to our dollars and cents. The Mexican *peso* ($) is divided into 100 *centavos* similar to the U.S. dollar and cents. Hotels and restaurants in Puerto Peñasco take American dollars. It is not necessary to change currency upon your arrival. If you are using Puerto Peñasco as a stopover for traveling further south, then exchanging your money is recommended. Cash and traveler's checks can be exchanged for *pesos* at banks, hotels, restaurants, and shops.

Credit cards are accepted as payment in some tourist restaurants and hotels but carrying plenty of cash in small bills is the best form of payment. Some merchants will accept a well-known *tarjeta de crédito* (credit card). They display Visa or Mastercard on the front window or on the cash register.

If you find yourself short of cash, banks will give a cash advance on your credit card with photo identification. Cash advances are usually paid in *pesos* rather than dollars. ATM machine locations are listed in Chapter 11, Business Services. Remember, if you purchase something on your card, the sales draft will reflect the *peso* amount. The bill does not charge against your U.S. account for a week or two. During the grace period, the *peso* may devaluate. When your statement arrives it will reflect a later exchange rate. It could be higher or lower than the day you purchased the item.

Some businesses add a service charge when a credit card is used. If a service charge is written on the sales draft as a credit card service charge, the amount can be disputed through Visa or Mastercard.

American Express travelers checks are recommended. Some merchants are familiar with American Express and will cash small demoninations ($50 or under) as long as you have proper identification. Sometimes they do not ask for identification. Travelers checks can be replaced quickly if lost, stolen or destroyed, take your receipts to the bank.

Personal checks are accepted for payment in very few places. If accepted, an additional charge is added for processing, usually $7. Most merchants and banks feel more comfortable when they know their money is guaranteed. Your best rule of thumb is to carry small denominations of cash and travelers checks.

Suitable Casual Attire

I want to stress the importance of dress in any foreign country, including Mexico. Improperly dressed Americans can be an embarrassment, if not to themselves, but to others.

The best way to fit in is to dress the way the locals do. It is not necessary to buy a new wardrobe, just be reasonable. Take notice of how the men and women are dressing in town then follow their example. Long shorts are acceptable attire in Puerto Peñasco if worn with shirts or cover-ups. Swim suits, bikini tops, "cheeky-shorts" and bare chests are not appropriate attire away from the beach. Please do not wear wet swim suits into any public place without covering up. This includes adults and children. Walking around barefoot is also frowned upon, and considered bad taste. Although restaurant owners will not say anything, they disapprove of inappropriately dressed customers.

Unfortunately, college students and many adults have been coming to Puerto Peñasco for years without regard to their behavior. Many partake in excessive drinking, loud and obnoxious behavior, sleeping around and putting themselves at risk for getting sick with a hangover and/or contracting sexually transmitted diseases. One encounter without using good judgment can affect you the rest of your life, or end it prematurely. Unfortunately, "ugly Americans" have given the local residents a negative impression of all Americans. Please be respectful. Remember you are a guest in someone else's country. You are in a sense an ambassador; please be a good representative.

Courtesy And Safety

Should you encounter any problems when crossing the border or while in Puerto Peñasco, go to the Chamber of Commerce office located behind the Jim Bur shopping center (Map D11), or dial (in Mexico) 011-91-800-00148. In the U. S. call 1-800-4-SONORA.

The people of Puerto Peñasco welcome visitors to the region and

> *A journey is a person in itself*
> *no two are alike.*
>
> *And all the plans, safeguards, policies*
> *and coercion are fruitless.*
>
> *We find after years of struggle,*
> *we do not take a trip:*
> *the trip takes us.*
>
> -John Steinbeck

want your trip to be pleasant and trouble-free. Mexico and all its people appreciate travelers who abide by their laws and respect their customs, so before you leave home please be aware of some of their regulations:

1. For safety reasons, please do not drive vehicles (automobiles, motorcycles, ATC's, sand buggies, etc.) along the beaches within the city limits. Areas include Sandy Beach, Cholla Bay, Playa Bonita, Playa Hermosa, Playa Miramar, Playa de Oro, Las Conchas, Playa Encanto, Dorado, and Morúa Estuary.

2. Motorcycles, ATC's or similar vehicles should not be driven by persons under 18 years of age at any time.

3. Please help keep the city and the beaches clean by throwing trash and cans in special designated areas marked for trash dumping or take it back to your hotel.

4. Respect the right of hikers, skiers, campers and others so they can enjoy their activities undisturbed.

5. Travel only where motorized vehicles are permitted. Avoid streams, wetlands, meadows, muddy roads and trails, steep hillsides, wildlife and livestock. Drive responsibly and protect the environment.

6. Educate yourself by reading this guidebook thoroughly.

7. Obtain travel maps and rules from public agencies if you are heading out into the desert or the Pinacates.

8. Comply with signs and barriers and ask the owners permission before crossing private property.

Protect Your Eyes From The Sun

The summer sun is very intense especially between the hours of 11:00 a.m. and 3:00 p.m. It is wise to take extra precautions to protect your eyes, particularly if you plan to spend the day on the beach, boating or fishing.

Most sunglasses block ultraviolet rays but some of the plastic varieties fail to block infrared rays. Both ultraviolet and infrared rays can damage eyesight. Green or gray lenses of high-quality optic glass provide protection from both. The best color value evidently is transmitted by natural gray lenses, which view all colors evenly with true value.

Leading manufacturers suggest a test for sunglass efficiency which you can do yourself in the store before you purchase the glasses. Put on the pair being considered and look in the mirror. If you can see your eyes easily, the lenses are not dark enough for adequate protection from sun glare. Yellow lenses are for hazy days only. They do the opposite of what sunglasses are intended to do. Yellow lenses magnify light intensity instead of diminishing it.

Polarized lenses eliminate excessive glare by means of a polarized layer of material sandwiched between two pieces of glass which then are pressed into the appropriate curvature. They can be made into a prescription. The polarized layer helps when looking downward but not when looking ahead, such as at a 90° angle. Then, we have to depend on the outside layers of colored glass, (or plastic) to do the job. Plastic lenses serve their purpose only to a degree because they are soft and very easily scratched, so high-quality ones of optical glass are well worth the added cost.

The modern range in protective glasses is too complex to more than touch on here. Suffice it to say that sunglasses can be obtained with photo chromatic polarized lenses (which change from light to dark depending on the intensity of the sun's rays) and that many types are made as bifocals.

One should also consider, particularly in tropic climates, the fact that light can leak in around the edges of sunglasses. For this reason glasses that enclose the entire eye area, similar to what skiers and mountain climbers use, provide added protection. Such "goggles" may be considered unattractive for fishing, but they are excellent protection from flying hooks.

Finally, to prevent dropping glasses overboard, cords, elastic and other-wise, are available that go around the neck and fasten to the frames. They allow you to pull off your glasses and let them hang against your chest.

Tourist Information

Camara Nacional de Comercio Servicios y Turismo de Puerto Peñasco (Chamber of Commerce), Blvd. Fremont y Plaza del Camarón, Apdo Postal 248, 83550. North of the police station behind the park, open during weekly business hours, 011-53-638-32848, Fax 011-53-638-34468. Map D11.

Consulate of Mexico/Phoenix Office, 1990 W. Camelback Plaza #110, Phoenix, Arizona 85035, 602-242-7398. Contact this office if you need FM2 and FM3 cards.

Consulate of Mexico/Tucson Office, 553 S. Stone Avenue, Tucson, Arizona 85705, 602-882-5595, Fax: 602-882-5595.

FM3 Preparation/Translation Service, 104-C Juarez Blvd., Puerto Peñasco, across from Thrifty Ice Cream in Old Port, 011-52-638-36209. Will assist you and save you trips to immigration. They prepare, translate, and notarize all types of documents. Map F32.

Immigration Office in Puerto Peñasco, Blvd. Juárez & Calle 18, 011-52-638-32526. Hours are Monday to Friday from 8 a.m. to 3 p.m. Pick up paperwork for FM2 and FM3 cards if you are planning to work or retire in Puerto Peñasco. For a FM3 card you will need the original paperwork and three copies of each of the following: (1) American passport. (2) Papers showing ownership of your home or condo. (3) Four front pictures and four right side facing pictures taken recently. (4) Birth certificate. (5) The last statement from your bank translated into Spanish. (6) Marriage Certificate translated into Spanish. (7) A letter from your employer on letterhead verifying employment and monthly income translated into Spanish. The cost is around $75 dollars. These requirements are just to live in Mexico, not to work. Please be advised that requirements for FM3 cards change constantly so be prepared to provide some or all of the above information. Completion of initial FM3's or yearly reissues can take up to several months. Map B41.

Internet Address, frequently updated information for visitors provided by Mike W. O'Neal, http://www.goodnet.com/~rockypt.

Mexican Government Tourism Office, In the U.S., 10100 Santa Monica Blvd., Suite 224, Los Angeles, CA 90067, 310-203-8191, Fax: 301-203-8316.

Mexican Tourist Bureau, in the U. S. call 602-947-7022.

Questions and Complaints Crossing the Border, Go to the nearest information center, office in charge, employee of the *Contraloría General de la Federacón,* the local tourism office, or dial toll free: *Contraloría,* when in Mexico, 011-91-800-00148, or *Tel-Tur* 011 91-800-62555. When in the U.S. call the **Sonora Tourism Office,** 1-800-4-SONORA, 1-800-476-6672.

Sonora Department of Tourism, 011-52-638-34129.

Travel Fax Program, "Travel Fax" is provided by Sonora's Department of Tourism and Realty Network, Inc., 19848 N. Cave Creek Road, Phoenix, Arizona 85024, 602-569-1125, Fax: 602-569-2399. To access the travel information from your Fax machine dial 1-602-930-4815 and follow the recorded message. The ID number for Puerto Peñasco, Sonora, Mexico is #2032. You will receive a brief description of Rocky Point, a map, and local travel information.

U.S. Customs, P.O. Box 7407, Washington, DC 20044.

U.S. Customs Port Director, in the U. S. call, 602-379-3514, 602-379-3516.

Bonel Travel Agency, Nicolás Bravo #12, 011-52-638-33555. Will arrange your pleasure or business trip in Mexico or to any other part of the world. Airline ticket reservations, hotel and car reservations, organized excursions and tours. Ask for the city tours. The only agency in town authorized by the Mexican Government. Secretaría de Turismo, Jorge Bonillas. Map B38.

The fish market in Old Port offers fresh seafood daily. Several fine gourmet restaurants and ocean front taco stands cater to discriminating tastes.

Puerto Peñasco's fishing fleet provides the majority of the towns fresh seafood. Peak fishing months for shrimp are September to December.

Destination: Fun

For my part, I travel not to go anywhere, but to go.
I travel for travel's sake. The great affair is to move.
 -Robert Louis Stevenson

Mileage From Rocky Point To:

Sonoyta	100 Kms.	62 Miles
Lukeville	104 Kms.	65 Miles
Ajo	164 Kms.	98 Miles
Caborca	256 Kms.	159 Miles
San Luis	294 Kms.	182 Miles
Mexicali	365 Kms.	226 Miles
Yuma	418 Kms.	260 Miles
Nogales	365 Kms.	226 Miles
Tucson	341 Kms.	212 Miles
Phoenix	341 Kms.	212 Miles
Flagstaff	580 Kms.	350 Miles
Hermosillo	529 Kms.	260 Miles
Guaymas	665 Kms.	340 Miles
San Diego	706 Kms.	439 Miles
Los Angeles	869 Kms.	540 Miles
Las Vegas	806 Kms.	501 Miles

Experience Mexico

Mexico is an exciting cosmos of contrasts. The culture and ambiance are a blend of medieval Spanish, native American and 20th Century civilizations. Underneath all this lies ancient Aztec, Zapotec, Toltec and Mayan civilizations with all their beliefs and customs. This merger of traditions, religions, and philosophies makes its people unique, which is why you see all those brown faces.

Mexico settlers married into the indigenous population and accepted new approaches to life.

Mexico is a *mestizo* nation. Its people are a fusion of Indian and Spanish, both biologically and culturally. Mexicans identify themselves as a mixture of both the Aztecs and the Spanish. There are no hyphenated Mexican names. Thus terms like African-American and Native-American have cultural nuances unique to the United States and make little sense in a Mexican content.

To Mexicans, wealth and prestige command respect, which comes from the early Spanish aristocrats who conquered Mexico in 1521. They have a strong class consciousness that we do not have. Mexicans tend to admire anyone from a higher social class and are uneasy mixing with a different class, whether it be higher or lower.

Mexicans feel that Americans are in a different social class. Many times it does not matter that the Mexican is as wealthy as you, because there are no exact counterparts to your respective social classes.

Ajo, Arizona

The four-hour trip from Phoenix or Tucson takes one through Ajo, down to Why, crossing the border at Lukeville, Arizona. The scenery in this area is considered some of the most beautiful in Arizona. The narrow, hilly highway passes through the Organ Pipe Cactus National Monument which offers excellent camping facilities and miles of unique desert growth. Near Lukeville the highway crosses a portion of The Devil's Road, *El Camino del Diablo.* The Devil's Road is the historical Spanish route along which hundreds of miners and pioneers lost their lives. A brief historical overview of this area can also be found in the history chapter of this book.

Ancient Ajo was a wild and primitive land. Indian presence in the Ajo area dates back eleven thousand years. Ventana Cave, where archeologists have uncovered evidence of human habitation, is located east of Ajo near Santa Rosa on the Indian Reservation. Child's Mountain and the Crater north of Ajo is approximately six million years old. The Coffee Pot Mountain area, eighteen miles east of Ajo, is approximately nine million years old. The Indians believe that Ventana Cave is the home of the Devil Wind God. Whirlwinds in the desert are called "Dust Devils."

One frequently hears that the town of Ajo was named by Mexican miners after the abundant wild garlic found in the area. This is probably not the real story. *Au-Auho*, a Papago Indian word was translated into the English word "paint." It is thought that originally the Papago Indians, now known as Tohono O'odham, used to come to this site to drink from a spring and to collect red oxide and green carbonate copper ores used for body paint. When the Spanish and Mexicans first arrived in southwest Arizona, they noted the paint colors and asked where the copper ore originated. Another native tribe, the Pima, told them of the Ajo copper source. The Pima word for paint is *au'auho*. So the Pima word was "Hispanicized" to suit Spanish phonetics, and *au'auho* was shortened to *au'ho,* which became Ajo. It is, coincidentally, the Spanish word for garlic. Anglo-Americans recorded and spread this early use of the name Ajo. The garlic coincidence was furthered by the presence of a lovely desert lily, an annual spring wild flower of the Ajo area. It has an edible bulbous root which supposedly tastes like garlic. It is reported that it actually tastes not at all like garlic and more like a mild spring onion. The settlement has been known as Ajo since 1854.

Hohokam Indians, "the people that went away," are believed to be the first in the area, dating from the 12th century AD. to the 16th century AD. The Papago Indians, renamed Tohono O'odham, are likely descendants of the Hohokam. They made regular trips to the Gulf of California to collect sea shells for tools, and ornaments. Temporary villages were located at The Lost City in Growler Valley, about twenty miles west of Ajo. These villages were inhabited in the spring and fall when the Indians made their semi-annual trips to the sea of Cortéz. Father Kino helped the Indians establish pearl fishing and today there are piles of oyster shells in the ruins of this old city.

The Tohono O'odham reservation stretches across 2,500,000 acres of land beginning twelve miles east of Ajo and continuing across the desert toward Tucson.

The first known victim of the *Camino del Diablo,* the Devil's Road, was the Spanish Conquistador Melchoir Díaz. He was part of the Coronado expedition of 1540 and third in command to Coronado. This expedition had been sent to find a legendary city of Gold, The Lost City of Cibola. Díaz was commanding a troop of lancers who rode to the Yuma Indian lands on the Colorado River. On the return trip, Díaz was mortally wounded with his own spear while chasing a coyote on horseback. The lance point dug into the ground and the momentum sent the wooden spear shaft through Díaz's middle. Carried on a litter, he lived until the group of lancers reached the Sonoyta River where Lukeville, Arizona is today. For their own safety the troopers buried Díaz in an unknown grave. Díaz Peak on the southern edge of the Ajo Mountain Range was named for him. The Indians considered him a god-like person who could not die.

Quitovaquito, just south and west of Ajo, was one of Father Kino's regular camping spots. It is now located on the present day Organ Pipe Cactus National Monument. Father Kino reestablished the Camino del Diablo originally founded and traveled by Melchoir Díaz in 1540. He traveled to the present Gila Bend area in 1700 and his trail became the main southern route west from both Mexico and the eastern United States. Father Kino's mission in Ajo was to teach and above all, civilize the natives. He taught agriculture, irrigation, stock raising, carpentry, building construction and boat building.

Ajo and the New Cornelia Mine are located at the eastern end of the little Ajo Mountains. Silver was not reported to be found at Ajo until thirteen years after Kino's death, about 1725.

Gunsight may be the oldest ghost town in the state of Arizona, located seventeen miles southeast of Ajo. A population of 1,500 people once lived in the town site. Some old building foundations, walls, and the shaft heading are all that remains today. The town claims were voided by the U.S. Government because they were located on the Indian Reservation. Around 1878, four Yuma men found a piece of silver while they were camped on a slope. They started their claims by digging a 43 foot shaft and shipping the ore to San Francisco. The mine was worked for fifteen months and was sold for $100,000.

How Gunsight got its name is not really known. Legend has it that one of the men needed a sight for his gun and made it out of pure silver found at the mine. Another story is that a nearby mountain resembled a gun sight.

In its heyday the Silver Gert Mining Company in Gunsight employed 40 men, housed in eight buildings constructed around 1892. An Indian village provided the Gunsight residents with vegetables and dairy products. A stage ran three times a week to Gila Bend. On Mondays and Thursdays it went from Gunsight to Tucson.

Reports show that the mine shaft was 840 feet deep with some tunnels a hundred feet in length. Reports on how much silver was mined is unknown.

Forty two miles of track was laid from Gila Bend to Ajo in seven months with the first train arriving in Ajo in February of 1916. This train was pulled by a steam engine borrowed from the Southern Pacific Railroad.

During prohibition in the 1920's, enforcement of the act was difficult. During this time the roads from Ajo to the border were wagon roads or old horse and mule trails. The desert was vast and provided many places to hide caches of potent brew. Stills were built in far away corners of the desert. Liquor was transported in large leather bags carried on either side of horses or mules. The hard living, hard drinking men of the southwestern desert were not about to give up their "fire water."

Before 1930 the Bureau of Internal Revenue was responsible for enforcing the law. When the Department of Justice took over, the agents were then known as Federal Men. The Mexican economy soared with the sale of booze, while the American economy dragged. The Americans made liquor, corn whiskey and beer for personal use. Mexicans produced mescal and tequila.

The road to Gila Bend was paved in 1938. The highway to Tucson became a state highway in 1943. The road was paved to the edge of the Indian Reservation, and from Tucson to the eastern edge.

It was 1948 before the 100 miles across the reservation was paved. The Gilbert Construction Company paved the road by 1951 at a cost of $1,500,000. An old legend says that even the buzzards flew to Tucson by way of Gila Bend. Highway 85 south from Ajo was completed in 1945. It passed through the Organ Pipe National Monument all the way to Lukeville.

Why, Arizona

Why is located ten miles from Ajo, where State Road 85 meets State Road 86, resulting in a "Y." The "Y" had to be changed into a word when the post office set up a branch office there. It is not a town, but it is a *place*. A trademark of the name from the State Attorney General's Office was requested.

Mrs. Peggy Kater and her husband, James, were the first settlers on this junction road. Within a few years eighty additional homes were built. The Why Utility Company was established to provide water to the residents. Every home owner who has a water meter has a vote in electing board members to run the company. Mrs. Kater asked the Bureau of Land Management to set aside an area where winter visitors could park and stay as long as they liked. The bureau gave the residents 80 days to build roads, sewage facilities, water and electricity. Many residents volunteered and the work was completed in 30 days.

The Coyote Howls Campground was completed and is managed by the Utility Company. It now encompasses 400 campsites with three lavatories and washrooms. Community Centers, a Fire Station, Border Patrol Headquarters, and Pozo Redondo home sites have made Why a nice place to live. Most of the land is privately owned and further expansion is not possible unless the Bureau of Land Management turns over more land for development.

Gringo Pass And Lukeville, Arizona

The gateway to Puerto Peñasco is Lukeville, Arizona, on the U.S. side. Sonoyta, in the state of Sonora, borders on the Mexican side.

Lukeville is located in a natural pass between the Puerto Blanco and Ajo Mountains and the nearby Quitobaquito Springs and Sonoyta River. This pass and the spring were used by Indians before the Spanish arrived in Mexico. The spot where the International Border crossing gateway now stands was a stagecoach stop between Spanish Mexico and California.

An American named Syde Kalil homesteaded on the Arizona side of the International Gate before W.W.I. Kalil was considered a "patriarch" of the area which was called Kalitown. Charlie Luke, a man who had also homesteaded in the area, pulled some strings and got the U.S. Post Office to officially designate the site as "Lukeville." This took place after W.W.I.

The town has no room to expand. Mexico is located to the south, and the Organ Pipe National Monument surrounds the other three sides. The entire town covers only 60 acres.

Lukeville remained an unimpressive stop-over on the way to Rocky Point until 1970, when Phoenix entrepreneur Alfred Gay, who a few years earlier had bought the land and facilities adjoining the Arizona side of the Gate, began to develop the area as a resort in itself. Naming the development "Gringo Pass" after his company, Gringo Pass, Inc. Gay put up a shopping center that includes a post office, grocery store, general store, laundromat, restaurant, apparel and gift shops, a gas station and other facilities. Mexican automobile insurance is sold at the General Store.

Other Gringo Pass facilities include a motel on the left as you approach the border gate and a trailer park. Legend has it that the site of the trailer park incorporates the ruins of the old stage coach where Pancho Villa is said to have had a shoot-out with *federales* during the Mexican revolution.

Lukeville is now a very attractive place to rest. Take the opportunity to "gas up" with American brand gasoline, and purchase needed supplies.

Sonoyta, Mexico

Sonoyta was founded by Father Eustebio Francisco Kino in 1699, and fringes the border on the Mexican side. Sonoyta is a Papago-Indian word and it means "The Place Where Corn Will Grow."

Sonoyta lies in a fertile meadow of the Sonoyta River, at the southern edge of the Pápago Indian Reservation, and about midway on the ancient road from Caborca to Yuma, appropriately and accurately named *El Camino del Diablo,* The Devil's Road.

From the death of Melchoir Díaz in 1541, until the middle of the 19th Century when gold fever drew a steady stream of immigrants from Sonora to California, the bleached bones of animals and men were scattered with profligate abandon along almost the whole 225 miles of *El Camino del Diablo.* Along this long stretch of parched desert, the Sonoyta meadow was the only stopping place with a dependable water supply and adequate food.

Highway 2 is a road which roughly follows the ancient route from Sonoyta to Yuma. Today, all roads to Sonoyta are paved. Sonoyta is about 45 miles south of Ajo on Arizona's State Route 85 and about 127 miles southeast of San Luis del Río Colorado on Mexican Federal Highway 2. Now it continues to Mexicali in Baja California.

Father Kino was interested in Sonoyta primarily as a way station on the overland route which he hoped to establish between the Sonora missions and California. Father Kino established a cattle ranch at Sonoyta in February 1699. Two years later he built Sonoyta's first church and said the first Mass on April 5, 1701. It fell to ruins around 1750. He named the mission, ranch and Indian village *San Marcelo.* A new church was built by Father Enrique Ruhen in 1751 and lasted only one year when a Pima Indian uprising reached the outpost. Father Enrique Ruhen was killed, the church was stripped of its sacred ornaments and the building was set on fire.

In 1907 the people of Sonoyta had no post office, school, teacher, church, priest, doctor, and no regular, or frequent, communication with the outside world. Main Street consisted of the house of "The Singing Bird," Señor Medina's store, a mescal establishment owned by 76 year old Señor Jesus Molina, and about six small adobe houses. The singing bird was a young Mexican woman who warbles tunefully. When someone became ill the family took care of them with the best medicines they happened to have.

When mothers gave birth, the other women took care of them. Up until this time no epidemic had passed through his tiny town.

Commercial, tourist and industrial activities running through the same door have brought this town into the 20th century. Two main roads and several highways intersect in Sonoyta. The Mexicali - Caborca highways cross the center of the city. So do the Lukeville "Sister city of Sonoyta" highway, and the Puerto Peñasco highway. Sonoyta is a bustle of activity and provides just about everything you are looking for – gas stations, banks, drug stores, curio shops, restaurants, and colonial style hotels.

About two miles from the border you will come to the business district of Sonoyta. When you reach the bottom of a long hill, you will see a statue of a Mexican general. Stay to the left. A large triangle-size central park with trees and a new tall structure which looks like the Washington Monument, are located on your left. Follow the sign to Rocky Point directing you to the right, then off toward the west.

Mexico has slow speed limits in town. Most car speedometers show speed in kilometers/hour. If your automobile does not have a kilometer conversion, one kilometer equals 5/8 of a mile. Just cut the speed limit sign number in half, i.e. 40 kilometer/hour = 20 miles/hour. All mileage signs in Mexico are measured in kilometers, 10 kilometers is 6.2 miles. Please respect these speed limits when driving in town and out on the highway. I was told the new police cars are being paid for by the *turistas* (tourists). Watch your speed and come to a full stop at all stop signs and traffic lights.

Puerto Peñasco, Mexico

Emerging from a flat desolate desert, Puerto Peñasco is a refreshing sight. In 1826 a British lieutenant named Robert William Hale Hardy traveled along the coast of the Gulf of California. Lt. Hardy came upon a calm, blue-green bay protected by a large mountain resembling a huge whale. Rocks were formed through the centuries by erosion, the tides formed a long rocky out-thrust. This bold outcropping of rock gives the town its common name – Rocky Point.

The Spanish translation is *Punta Peñasco*. The town was established around 1928 when Mexican fishermen discovered rich shrimp beds just off the coast and American John Stone constructed the first hotel.

The fishermen here are forever optimistic about bigger and better catches but many have taken up other business ventures. Although the season becomes shorter and the catches become smaller, they work hard from September through May. September, October, November and December are the peak fishing season months. During the late spring and summer they beach their fleet and spend long hours scraping, painting and tinkering with engines. Two ice plants, three packing plants, a railroad and an international airport supply the shrimp fleet.

The oldest business district is perched right on the tip of the rocky outcrop southwest of downtown. There is a bank, school, church, city hall, post office, the former New Cortéz Motel, now known as the Viña del Mar, and scores of stores, restaurants and curio shops. Some of the townspeople live right on the rock, but many more live north and east on the flat land near the main road and central business district. The population of Puerto Peñasco, as of a 1996 calculation, is 37,000 inhabitants.

Dirt roads are commonplace in this area and at first seem to guarantee the ruin of your car but soon lose their hostility and become quaint and fun to drive on. With the continued development of tourism, the government has plans to pave all the major streets in the downtown area so watch for continued construction.

Cholla Bay And Sandy Beach, Mexico

Cholla Bay and Sandy Beach are about four miles from town. Arriving from the border, a large sign on the right hand side of the road points the way. Another road mark to look for is the twelve foot high, white sign located on your right about two city blocks north of the first flashing stop light as you enter town from the border. See the Puerto Peñasco street and area map located in the back of this book for directions.

After crossing the railroad tracks, you will be entering what is now known as "Rodeo Drive" or the "Cholla Mall." Here tee-shirt and curio shops line the road for several blocks. Continue in a northwesterly direction. Ahead of you, the first point of rock from Puerto Peñasco are the Cholla Mountains. Sandy Beach is left of this point, Pelican Point and Cholla Bay are to the right. Well placed painted signs direct you to each area.

The entire length of road to Sandy Beach and Cholla Bay is narrow and sandy, and resembles a washboard. The top speed is about 20 mph. If you pull off the road you may sink to the floorboards in soft sand. A road grader makes this trek on a regular basis leveling the soft dunes and bumps. If you are fortunate enough to follow one, the ride will be much smoother.

Until recently, Sandy Beach was the cheapest way to go for camping on the beach. At $3.00 per night, bathrooms were few and far between. Hot summer winds are brutal on tent poles and the drone of all-terrain vehicles early in the morning is not a welcome sound, especially for those who imbibed a bit too much the night before. The Reef restaurant and bar is located in this area. Plans have been finalized to commercially develop this area and prohibit overnight camping.

Besides the beach that skirts the bay, the most popular place here is JJ's Cantina, which seems to be considered the center of town. JJ's is always open and obliging with homemade tacos or your favorite beverage.

Sport fishing is attracting more enthusiasts every year. Boats are available for hire. See Chapter 15, Recreation, for more information on boating and fishing in this area.

Las Conchas, Mexico

The community of Las Conchas is located approximately two miles out of town. Follow Blvd. Fremont to the sign directing traffic to the right, the entrance is about one half mile.

Twenty years ago Las Conchas was developed to provide an exclusive guarded community located on the beach which extends almost five miles along the coastline. You will see many expensive, unique, and one-of-a-kind custom built homes in this area. Many are vacation homes and are used as weekend rentals. There are, however, more people retiring in this small inviting community and live here year round.

Playa Encanto, Mexico

If you continue on Blvd. Fremont another seven miles out of town, a sign will direct you to the right toward the private community of Playa Encanto. It is another seven miles to the top of a small hill. The road follows the beach which, in the author's opinion, is one of the most beautiful and serene in all of Puerto Peñasco. Private homes dot the shoreline which is much less developed than Las Conchas. Generators provide electricity to the exclusive beach front homes and water is brought in by trucks and stored in cisterns located on the rooftops.

This beach is worth the drive. It stretches for miles and is excellent for shell collecting and strolling during the early morning hours or at sunset. There are no facilities in this area. If you plan to spend the day, take plenty of water, food, and attire for cool winter winds or hot summer days. If you are spending a day on the beach, shelter is not available anywhere. Day trippers are welcome and public access is located near the entrance. Please be advised camping and all terrain vehicles are not allowed. The residents of this area ask your cooperation in keeping their community clean and quiet.

El Dorada and Miramar, Mexico

If you stay on the main road and continue toward Caborca, you will see the entrances to El Dorada and Miramar. Both are new developments located on the beach. Spending a quiet day strolling, shell collecting, or just relaxing is the best way to enjoy these two beaches. Neither provide facilities, so make sure you bring shade, food and water. All areas have public access to the beach.

Transportes De Sonora Coop, 1942. The railroad was being built from Puerto Peñasco North to Mexacali. Busses transported railroad workers from Santana, about 400K south, up to Peñasco as frequently as 10 times a day. Photo courtesy of Guillermo Munro.

Cholla Bay is the largest foreign occupied residential development in Mexico. Americans such as the prominent Babbit family and Phoenix Mayor Skip Rimsa own beach homes in Cholla Bay.

Both of these photographs were taken from the same spot above Old Port looking toward Pelican Point near Cholla Bay in Rocky Point. The photo above (courtesy of Guillermo Munro) shows the New Cortéz Motel being built in the early 1940s. The old Hotel Peñasco (oblong building) can be seen in the upper right hand corner. The photo below shows the New Cortéz Motel remodeled and renamed the Viña Del Mar. In the center of the photograph is the Costa Brava Hotel and Restaurant which sits on the Malceon facing the ocean.

Behind The Wheel

The automobile-a walking stick; and one of the
finest things in life is going on a journey with it.
-Robert Holliday

Mexico Route 8 from Sonoyta to Puerto Peñasco is paved and maintained reasonably well. Caution signs warn of *vados* (dips) and others show a silhouette of a cow to warn of livestock. This stretch of roadway can be very busy on holidays and weekends. Drive with caution and use your headlights, even during the daylight hours. Construction was completed on the stretch of highway between Sonoyta and Puerto Peñasco to make this a two lane highway with wide shoulders. ***Please drive carefully***. Rules are very strict about drinking and driving. ***Don't do it***. Assign a designated driver before starting out.

A few small settlements are scattered along the 62 mile stretch of highway from Sonoyta to Puerto Peñasco. The only services provided are cold drinks and a tire repair shop on the left side of the roadway about half way between Sonoyta and Puerto Peñasco. Telephone service is not available. The speed limit along this stretch of highway is 80 kilometers or 50 miles per hour.

Once out of town you see desert country similar to the Arizona side. Fifteen miles south of the border you are still surrounded by rocky ridges and peaks. Vegetation is dense: organ pipe, senita, saguaro and Cholla cactus plus mesquite, creosote, ironwood and Palo Verde.

On the roadway, many Mexican drivers make an effort to help you out when you wish to pass. They use their lights as a signal. You can recognize these signs and use them yourself. When a left turn signal is used, it means *siga,* (safe to pass). A right turn signal means *alto,* (do not pass). The "Danger Ahead Of You" signal is given to oncoming cars by blinking the headlights or both turn signals in addition to honking the horn.

Puerto Peñasco has four stop lights but only two are used regularly. They are small and can easily be overlooked by mistake. Similarly, *ALTO* (stop signs) will appear in the most unlikely places and can be completely ignored by passing traffic. Casually running a stop sign can happen very easily, so pay attention and stay alert. Speed laws are pretty well maintained. Please respect the speed limit while driving anywhere in Mexico.

A word of caution in Puerto Peñasco. Highway patrolmen "hang out" on foot beneath the large shade tree on the south end of town waving down *turistas* who do not come to a complete stop at the railroad tracks. They also monitor speeds through the two school zones on each end of town. These zones are posted with signs in the center line just like in the United States.

What do you do when you are stopped? Act pleasant, determine what the problem is, and then decide whether to pay or not to pay. Generally, the policeman is right, you were speeding, or you did miss that stop sign. If this is the case, it is easier to bargain for the fine and be on your way. A fine of five or ten dollars and a promise to pay more attention next time is usually adequate settlement. Many patrolmen speak some English, so playing dumb is not recommended. You can also resolve the ticket with the policeman at the police station.

You may encounter a situation in which a *mordida* (bribe) is demanded. If you are charged with an offense that you are certain you did not commit, ask for documentation of the rule you violated. If necessary, ask to speak with someone with higher authority such as the Chief of Police.

What To Do In Case Of An Accident

Every accident is judged on its own merit. There are set fines for violations such as speeding, running stop signs, wrong way driving, etc.

You are taken to the police station if you get stopped for drunk driving. Paperwork is filled out and you will be charged from $45 to $80. If you are sent to appear in front of a judge, you may be expected to pay double and/or be sent to jail for two days. If you are found not guilty you will be allowed to leave.

Proper registration, titles, or proof of ownership for all vehicles, ATV's, boats and jet skis should be carried with you at all times.

Parking

Tickets are not issued in Mexico for parking violations. Your car is not towed away unless you are parked in a tow-a-way zone, but they may remove your license plates from the car. By removing the plates, it makes it very difficult to drive around without them. The only way to get them returned to you is by going to the nearest federal bank and obtain a receipt that shows you paid the fine. Take it to the central headquarters that houses all confiscated license plates and your plates will be returned. In Puerto Peñasco go to the police station.

Gas Stations

The selection is easy – PEMEX is the only selection. Several are located in the downtown area and one is located in the center of Old Port. Oil and gasoline prices are controlled by the government. There are several brands of oil including a number of American made brands. Mexican-produced brands are as good as their U.S. counterparts. *Pemex-Sol Special* is the only one sold in Puerto Peñasco.

Gas stations provide attendants to assist you. Gasoline in Mexico is sold as "unleaded" (*Magna Sin*) and "regular" (*Nova*). Prices fluctuate constantly like they do in the United States. Pump measurements are written in *litros* (liters), which is 0.26 of a gallon. Nineteen *litros* equal five gallons; 38 *litros* equal 10 gallons, and so on. You may also want to put the tanks capacity in liters on top of the gas cap or near the filler neck with paint or label tape.

Capacidad 40 litros (capacity 40 liters) which will let the attendant know what the capacity is.

Prices are usually posted by the door on the outside of the building or near the cashier in dollars per gallon. Diesel fuel is widely available and about one-third cheaper than regular or unleaded gasoline.

Shortages in fuel are unlikely, but stations do run out and pumps do go dry. It is advisable to buy gas before and after you cross the border. If you must purchase gasoline, your only concern is the price. You will find a complete list of gas stations in Chapter 11, Business Services.

Miles And Kilometers Conversion Chart

Kilometers to Miles		Miles to Kilometers	
1	0.62	1	1.61
2	1.24	2	3.22
3	1.86	3	4.83
4	2.48	4	6.44
5	3.1	5	8.05
6	3.72	6	9.65
7	4.34	7	11.26
8	4.96	8	12.87
9	5.58	9	14.48
10	6.2	10	16.09
20	12.4	20	32.18
25	15.5	25	40.23
50	31	50	80.45
100	62	100	160.9

Car Repairs And Servicing

The Green Angels or *Angeles Verde's* are green repair trucks that patrol all major routes in Mexico and drive the highway between the border and Puerto Peñasco from 8 a.m. to 8 p.m. daily. Each truck carries two English speaking mechanics who will help fix your car if they see you stranded along the roadway. The labor is free, but you must pay for parts or gasoline. They offer tourist information, first aid supplies, free towing and mechanic aid for your vehicle. To summon a Green Angel, pull off the roadway and lift the hood of your car. If you have a VHF or CB radio try reaching them on Channel 9 or 16.

If your car should break down, pull off the road on a flat, shrub-free surface. Set out flares or put rocks in the roadway, a universal sign of trouble ahead. Red Tecate beer cans, found in plentiful supply along most roadways, make excellent reflectors.

Raise your hood and stay with your car. You should always be prepared. Take plenty of supplies when traveling across the border. It is advisable to bring extra oil, water for drinking or radiator leaks, a tool box, flares, a flashlight, snacks, a small shovel, small portable tire pump, battery cables, and a tow rope.

Rough roads can play havoc with your car. Check your under body beforehand so you know where the low points are. If you puncture a gas tank, you can seal it by scraping a bar of soap across it to fill the hole. Don't carry your spare underneath the car or you may have no way of getting to it if you car gets stuck in soft terrain.

When driving through sand, don't hesitate or you will sink. Avoid downshifting if you can. It is best to lug your engine so the tires don't spin. Once stuck, as long as you have a pump, let the air out of your tires down to 10 psi. Wet the sand with buckets of water. Slide branches or rocks under the jacked up tire for additional traction.

If you are unfortunate enough to break down in Puerto Peñasco, you will find that the best garage may look like a nomad hut in the middle of a junk yard. Rest assured this is the normal way of things all over Mexico and appearances don't count in regard to the average mechanic.

The best way to find a reliable *mecánico* (mechanic) is to ask a local resident whom you have met. A gringo who lives in the area may have knowledge of someone dependable. You can contact the

> *Note:* Local mechanics dream about having a good set of automotive tools. Gringos have traded quality tools for repair jobs, saved money, and done the mechanic a favor.

Rocky Point Times Newspaper office for references. You may also refer to the mechanics listed below. Many mechanics learn their trade on heavy equipment and have years of experience.

Some precautions and procedures should be established if you need to have repairs and must take your car to a mechanic in Puerto Peñasco.

Always ask for an estimate before the work is started. Should there be major repairs, ask for a written estimate. *"¿Más o menos, cuánto va a costar?"* (More or less, how much will it cost?).

It is common to be asked to pay for parts in advance. Small garages operate on almost no overhead. Reconditioned parts are installed if new ones are not available, so be clear on what kind of part will be used. It is standard procedure to ask for a *recibo* (receipt) for purchased parts paid for in advance.

Stay in obvious attendance once work begins. If the owner is present the *maestro* will feel more obligated to do the work himself rather than delegate it to a young apprentice. Should you leave your car unattended, remove all valuables.

Garages will attempt to do almost any job – whether they have the knowledge or tools necessary to do it properly. Feel free to lend a hand or offer advice if you feel it necessary.

It is standard practice to siphon gas from the tank to clean parts. Check the car thoroughly to make sure the cap is on, the tank has gas, and the oil registers full.

Take the car for a test drive <u>before</u> you leave. The *maestro* will probably want to go along to see you are satisfied and won't leave without paying.

Don't hesitate to ask questions about repairs or what is listed on the final receipt which should include the labor and part charges. If your car poops-out after you have paid for a repair job, don't hesitate to return it to the shop and complain. Stay calm, most garages are apologetic and gracious when asked to make a job good.

Automotive And Boat Repair Businesses

Arizona Auto Repair Parts & Service, Blvd. Benito Juárez at the stoplight on Calle 20 Simón Morúa. Map B27.

Atlas Auto Parts, Ave San Luis south of Calle 22 downtown. General automotive repair, English spoken. Map A28.

Automobile Repair, Located across from the Corona distributor at #53 Constitucion. Pancho Flores, 011-52-638-32928. Fifty years experience specializing in sand buggies, VW's, Jeeps and older cars and trucks. Reasonable rates. English spoken (Recommended).

Autoservicio Baja 1000, Blvd. Fremont, 011-52-638-33370, 33313. General mechanics, auto parts, tire align and balance. Fuel injection service and car wash. Map D18.

Auto Parts, Ave 14 & Calle 21. Map B11.

Auto Servicio y Refaccionaria Sonora, Blvd. Benito Juárez No. 160, 011-52-638-32398, 32399. Auto parts, gas station, grease jobs, wheel alignment, and mechanic shop, guaranteed workmanship.

Comex Farreteria Mobil, Blvd. Benito Juárez & Calle 17 Melchor Ocampo. Auto parts and accessories. Map B46.

La Estrellita, Benito Juárez Blvd., 011-52-638-32726. Gas station, auto parts, electrical supplies, oil products. 24 hour service, since 1957. Map B26.

Peñasco Repair & Maintenance, office located in the Peñasco T-shirt Co. in Old Port. Kurt & Mary Yardley, 011-52-638-35286. English spoken. All types of repair on RV's, cars, trucks, motor homes, and water craft. Map F26.

Provedora de Pesca Superama, Blvd. Kino y Guillermo Prieto (one block from La Curva Restaurant), 011-52-638-33700. Motor boats, parts and fishing equipment. Yamaha dealer, wave runners, generators, outboards, spark plugs for ATC's and motorcycles.

Refacciones y Accesorios Sonoyta, Fray Eusebio Kino No. 108 in Sonoyta 011-52-651-21764. Blvd. Juárez y Ferrocarril in Puerto Peñasco 011-52-638-32676. Auto parts and mechanic shop, Juan Ruben Murillo, Manager.

Richie Auto Parts, Blvd. Benito Juarez & Calle 21. Map B4.

Rocky Point Tires, Blvd. Benito Juarez across from the high school two blocks south of Cholla Bay Road. Used tires for cars, trucks, ATV's. Sodas, ice, cigarettes, and fire wood.

Super Servicio Salcido Gas Station, heart of the city on main street, 011-52-638-21141, 011-52-638-11091. Auto parts and diesel fuel, open 24 hours. Map B37

Why

Joe Flores & Sons, Box 9788, Why, Arizona 85321, 520-387-9921, 5422. Towing and Mexican Insurance. Open 7 days a week.

Ajo

Napa Auto Parts, 2050 N. Highway 85, Ajo, Arizona 85321. Located 2 miles north of the red traffic light in the center of town, 520-387-6962, 6907. Monday to Friday 8:30 a.m. to 6:00 p.m., Saturday 9:00 a.m. to 3:00 p.m. 24 hour emergency parts and service. Small engine parts and supplies, auto and RV repair. Marine supplies. Reasonable prices and excellent service.

Recreational Vehicle Travel

Travel broadens the mind.
-Proverb

Many "snowbirds," as well as families, are finding that Puerto Peñasco is an ideal winter getaway. R.V. Parks with 200 plus spaces are nearly full from October to May. Many come from as far as Alaska, Canada, Oregon, Minnesota, and Wisconsin and stay as long as four or five months. You should make advance reservations if you are going to visit during the winter months. Rocky Point R.V. parks provide everything the traveler needs to live comfortably and cheaply. Ask for senior discounts if the park belongs to AARP or Good Sam Travel Club.

Recreational Vehicle Vacation Packages

Peñasco R.V. Club, 35 N. Elliott Road, Ajo, Arizona 85321. In the U.S. call, 1-800-850-9248, 520-387-7894. Our RV caravan trips are sure to take away the mystery and uncertainty of traveling to Mexico. Bring your own RV and we do the rest. Each trip is a Friday night through Sunday night trip.

Recreational Vehicle Parks

ON THE BEACH
Playa Bonita R.V. Park, next to Playa Bonita Hotel, 011-52-638-32586, 35566, 32199. 260 spaces located right on the beach, full hookups, showers, restrooms, use of recreation room with satellite TV, laundry room, crystal bottled water, boat ramp, billiards room. Map E21.

Playa De Oro Trailer Park, Between Las Olas Condos by the Pitahaya bar and north of Calle 1, 011-52-638-32668. 300 spaces located on the beach, complete hookups, showers, laundromat, recreation room, grocery store, restaurant, boat launching and storage. Good Sam Park. Map G24.

Playa Miramar Trailer Park, Matamoros & Campeche, Apdo. Postal #2, 011-52-638-32587, 32351. 100 camping spaces on the beach complete with hookups, laundry room, pure well water, ice available, showers, recreation room, restrooms, satellite TV hooked up to every space. Good Sam Park, AAA approved. Map G5.

Playa Elegante RV Resort, Apdo. Postal #101, Puerto Peñasco, Sonora, 83550. Located just east of the Pitahaya Bar, 011-52-638-33712. South of town on a beautiful shell beach, golf course with senior citizen discount on regular spaces, complete hookups, public telephone, pure well water, recreation hall, boat launching, satellite TV, clean and modern, laundromat, snack shop, sun deck, storage, ice, security. Senior citizen discount. Map G27.

Sunrise Executive RV Park, P.O. Box 625, Lukeville, Arizona. Located by Playa Miramar south of town, 011-52-638-34450, in U.S., 602-483-9307 or 602-540-2176. Only 16 spaces, short walk to the beach, swimming pool, Jacuzzi, laundry room, satellite receiver, recreation room, additional showers and restrooms, water, electricity and waste hookup, gravel base with patio and barbecue grills. Map G8

El Mirador Trailer Park, 011-52-638-33291, 32322, west of the Pitahaya Bar. Full hookups, laundry room, showers, billiards. Restaurant Mar De Cortéz and adjoining Buchanans Bar. English spoken. Map G23.

Local beach vendors sell jewelry, hats, blankets, food, hand-carved wood objects, and clothing. If they don't have what you want, they will find it for you, just ask!

NEAR THE BEACH

San Rafael RV Park, P.O. Box 58, east of Playa De Oro, 011-52-638-32681, 35044. New with all modern facilities open all year. Complete hookup, laundry, gift shop, showers (hot and cold), restrooms, barbecue pits, ice cubes, 24 hour security guard, management speaks English. Map G28

Señorial R. V. Park, north of the Playa de Oro R. V. Park on Calle 1, 011-52-638-33055. Map G21.

Recreational Vehicle Repair
(See Chapter 4 - Behind The Wheel)

Recreational Vehicle Storage
(See Chapter 11 - Business Services)

SIGNS TO WATCH FOR WHILE DRIVING IN MEXICO

Alto - Stop

Crucero pligroso - dangerous crossing

Cuidado - caution, careful

Cuidado con eltren - railroad crossing

Curva peligrosa - dangerous curve

Derecha - right

Izquierda - left

Despacio - slow

Desviación - detour

Direccion prohibida - no entry

Un solo sentido - one way street

Entrada - entrance

Estacionamiento prohibido - no parking

No obstruya la entrada - do not block entrance

Obras - road work

Parada - bus stop

Peatones - pedestrians

Peligro - danger

No rebase - no passing

No estacionarse - no parking

Prohibido entrar - do not enter

Zona azul - limited parking

ROAD SIGNS

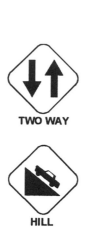 **TWO WAY**

 TRANSITION

 ROAD NARROWS

 NARROW BRIDGE

 SLIPPERY

 HILL

DIP

RAILROAD CROSSING

 WORKMEN

 SCHOOL

 SLIDE AREA

 SIGNAL

 **CATTLE**

 ALTO **STOP**

 CEDA EL PASO **YIELD**

 ADUANA **INSPECTION**

 100 MAXIMA **SPEED LIMIT (KM)**

 CIRCULACIÓN **ONE WAY**

 SOLO IZQ **LEFT TURN ONLY**

 CONSERVE SU DERECHA **KEEP RIGHT**

 DOBLE CIRCULACIÓN **TWO WAY**

NO **NO LEFT TURN**

NO REBASE **DO NOT PASS**

NO **DO NOT ENTER**

PARADA **BUS STOP**

 PRECAUCIÓN **SLOW DOWN**

1 Km **GAS STATION**

HOSPITAL

CAMPING

Sleeping Over

Hotel: A refuge from home life.
-George Bernard Shaw

Puerto Peñasco has a wide variety of comfortable hotels to choose from in all price ranges. The best bargains are found the farthest from the beach. They offer more personal service and better prices than their larger competitors who cater to *turistas.* Some of the newer hotels provide first class comfort. Remember, you are in Mexico so don't expect the same quality and service you find in the United States.

To really enjoy Mexico you can capture the ambiance by sleeping in a room with Mexican cement floors, miss-matched furniture, hand made tiles lining the bathroom and listening to Mariachi music filtering in through an open window. This is what traveling is all about – experiencing the unusual and different far away from home. By buying this book, you have already begun some important preliminary research. Now all you need to do is make the final decision.

Reservations are recommended, especially during holiday weekends. Many hotels and condos are reserved one year in advance. Sometimes the room rates are posted in the lobby. Ask if season discounts are available. If you have an advertisement to show that a discount is offered during the summer or winter months, the establishment will be more receptive to giving you the lower price. Mexicans think that all *gringos* are wealthy and can pay the full asking price. Effective bartering can sometimes help in getting a better rate.

The next thing you need to do is "check it out." Ask to look at the room before agreeing to take it. The Mexican people are very proud of their business and will make every effort to comply with your request for something larger, smaller, or away from traffic or noise.

Hot water is not always readily available, especially in the morning and evening hours. Sometimes the water is shut off because of problems or repairs. At times the water and electricity are turned off throughout town and lasts hours or days. I was settled into a condo for a week of sun and fun when the property manager notified me the unit needed to be hooked to an individual electrical meter. The electricity and water would be turned off for a few hours. Twenty-four hours later the electricity came back on, six hours after that the water was turned on. Be prepared for these types of inconveniences, it's the way of the land.

Reservation Agencies

Alberto's Reservations, P.O. Box 205, Lukeville, Arizona 85341, 011-52-638-35656. Condos, and beach front homes, at Playa Encanto, Peñasco Beach Club, Fiesta De Cortéz and Condominio Pinacate at the Marina Peñasco. Call or Fax. Map E18

Casa de Carolina Rentals, P.O. Box 589, Lukeville, Arizona 85341, 011-52-638-35482, in the U.S. call: 602-248-0007. Beach front condo's, ocean view apartments and R.V. spaces. English spoken.

Cindi's Sea of Cortéz Vacation Rentals and Property Management, located on the right as you enter town just north of the baseball stadium. P.O. Box 557, Lukeville, Arizona 85341, 011-52-638-35145. Rentals available every day of the week. A worry free vacation and worry free vacation property management.

Brooks Real Estate and Property Management Rentals, P.O. Box 785, Lukeville, Arizona 85341, located on Ave Armanda Nacional down from the Marina Peñasco resort, 011-52-638-35080, Fax: 011-52-638-35080. Dee Brooks broker and owner. Condos, homes, commercial and private land available. Map E32.

Oceano Rentals and Property Management, located on the fork of Ruiz and Blvd. Juarez as you enter Old Port. Lupe Lopez office manager, 011-52-638-35413, Charlie & Sue Salem, in the U.S. call 602-935-3152, Fax: 602-935-3152. Map F5.

Pathfinder Travel, Blvd. Benito Juarez No. 154-4D, 011-52-638-34420, Fax: 011-52-638- 34032. Travel agency and real estate advisors, airline reservations, hotel reservations, rental houses, tourist information. Map A16.

Rocky Point Rentals, Phone Tim Aikin, Phoenix, 602-860-0372.

Rocky Point Reservations, P.O. Box 87540, Phoenix, Arizona 85080. In the U.S. call 602-587-0345, or 1-800-42-ROCKY, Fax: 602-587-0344. Kim Harney. Established in 1987. Condos, hotels and motels on or near the beach.

Romantic Travel, Inc., 10833 N. 29th Drive, Phoenix, Arizona 85029. In the U. S call 602-789-9124, Fax: 602-789-9124. In Mexico call 011-52-638-35816. Ron & Marsha Kornegay. Rocky Point beach front homes in Las Conchas, Playa Encanto, Playa Navidad, Playa Dorada and Playa Miramar. Two, three and four bedroom private homes on the beach.

Servi Rents, Apdo. Postal #41, Puerto Peñasco, or P.O. Box 770, Lukeville, AZ 85341. 011-52-638-33225, Fax 011-52-638-33433. Servi Rents provides information on many rentals and property which is for sale in the Rocky Point area. Many are located in the Las Conchas community. Most rentals do not provide sheets and towels and a deposit is required. A listing of their properties is printed monthly, stop by their office during business hours. Map B48.

Travel Made Simple, Sue Schmidt, P.O. Box 14574, Tucson, Arizona 85732, in the U. S. call, 520-751-4425. All inclusive packages from Green Valley, Arizona.

Quick Reference for Hotels, Motels, Condos and Suites
Based on double occupancy per night

$	Budget	*$18 to $39*
$$	Moderate	*$40 to $90*
$$$	Costly	*$91 to $250*

On the Beach
$$$ - Condominio Pinacate, Map E28
$$$ - Plaza Las Glorias, Map E26
$$$ - La Casa Blanca, Las Conchas Community
$$$ - La Paloma Del Mar, Las Conchas Community
$$$ - Mar Brisas Resort, Map G4
$$$ - Peñasco Beach Club, E24
$$$ - Viva Casitas, Las Conchas Community
$$ - Las Olas Condos, Map G12
$$ - La Palapa Condominiums, Map G32
$$ - Playa Bonita, Map E19
$$ - Granada Del Mar, Map G26
$$ - Manny's Beach Club, Map G10
$$ - Hotel Vista Del Mar at Cholla Bay

Near the Beach
$$ - Playa Inn Suites, Map D31
$$ - Motel Señorial, Map E7
$$ - Fiesta de Cortéz, G3
$$ - La Palapa Condominiums, Map G32
$ - Playa Hermosa, Map E22
$ - Motel Playa Azul, Map E11
$ - Margaritavilla, Map G1

Old Port
$$ - Viña Del Mar, Map F56
$$ - Costa Brava, Map F55
$$ - Bella Vista Suites, Map F40

Downtown
$ - Paraiso Del Desierto, Map B8
$ - Mar Y Sol - North of Cholla Bay Road
$ - Posada De Leon, Map A3

$ - Hotel Villa Granada, Map C7

$ - Motel Davis - West of railroad station

$ - Motel Elisa - West of railroad station

$ - Hotel El Ranchito - North of Cholla Bay Road

ON THE BEACH

$$$ - **Condominio Pinacate,** next to the Plaza Las Glorias Hotel at the Marina Peñasco Resort at Playa Bonita beach. Contact Alberto's Reservations 011-52-638-35656, or Rocky Point Reservations at 1-800-42-ROCKY. One, two, three bedroom condominiums, two and three story villas available. Completely furnished, full kitchen facilities. Cable TV, stereo's, and VCR's in most units. Map E28.

$$$ - **Hotel Plaza Las Glorias,** on the Esplanade at the end of Calle 13. Turn right past the covered walkway, 011-52-38-36010, 36027, From the U.S. call 1-800-342-2644, Fax: 011-52-638-36015. Four star resort. One or two beds, rooms with balconies facing the ocean, pool, Jacuzzi, restaurant, bar, color satellite TV. Airline employee discounts may be available. Call the toll free number in advance. Map E26.

$$$ - **La Casa Blanca,** Las Conchas, 011-52-638-20061, in Arizona call, 602-991-1536. A little over 20 years ago the area now known as "Las Conchas" was developed, providing an exclusive guarded community surrounded by beach front serenity on the Sea of Cortéz. La Casa Blanca, "the white house" was one of the first homes constructed in the development. This palatial mansion is built on three contiguous lots and includes a massive Spanish courtyard and fountain with almost 200 feet of private sandy beach. Five bedroom suites with entrances to the courtyard, each with a fireplace and private bath. The lavish master suite has an elegant sunken tub, separate shower and private dressing area overlooking the ocean. The game room has a 52" television with satellite programming and a stereo system. Complete kitchen, large dining room and separate bar. A huge patio with two palapas, two cooking areas with gas grills and two heated Jacuzzi spas.

$$$ - La Paloma Del Mar an Oceanfront Estate, Las Conchas. Realty Network, 19848 N. Cave Creek Road, Phoenix, Arizona 85024. In the U.S. call 602-569-1125, Fax: 602-569-2399. You can create your own dream vacation, corporate retreat, or wedding at La Paloma Del Mar by renting the entire estate or a single guest house. The estate consists of a main house with 3 bedrooms and 3 half baths, and 3 separate guest homes. Amenities include walled tennis court, 5 miles of sandy beach, basketball court, barbecue grill, beach volleyball and putting green with a view. Filtered water is offered to all homes. Optional services can include: telephone and fax service, catering and kitchen or housekeeping staff.

$$$ - Mar Brisas Resort, Ave. Campeche Y Matamoros, near Manny's Restaurant. P.O. Box 559, Lukeville, Arizona 85341, 011-52-638-32785. Nestled next to the cliff above the beach, this resort provides spectacular views, ocean views, and security guard. Close to the fish market, dining establishments and R.V. parks. Town homes offered for rent. Upstairs: Sunken living room, fireplace, TV, fully equipped kitchen, half bath and balcony, master bedroom with king-size bed, TV, full bath. Downstairs: Bedroom with two twin beds, full bath, family room with queen size sofa bed, sliding glass door entrance. Linens and towels supplied, VCR available, air conditioning, (up to 4 guests). Refundable deposit required.
Sales information - Retirement living, investment purchase or income potential. 1700 square feet of living area. Washer/dryer hookups. Ownership guaranteed through a bank trust. Resort fees, $75 per month includes water and night security guard. Unfurnished, furnished, terms available. Map G4.

$$$ - Peñasco Beach Club, Paseo Balboa & Calle Mar de Cortéz, next to the Plaza Las Glorias Hotel on Sandy Beach. P.O. Box 245, Lukeville, Arizona 85341, 011-52-638-35656, 34268, Fax: 011-52-638-33374. Map E18.

$$$ - Viva Casitas Condos, P.O. Box 12833, Scottsdale, Arizona 85267. In the U.S. call 602-788-8580. George Cullom. The

Casitas were originally built as individual, vacation rental homes. Four Casitas, side by side, located in the private community of Las Conchas about one hundred feet from the beach. Each bedroom has a king size bed, all bedrooms and bathrooms are the same size. All supplies are furnished including linens, towels, soap, kitchen utensils, pots and pans, coffee maker, blender, toaster and barbecue. Kitchen has a small refrigerator and 3-burner stove/oven.

$$ - **Las Olas Condos,** next to Manny's Beach Bar. Managed by Roger Weiland, P.O. Box 152, Puerto Peñasco, 011-52-638-32565. 33808. Beach front patios with barbecue's. Clean, comfortable, close to restaurants and bars. Two bedroom, two bath with kitchen. Map G12.

$$ - **La Palapa Condominiums,** P.O. Box 646, Lukeville, Arizona 85341, 011-52-638-33866, in the U.S. call: 602-866-2419, 602-993-3686. Beautiful ocean view 2 story, 2 bedroom, 2 bath units including fireplace and fully equipped with everything you need for a relaxing visit. Community palapas, barbecue, coin-op laundry. Weekly rates available. Map G32.

$$$ - **Playa Bonita,** Paseo Balboa No. 100, P.O. Box no. 282, 011-52-638-32586, in Arizona call 602-994-4475. Located on Playa Bonita beach. Restaurant Puesta del Sol is open for breakfast, lunch, and dinner. Happy hour every day on the patio. Air conditioning, color TV satellite system, carpeted rooms, and a fresh water pool. Ocean view rooms with one or two queen beds. Make reservations in advance to guarantee a room. Map E19.

$$ - **Granada Del Mar,** Ave Michoacan Apdo. Postal 278, Puerto Peñasco, 83550. Right on the beach next to the Pitahaya Bar. Roberto Fleischer manager, 011-5-638-32742. Double beach front rooms with or without kitchen. Map G26.

$$ - **Mannys Beach Club,** Ave Coahuila y Calle 1, right on the beach next to the Miramar R.V. park, 011-52-638-35497, Fax: 011-

52-638-35481. Office location on main Blvd. Benito Juarez at the corner of 12th street next door to the office of Rocky Point Times. Map G10.

$$ - Hotel Vista Del Mar at Cholla Bay, on a hill overlooking the ocean above Tucson beach, 011-052-638-34373. Go to JJ's Cantina to inquire about rooms. Fourteen rooms right on Tucson Beach are large and clean, bedspreads and drapes need replacing. Picnic tables on every balcony, indoor-outdoor carpeting is torn and worn. All rooms require key deposit.

NEAR THE BEACH
$$ - Playa Inn Suites, off Fremont Blvd. on Sinaloa, 011-52-638-35015, Fax: 011-52-638-35016, in the U.S. 1-800-952-8426, in Arizona 602-899-3722. Just a short walk to the beach. Convenient and close to shopping, deep sea fishing, jet skiing, the fish market and boat harbor. Offers two room suites. The two bedroom suite has two queen beds, in the living room area there is a comfortable sofa sleeper plus a full kitchen including a refrigerator, stove, microwave oven, coffee maker, and hair dryer. Swimming pool and restaurant. Enjoy a complimentary continental breakfast and afternoon "social hour" daily. Map D31.

$$ - Motel Señorial, turn right at the overpass light, cross tracks, two blocks past traffic light, on the left side of street, 011-52-638-32329, 32065, 32120, Fax: 011-52-638-33055. For information and reservations in the U.S. call Amigo Enterprises 602-933-3300. Color satellite TV, 72 air conditioned rooms, telephones, swimming pool, restaurant, and bar. Map E7.

$$ - Fiesta de Cortéz Suites and Hotel, 9414 E. San Salvador, Ste. 204-12, Scottsdale, Arizona 85258. For reservations call Fiesta Beach Travel 1-800-713-6259, Fax: 602-860-1343. "A pleasant encounter with nature in a comfortable atmosphere, ideal for a relaxing vacation." Suites are fully equipped with kitchenettes, spacious dining-living rooms, king size beds, 2 twin beds, and satellite color TV's. Enjoy the semi-Olympic swimming pool, and restaurant with sport club and bar. Close to the beach. Map G3.

$$ - **La Palapa Condominiums,** Les & Pat Foss, P.O. Box 646, Lukeville, Arizona 85341, 011-052-638-33866, in Arizona call 602-866 2419, or 993 3646. Just past the municipal building at the Banamex bank building stay to the left. Follow the street to the top of the hill and turn left at the Casa de Carolina sign, go one block. Featuring two bedrooms, two baths, kitchen and dining room, living room with fireplace, ocean view terrace, central heat and air conditioning, and private garage. Map G32.

$ - **Playa Hermosa,** Turn right at the overpass light, cross tracks, to the top of the hill on your left just east of the Plaza Las Glorias Hotel. 34 air conditioned rooms. Map E22.

$ - **Motel Playa Azúl,** Turn right at the overhead light, cross the railroad tracks, on your right past the stop light, 011-52-638-36296. New motel with 24 rooms, one city block from Sandy beach. Air conditioning and television. Map E11.

$ - **Margaritavilla, The Pirate Diver's Den,** Ave 10 Campeche, on the way to Playa Miramar, 011-52-638-35344. Open Friday, Saturday and Sunday 7:00 a.m. to 1:00 a.m., Monday to Thursday from 11:00 a.m. to 1:00 a.m. Cheap drinks, good food, classic rock, Reggae, darts, foozball, and Ping-Pong. The second oldest building in town. These buildings once housed the town jail and the original home of The Crystal Palace, Puerto Peñasco's place of legal prostitution. Now a small hotel, bar and restaurant, rooms go for $20 per night with air conditioning, carpeted floors and bared windows. Restrooms and showers are located down the sidewalk in the center corner of the L-shaped building. Map G1.

OLD PORT
$$ - **Hotel Viña Del Mar,** Ave 1ero Junio, Old Port, 011-52-638-33600, 33601, 33602, Fax: 011-52-638-33714. One of the first

hotels built in Peñasco. Right on the cliff ledge, overlooking the Sea of Cortéz. Maria Restaurant, comfortable accommodations, sea pool, swimming pool and Jacuzzi, boutique and gift shop. No sandy beach area but this hotel is located right on the edge of the shopping and restaurant area of Old Port. Double beds, single beds, ocean side junior suite with two double beds and living room available. Large groups and conventions welcome. Visa and Mastercard honored. Map F56.

$$ - **Costa Brava**, Malecón Fundadores y Paseo V. Estrella, on the waterfront in Old Port, 011-52-638-34100, 33130. From the comfort of your hotel balcony, view the beautiful sunsets of Rocky Point. Three stories, air conditioned, telephone and satellite TV, no sandy beach. Bar and restaurant. Map F55.

$$ - **Bella Vista Suites**, Old Port, 011-52-638-32007, in Arizona call, 602-587-0345. Ask about our mid-week specials. Fantastic ocean panorama from a huge rooftop patio. Beautiful clean rooms complete with kitchens, dishes and everything you need for a do it yourself weekend. Just bring yourself. Map F40.

DOWNTOWN
$$ - **Hotel Paraiso del Desierto**, Constitución and Simón Morúa, as you enter Puerto Peñasco from Lukeville, turn right at the second stop light in the middle of town. The back of the hotel faces the railroad tracks, in Tucson, 520-293-6139 from 6:00 a.m. to 10:00 p.m., 011-52-638-32175, 36175, 32818, Fax: 011-52-638-35272 P.O. Box 463, Lukeville, AZ 85341, 1700 W. Prince Rd. 1028, Tucson, Arizona 85705. Satellite TV in every room, 67 air conditioned single or double bedrooms and suites. The Galeón restaurant is located near the lobby. Separate adult and children's swimming pools. Two twin beds with 2 persons, queen size beds, two full beds, two queen size beds, suites. Children over 12 count as an adult. The rooms around the pool area can be noisy. Ask for something in the next building on the second floor or toward the back. Clean, comfortable, and newly remodeled. Restaurant on the property. Map B8.

$$ - **Motel Mar Y Sol,** The first motel entering Puerto Peñasco on the left side of Highway 94 about 2 miles north of town, 011-52-638-33188, 33190. Air conditioned units and charcoal broiler area for outdoor cooking. Sports bar upstairs.

$ - **Posada Del León Motel,** López Mateos, in front of the Parque de Beisbol on your left as you enter town from Lukeville, 011-52-638-33997, 33445. 24 hour desk service, clean, air conditioned rooms and suites, satellite and color TV, restaurant and bar available. Single (1 double bed), double (2 double beds), one suite with kitchenette. Map A3.

$ - **Hotel Villa Granada,** Ave Francisco I. Madero, turn left just before the overhead walkway light, 2 blocks west, 011-52-638-32775, in Arizona call 602-993-3646. This old two story inn looks like something out of a John Wayne movie. Built around the 1950's, it's ambiance is typical Mexico. The restaurant has been opened up into a bar overlooking a new pool. Air conditioning and heat, large rooms, 3 apartments, restaurant, lounge, and pool table available. With all of it's grace, this hotel is rundown. Map C7.

$ - **Motel Davis,** Calle 14, turn right at overhead walkway, cross railroad tracks, turn right at the light, turn left at the first street, hotel is on the left, 011-52-638-34314. Recommended for the budget traveler, quiet street, tile floors, hot water, very clean, sheets and bedspread smell of soap and bleach. Mattresses are lumpy so roll out a sleeping bag to smooth out the dips. The air conditioning unit was noisy and not efficient enough to cool.

$ - **Motel Elisa,** West side of downtown area. Small, local family-owned hotel, clean, hot running water. Doubles, some rooms have extra single beds.

$ - **Hotel El Ranchito,** Artículo 123 & Francisco Márquez, turn right at Cholla Bay Road, one block west turn right, one block north, 011-52-638-35103, in Arizona call, 602-231-0621. Owned and operated by the Nuñez family. This quaint two story hotel has an enclosed courtyard with bougainvillea covered patios. Clean with swamp coolers and fans, doubles and triples.

SONOYTA

Motel Excelsior, Blvd. De Las Americas 40, in the center of the shopping district in downtown Sonoyta, 011-52-638-21041, 21044, 21045, 21049. The best motel in town. Satellite color TV, telephone in each room, swimming pool. Double with two. Restaurant next door. Map I12.

Motel San Antonio, Blvd. De Las Americas 35, across from the monument at the "triangle" in the center of the business district, 011-52-638-21027, 21548. Newer hotel, clean and comfortable. Map I15.

Motel Sol Del Diesierto, Blvd. De Las Americas 11, 011-52-638-21189. Map I94

The new four star Plaza Las Glorias Resort, completed in 1996, sits on the edge of Sandy Beach in the center of Rocky Point.

Eateries

*To eat what you don't want, drink what you don't like
and do what you'd rather not.*

-Mark Twain

One of the greatest pleasures in this small town is the abundance of gourmet food. Puerto Peñasco offers an incredible range not only in what to eat, but where to eat. I have been known to plan a trip just to nibble nachos at a small shack on the beach during sunset, or lose myself over a plate of chicken tacos smothered in guacamole and three kinds of salsa that squeezes out over my fingers when I take that first enticing bite. I encounter many enjoyable surprises by being adventurous. My best advice is to search out the unfamiliar. This is the town in which to do it.

Choosing The Right Place

Depending on your mood and the type of atmosphere you are looking for, selecting a place to dine can be a challenge. There are many good restaurants to choose from and new ones are opening every month.

Menus are usually posted outside the door, feel free to look at the menu before being seated. Although many *meseras* (waitresses) speak English, translations are usually entered next to the Spanish version with the prices listed in pesos and in dollars. You can pay for your meal with U.S. dollars.

The most common type of restaurant is the *lonchería* or *comedor* that provides a constant output of good, inexpensive food. Usually lacking in atmosphere, comfort and fast service, they have a view of the street or a parking lot. This type of restaurant is the most reasonable choice for the adventuresome budget traveler.

Fondas are eating stalls found around a market, on the edge of a carnival and on the city streets. In Puerto Peñasco these *fondas* appear along the main street downtown and in Old Port. These eateries are very economical. In the early afternoon and evening, business is brisk. Tables, chairs, and tourists appear out of nowhere. Local families eagerly cook chicken, beans, soup, and *tacos* served with bowls full of condiments to accompany your favorite "comestibles." If you are apprehensive about eating at these *fondas,* check out the other customers. If you see the *gringos* that were sitting next to you on the beach devouring plates of food with enthusiasm, by all means go ahead and enjoy.

Drinking Water Is Purified

Yes! You can drink the water served in restaurants!

There are eight water purification plants in Puerto Peñasco. The water provided in the bars and restaurants is purified, so drink and enjoy. The system of administration in Mexico is educating food vendors in the rites and rituals of sanitation.

Nasty bacteria can be picked up in any restaurant, inside or outside the country. The current theory is that the bacteria living inside a person's body have adapted to their owner. Your bacteria doesn't travel well away from home and becomes subjected to a new type of bacteria. Unfortunately, during the adaptation process, which can span from a few days to a few weeks, travelers may not feel as robust as usual. This is one of the gambles of being away from home. If the risk is too much for you then restrict your range of traveling and carry a cooler filled with *gringo* food.

A good rule of thumb; if the place is full of customers hungrily diving into their food, and savory odors bring eager rumbles from your stomach, it's probably a good place to eat. Many of the hotels have restaurants which provide good budget meals.

In Old Port near the fish market you will find the higher priced *tourista* seafood restaurants. Compared to the United States, these restaurants serve memorable meals for surprisingly reasonable prices. Besides being inundated with food smells, there seems to be a constant state of pandemonium. Tourists chatter while pitchers of Margaritas steep on the table, waiters slip on discarded limes rushing from the kitchen with steaming plates of flounder, sautéed shrimp, fish *tacos*, and smothered sea scallops. I have always watched in awe at this wild, private *fiesta* and wonder if this is always the normal mealtime hubbub.

Tipping

Tipping in Puerto Peñasco is the same as it is in the United States. Tips of 10 to 15 percent are recommended. A Tax of 10 percent is added to all food bills. In Mexico, service charges are seldom added to the hotel, restaurant, or bar bills. But as tourism grows, this policy may change – ask your waitress. Waiters, maids, porters, and other workers whose wages are low must rely on tips for their living. Among the few exceptions are taxi drivers, who aren't tipped unless they have performed some special service.

Test Those Taste Buds

If you are open to trying new foods that are uniquely different you will find the food in Puerto Peñasco tasty and very enjoyable After years of traveling throughout Mexico, I'm still learning about new foods and flavors. If this is your first visit, you could be overwhelmed by the variety of dishes that are offered.

Most *turistas* think in terms of *tacos, enchiladas* and *chili rellenos* the way they are served at Taco Bell. Don't make the mistake of ordering the same thing all the time. Ask your English speaking *mesero* (waiter) to make a recommendation or explain certain foods you're not familiar with. The fun in traveling, is exploring and trying new things.

An incredible amount of time goes into the preparation of many local dishes. A *mole* sauce can take up to a week to prepare and contains 35 different ingredients. *Maíz* (corn), worshipped by the Aztecs and cultivated for about 4,000 years, is considered the "staff of life" in Mexico. From *maíz,* many popular dishes are prepared.

Tortillas are round cooked cakes of corn meal or flour ranging in size from a few inches to the dimension of a small pizza. In many *fondas* you see women rolling, patting and frying them by hand. It's a long, hot, and toilsome task that occupies many waking hours. The process entails soaking kernels of corn in lime water to form a hominy which is ground into a *masa* (paste) shaped into a ball and patted by hand into *tortillas,* which are cooked on a metal griddle.

I prefer the corn tortilla when dining on tacos, but you will find flour tortillas used more often in local dishes in Puerto Peñasco. *Tortillerías* (*tortilla* factories) are located around town. My favorite is in Sonoyta a couple doors to the right of the *Licores y Curios Vásquez* shop at the "triangle." My trip is not complete unless I purchase a couple dozen (about $2.00) to eat at home. If they are frozen the same day, then removed from the freezer as needed and heated in the microwave for 15 seconds, they taste as if they came right from the grill. *Tortillas* are not only cheap but turn a simple plate of beans and chilies into a nourishing and healthy meal. Learn to use *tortillas* as eating utensils. It is proper to use your fingers and tear them apart, filling them with meat and beans to make *tacos.*

Frijoles (beans) are served with almost every meal, even breakfast. Local women always have a pot of *frijoles* sitting on the stove. When combined with *tortillas,* the balance is complete protein. They are filling and will hold you for hours.

Carne (beef), also known as *bistec,* or *bistek,* a general term for steak. Some of the better restaurants around the fish market serve quality meats combined with fresh seafood.

Huevos (eggs) dishes are common and always temptingly good, when scrambled eggs are combined with meats, vegetables and chilies. *Huevos con chorizo* are eggs mixed with sausage which have a spicy strong greasy taste. My all time favorite is *huevos rancheros.* Two eggs served ranch style, sunny side up, placed on *tortillas* and smothered with sauce accompanied by beans and more *tortillas* for "scooping." The sauce can be red or green combined with onion and garlic. This delectable, savory dish is very filling and can curb hunger pangs for hours. *Huevos estrellados* are eggs sunny side up. *Huevos fritos duros* are eggs fried hard, usually dripping in butter and somewhat greasy. *Torta de huevos* are omelets and *Chilaquiles* are a type of omelet with many variations which can be quite spicy.

Chile (chili) is a very important and popular food. Usually served fresh, dried, pickled, cooked or raw in sauces, stews, soups, desserts, and mixed drinks. Chilies are hot peppers and are prepared in various ways. If you're bold, by all means try the many delicious sauces that are customarily served with meals. Many who add chili to their food eventually become very fond of it. If you are requesting the kind of chili sauce found in the United States, ask for *salsa or salsa picante* (hot sauce).

Queso (cheese) is sold under familiar names like: Camembert, Gouda, Parmesan, etc. The Mormon immigrants introduced one of the most well known cheeses called *Chihuahua* which is pale in color and tastes like mild cheddar. It keeps well without refrigeration but should be kept wrapped properly in paper or cloth. *Quesillo* is a white stringy cheese, usually served hot with tortillas as an appetizer. It is very filling and can be combined with a plate of nachos for a hearty meal.

Quick Reference for Restaurants
Based on single meal orders without beverages or appetizers

$	*Budget*	*$3 and under*
$$	*Moderate*	*$4 to $7*
$$$	*Costly*	*$8 and up*

On the Beach
$$$ - Cafe Plaza, Plaza Las Glorias, Map E26
$$$ - Puesta Del Sol, Playa Bonita Hotel, Map E20
$$$ - Gamma's, Map E17
  $$ - Manny's Beach Club, Map G11
   $ - JJ's Cantina, Cholla Bay
   $ - Rottweiler Bar & Grill, Map F50

Near the Beach
$$$ - Happy Frog, Map G13
$$$ - Pink Cadillac, Map G22
$$$ - Cocodrilos Bar & Grill, Map E23
$$$ - Restaurant El Mar, Señorial Hotel, Map E7
$$$ - Villa Las Palmas, Map E12

$$$ - Baja Willie's, Map G31
$$ - Marichi's, Fiesta Cortéz Hotel, Map G3
$$ - Margaritavilla, Map G1
$$ - Rocky Garden, Map G19
$$ - Mariscos Kenos, Map E51
$$ - Restaurant Tropics, Map G6
$ - Playa Hermosa, Map E22
$ - Licores Brisa La Ranita, Map D19
$ - Expresso Express, Map G9

Old Port

$$$ - La Casa Del Captain, Map F61
$$$ - Lily's, Map F41
$$$ - El Delfin Amigable, Map F9
$$$ - Bonita Maria, Map F57
$$$ - Costa Brava, Map F55
$$$ - Latitude 31, Map D31
$$ - Senior Amigo, Map F62
$$ - Old Port Deli and Restaurant, Map F20
$$ - Roberto's Italian Broiler, Map F47
$$ - Mariscos Kenos, Map F51
$$ - Blue Marlin Seafood & Smokehouse, Map F38
$$ - La Cita, Map F43
$$ - Cheiky's Pizza, Map F46
$$ - Danny's, Map F30
$ - Thrifty Ice Cream, Map F36

Downtown

$$$ - Mr Amigo, D29
$$$ - Posada De Leon, Map A3
$$ - La Fabula Pizza, Map B101
$$ - Mama Lusia, Villa Granada Hotel, Map C5
$$ - Aztlan, Map C26
$$ - La Curva, Map C22
$$ - Galeón, Paraiso Del Desierto Hotel, Map B8
$$ - Rocky Point Restaurant, Chinese Food
$$ - Restaurant Playas del Rey Map C21
$ - Asadero Sinaloa, Map A7
$ - Cenadura Zanitzito
$ - Asadero Sonora
$ - Neveria Zygle, Map B20

$ - La Flor De Michoacan, Map B109/A25
$ - Pollo Giro
$ - My Javy's Burgers, B29
$ - Pepeos II, Map A2
$ - Hansel Ice Cream, Map E9

Cholla Bay
$ - JJ's Cantina

Sonoyta
$$ - Excelsior Cafe, Map H12
$$ - Mr. Blaynes Restaurant, Map H92
$$ - Restaurant Bar Cimarron, Map H14
$$ - Restaurant San Antonio, Map H15
$$ - Restaurant Tierra Del Sol, Map H11

ON THE BEACH

$$$ - **Cafe Plaza Restaurant,** Plaza Las Glorias Hotel. One of the finest restaurants in Puerto Peñasco. Dine inside or outside. Menu offers shrimp cocktails, seafood embarcadero, homemade soups, salads, sandwiches and desserts. Chicken breasts are served breaded, barbecued, or covered with cheese. Fish is grilled, baked or stuffed with fresh seafood. Meats are quality cuts accompanied by a baked potato and side of vegetables. The medallion filet melts in your mouth. House specialties are offered daily. If a large tour group is in town, the restaurant offers an extensive buffet which is well worth the price. This restaurant offers an extensive wine list. Order by the bottle or glass. Quality champagnes and Dom Perignon wine are also available. Map E26.

$$$ - **Restaurant Puesta del Sol,** in the Playa Bonita hotel. Two levels facing the ocean, dining inside or outside for lunch or dinner. True Spanish architecture with high beamed ceilings, solid wooden tables and chairs with lime green accents. The restaurant is usually busy. Reservations are not necessary. Two of my favorite appetizers are: *Nachos*, (a meal in itself), smothered with cheese, salsa and guacamole, and the *Queso fondido* consisting of melted cheese served with soft tortillas and Mexican hot sauces. Menu selections

include three different types of baked oysters, *Calamares en su Tinta* (broiled squid with juice and herbs). Grilled seafood, steaks, and one of the best Mexican food combination plates south of the border. An all you can eat breakfast buffet is served on Saturday and Sunday mornings until 11:00 a.m. Chefs prepare omelets, *huevos rancheros*, fried or scrambled eggs to your liking, accompanied by bacon, ham, *frijoles*, pancakes, fruit compote, cereals, muffins, *tortillas*, fresh fruits, juice, and coffee. Map E20.

$$$ - Gama's, in *"La Explanada"* right on the beach next to the Plaza Las Glorias Hotel on the Esplanade. This family-owned restaurant has been serving quality seafood for years. Don't be turned off by the wood frame structure, picnic tables and sand floor. A meal here can be a meal to remember. You can order a fresh and flaky fried fish by the pound served with salsa and corn tortillas. Seafood specialties. Map E17.

$$ - Manny's Beach Club Inn Restaurant and Bar, Ave Cohauila y Calle 1, on the beach, 011-52-638-33605. American, Mexican and Seafood cuisine, with a wide variety to choose from. Indoor and outdoor bar and restaurant services available. The patio is thatched covered with a sand and shell floor. Needless to say this place is "laid back." Many *gringos* frequent this establishment. A sign on the wall says, "If our food/drink are not up to your standards - please lower your standards. No shoes, no shirt, no problem!" A bandstand provides a variety of entertainment. Map G11.

$ - JJ's Cantina, Cholla Bay. Always obliging with food or drink. Tacos, burgers and fast food.

$ - Rottweiler Bar and Grill, on the waterfront in Old Port. Come in and see the painted jungle and enjoy the sunset from our terrace. Burgers and hot-dogs cooked over an open grill. Map F50.

NEAR THE BEACH

$$ - Happy Frog Seafood, Calle 1 behind Las Olas Condos near Playa Miramar. Bring your appetite and be prepared for a feast if you dine here. This restaurant has the biggest shrimp and seafood dinners in town. Cooked to perfection; grilled, fried, baked, covered in coconut or served in foil with vegetables. All dinners include hot minestrone soup, home made coleslaw, rice and potatoes. Two or more orders of the seafood combination are served at your table "home style." Mexican food combinations are also available. Dine inside or outside on the upper balcony. Beer and mixed drinks are available. Map G13.

$$$ - Pink Cadillac Cantina & Cadillac Lounge, Playa Miramar on Calle 1 just north of the El Mirador R. V. Park, 011-52-638-35880. Decor from the 50's done in pink and black, checkered tile floor with pictures of Cadallac's surrounding the dining area. Lunch includes fries or potato salad featuring burgers, dogs sandwiches and fried chicken. Happy hour from 4 p.m. to 7 p.m. Dinner includes soup or salad, baked or fried potatoes from steak, fish and chicken. If you're hungry for something from home, this is the place. Map G22.

$$$ - Cocodrilos Bar & Grill, on Calle 13 on the left as you enter the Hotel Plaza Las Glorias complex, 011-52-638-36376. Terrace dining. International food, Mexican specialties, flavored margaritas, beer and wine. Map E23.

$$$ - Restaurant El Mar, the lobby of the Motel Señorial, Calle 13, on the way to Playa Hermosa, an art deco type building, 011-52-638-32065. Specialty is Chinese from Wanton soup, red barbecue beef to shrimp tempura. Also included are Mexican, American and seafood specialties. Banquet facilities available. Breakfast, lunch and dinner served. Take out available. Map E7.

$$$ - Villa Las Palmas Restaurant, Calle 13, Ave 6 across from Motel Señorial one block from the beach, 011-52-638-33951. The owners, Mike and Cindy greet, seat, and serve patrons. Have a cold draft beer or Margarita at the bar watching cable sports or sit in the dining room and feast on local delicacies. Mexican and American food with seafood specialties. Open for breakfast. Evening specials offered during the week. Map E12.

$$$ - Baja Willie's, located in the Playa Inn. Breakfast, lunch and dinner. Mexican and American food. Try the Cajun specialties. Map G31.

$$ - Mariachi's Restaurant, Fiesta De Cortéz Hotel. This restaurant has changed names more than any other establishment in Puerto Peñasco and still operates. Mexican, fish, chicken and beef. Breakfast, lunch and dinner. Map G3.

$$ - Margaritavilla, The Pirate Diver's Den, Ave 10 Campeche toward Playa Miramar, 011-52-638-35344. Open Friday, Saturday and Sunday 7:00 a.m. to 1:00 a.m., Monday to Thursday from 11:00 a.m. to 1:00 a.m. Cheap drinks, good food, classic rock, Reggae, darts, foozball, and Ping-Pong. The second oldest building in town. These buildings once housed the town jail and the original home of The Crystal Palace, Puerto Peñasco's place of legal prostitution. Cook your own or have the bartenders cook for your. Outside grill and seating. T-bone and rib-eye steaks, shrimp on a skewer, chicken, served with baked potato and salad. Hamburgers and hot dogs for smaller appetites. All drinks $1.00 except for Rick's special rum drink which is $2.00. A great place to relax and feel like you're at home. Map G1.

$$ - Rocky Garden, on Calle 1 in front of the R.V. parks at Miramar Beach, 011-52-638-35442. Breakfast, lunch, and dinner from 7:00 a.m. until 1:00 a.m. Summer hours Friday, Saturday, and Sunday only from 7:00 a.m. to 11:00 p.m. Breakfast huevos rancheros, shrimp rancheros, omelets, pancakes, and American favorites cooked to your specifications. Appetizers, salads, soups, seafood, Mexican, barbecue steaks, burgers, sandwiches, deserts, ice cream, fried ice cream and pumpkin moose pie. The shrimp salad is cheap and awesome! Meals served with chips, salsa and guacamole dip. The restaurant has its own reverse osmosis water purification system so all dishes are prepared with purified water. Dine inside or on the patio under the sun or stars. Sports bar located upstairs with a big screen TV. Happy hour 3-6 p.m. with free appetizers. Map G19.

$$ - **Mariscos Kenos,** on the road to Playa Hermosa, front restaurant "Villa Las Palmas." Hails itself as the best fresh seafood in town with low prices. Oysters, fish, shrimp, squid, snails, clams, red snapper, octopus, and Mexican halibut. Map E51.

$$ - **Restaurant Tropics,** Calle 1 across from the Sunrise R.V. Park. Happy hour specials, open from 7 a.m. to 11 p.m. Map G6.

$ - **Playa Hermosa,** behind the Plaza Las Glorias Hotel, 011-52-638-32576. Breakfast menu only. On a moments notice, "grandma" is ready to whip up anything you request. Map E22.

$ - **Licores Brisa La Ranita,** next to the liquor store and Baja 1000 on the Blvd. Fremont. Hot dogs, tortas, nachos, and drinks to go. Map D19.

$ - **Expresso Express,** next to Restaurant Tropics on Calle 1 at Playa Miramar, 011-52-638-34098. Jump start your day with a gourmet cafe, espresso and cappuccino at the beach. Gourmet coffee and tea, breakfast, lunch and desserts, Hawaiian shaved ice, tacos, and baby back pork ribs. Dinner by reservation. Curb service on the beach. Here or to go, call orders ahead. Map G9.

OLD PORT
$$$ - **La Casa del Captain,** in Old Port perched behind Viña de Mar Hotel on top of the point, 011-52-638-35698. The García family spent three years building this beautiful stucco and marble, Spanish style, two story home and restaurant. Dine on the verandah during the day or in the evening, overlooking the sea. Windows

and doors are arched, fanlights with beam ceilings accentuate the rose, tan, cream and rust accent colors blended with white. Serving meals fit for a king or queen, the Garcia's have been in the restaurant business for over twenty years. Their dishes are culinary delights. Mexican combos, house specialties with soup or salad, dishes from the sea. If you want a tasty, filling meal while watching the sunset overlooking the bay, this is the place. The entrance is a dirt road, located below the restaurant sign on the road to Old Port. Map F61.

$$$ - **Lily's,** across from the fish market in Old Port on the *Malecon*, 011-52-638-32510. Open daily from 7:00 a.m. till 11:00 p.m. Chili's are baked, stuffed with cheese and shrimp then smothered with a light delicate white sauce which takes all day to prepare. Served on the side are fresh steamed vegetables and rice. These plates of steaming food are like a work of art. Appetizers are served with all meals. Cocktails, beer and wine available. Gourmet meals, Mexican, American and seafood, desserts, fried ice cream special recipe, and appetizers. Breakfast, lunch and dinner. Visa and Mastercard accepted. Map F41.

$$$ - **El Delfin Amigable,** Ave Alcantar No 44 in Old Port, 011-52-638-32608. "The Friendly Dolphin" is an exclusive seafood restaurant serving home-cooked meals. Open 7 days from 11:00 a.m. to 10:00 p.m. Terrace dining overlooking the fishing boats. Newly remodeled, very unique configuration, stop in for a stroll to enjoy many old photographs from the archives of Mexico's history. Map F9.

$$$ - **Maria Bonita,** located in the Hotel Viña del Mar in Old Port. Breakfast, lunch and dinner. Specializing in Italian dishes served with salad and garlic sticks, Mexican combination dishes, shrimp prepared eight ways. The flan has been touted as being the best in town. Atmosphere is comfortable, outside seating right on the ocean, you can watch the sunset and listen to the waves crash over the rocks below. Map F57.

$$$ - **Costa Brava,** Blvd. Kino y 1 ero de Junio by the point in Old Port, 011-52-638-33130. One of the most popular restaurants in Puerto Peñasco especially with the locals and the *turistas*. With red and white accent colors, hundreds of business cards adorn the walls. Breakfast, lunch, and dinner is served including soups, salads, seafood, fish, beef, specialties, and Mexican combination plates. Map F55.

$$$ - **Latitude 31 Restaurant and Sports Bar,** on the left side of the street as you enter Old Port across from the anchor, 011-52-638-34311. On the side of the hill with a beautiful view of the Marina and sunsets – indoor and outdoor seating. Daily lunch and dinner specials. Map D33.

$$ - **Old Port Deli and Restaurant,** Old Port across from Pueblo Viejo. 011-52-638-33354. Open 8:00 a.m. to 9:00 p.m. Breakfast specials from 8:00 a.m. to 11:30 a.m. include bagels-n-cream cheese, egg-els (eggs on a bagel), breakfast burritos all served with coffee. Lunch and dinner deli sandwiches, salads, desserts, and your favorite New York-style bagels. Try their excellent tortilla soup! With advance notice deli trays and box lunches are prepared to your specifications. Now serving dinner specials on the weekends. Map F20.

$$ - **Roberto's Italian Broiler,** located just up from the fish market in Old Port. Open 7:00 a.m. to 10:00 p.m. 7 days a week. Breakfast, lunch and dinner. Fine Italian and seafood, lasagna, rotini, spaghetti, manicotti, shrimp cocktails, scampi, garlic flounder, scallops with cream sauce, and crab cakes. Hoagie, ham and cheese, flounder and cheese, meatballs with peppers and cheese, Italian sausage with peppers, and cheese sandwiches. The best $.75 hot dog in town. Map F47.

$$ - **Mariscos Kenos,** fish market on the Malecon. You don't want to miss this casual gathering place right on the ocean. If the place is

full, they borrow some tables and chairs from next door. Happy hour usually includes local bands that encourage aspiring singers to join in (and you don't have to be good). Song requests are welcome. Shrimp cocktails are served in three sizes. Six types of Mexican salsas line the table next to heaping bowls of fresh limes. Enjoy yourself here while watching the sunset. Map F51.

$$ - The Blue Marlin Seafood & Smokehouse, located behind Lily's across from Thrifty Ice Cream in Old Port. Specializing in smoked fish (Ahi) and tuna jerky. Fresh and frozen shrimp, fish, clams, oysters, and more. Full line of fish fillets displayed for viewing. Map F38.

$$ - La Cita Cafe, Paseo Victor Estrella in Old Port before the fish market, 011-52-638-32270. Open 7 days from 7:00 a.m. to 9:00 p.m. Satisfying the hungry palate since 1957, the owner, originally from the state of Puebla, really knows the art of cooking. La Cita Cafe just celebrated their 40th birthday on March 2, 1997. They were the first restaurant to install air conditioning. Authentic Mexican cuisine & seafood. Ranch-style shrimp and shrimp cocktail, along with breaded veal, are a few of the specialties. *Mole Poblano,* made with several *chilies,* chocolate, and peanuts is a favorite of many. Dine inside or on the terrace overlooking the Sea of Cortéz. Map F43.

$$ - Cheiky's Pizzeria, Calle 17, Old Port, 011-52-638-33627. The best pizza in Puerto Peñasco and the U.S. Great "American style" pizza sure to cure your cravings. Three sizes, pick your own toppings or try one of theirs. Delivery available, to-go orders, eat in or take out. Also serving the best hamburgers in town. Open until 1:00 a.m. Map F46.

$$ - **Danny's,** 20 de Noviembre across from the Hotel Peñasco in Old Port. Mexican and American food. Open for breakfast, lunch, and dinner. Map F30.

$ - **Thrifty Ice Cream,** Old Port across from the Catholic Church, 011-52-638-36303. All your favorite flavors. Eat in or take out, sundaes, floats, cones, pints or gallons. Map F36.

DOWNTOWN
$$$ - **Mr. Amigo Restaurant and Bar,** on the road to Las Conchas, Blvd. 9 Fremont, 011-52-638-35079. Large variety of Mexican and international dishes. Seven kinds of shrimp. Stuffed filet with shrimp, squid and oysters in a sauce. Beef, four types of chicken with potato salad, and Mexican combinations. Happy hour daily from 5:00 p.m. to 9:00 p.m. – the longest happy hour in town. Map D16.

$$ - **La Fabula Pizza,** 109 Barrera Avenue, 011-52-638-35033. If you like Chuckie Cheese you will love this place. The kids can entertain themselves while you wait for pizzas, beverages, sandwiches and snacks. Map B101.

$$ - **Mama Lusia,** Villa Granada Hotel. Specializing in typical Mexican dishes, making them light and healthful. Breakfast and lunch also available. All you can eat fish fry on Friday. Map C5.

$$ - **Aztlan,** Blvd. Kino north of La Curva restaurant, 011-52-638-32027, 33597. Restaurant is open for breakfast, lunch and dinner from 7:00 a.m. to 12 midnight serving sixteen different dishes all you can eat, buffet style. The morning we went there a business meeting was taking place in the dining room so they set up a table for us in the breezeway. Excellent service, clean restrooms. Bar is open from noon to 3:00 a.m. with live music, jazz and blues. Valet parking is available and includes a free car wash. Map C26.

$$ - **La Curva Restaurant and Bar,** Blvd. Kino y Ave San Luis, 011-52-638-33470. Open 7 days, Monday to Thursday 8:00 a.m. to

10:30 p.m., Friday to Sunday 8:00 a.m. to 11:00 p.m. Happy hour Monday to Friday 3:00 p.m. to 5:00 p.m. and Saturday 3:00 p.m. to 4:00 p.m. English spoken. A tantalizing array of Mexican, American and seafood cuisine along with many other dishes including steaks and chicken. Treat yourself to one of the famous "Especials" or their margaritas. Banquet facilities available for large groups and special occasions. Serving breakfast, lunch, and dinner. Try their shrimp crepes – you won't be sorry. This restaurant serves some fabulous, reasonably priced dishes, including appetizers. Map C22.

$ - **Galeón Restaurant,** in the Hotel Paraiso del Desierto. Seafood, steaks and Mexican food. Breakfast, lunch and dinner, specializing in seafood, chicken and Mexican specialties. A favorite breakfast meeting place for local business people. Excellent service. Map B8.

$$ - **Rocky Point Restaurant Chinese Food,** take the road to Las Conchas, turn left (north) on Sinaloa just past the liquor store, cross the railroad tracks, about two blocks down on your right, 011-52-638-35940. Special dinner combinations, chop suey, egg foo young, and fried rice. To go or dine in, deliveries available.

$$ - **Restaurant Playas del Rey,** Blvd. Kino, 011-52-638-33812. Open daily 12:00 noon to 10:00 p.m. Live music Friday to Sunday from 5:00 p.m. to 10:00 p.m. Happy hour everyday from 6:00 p.m. to 7:00 p.m. Mexican dishes, seafood, steaks and Chinese food. Dine in or take out. They accept Visa and Mastercard. Map C21.

$ - **Asadero Sinaloa,** as you enter town from Lukeville, one of the first two story buildings on your right. You can sit inside or on a stool at the kitchen counter "open-air" and watch the activities outside on main street. *Tacos*, beef or chicken served with bowls of fresh condiments heaping with sliced cucumbers, guacamole, two varieties of salsa and fresh limes. Map A7

$ - **Cenadura Zanitzito,** faces the tracks at the back of the railroad station. Open 24 hours. Mexican seafood, *pozole*, free coffee.

$ - **Asadero Sonora,** Constitution St., in front of the railroad station, 011-52-638-32929. Charcoal beef tacos, broiled chicken, cheese quesadillas, and typical Mexican food served with a variety of rich salsas, beans, *guacamole* and freshly made soft flour tortillas.

$ - **Neveria Zygle,** Avenida de la Bandera, next to Zygle Pharmacy. Ice cream cones, popcorn, chips, soft drinks, water and ice snow cones. Map B20.

$ - **La Flor de Michoacan,** Calle 17 and Juan de la Barrera, downtown. Large selection of fresh fruit drinks and slush's, fruit and cream bars – try both. A taste treat for ice cream and fruit lovers. Map B109 / Map A25.

$ - **Pollo Giro,** B. Juarez Blvd., & A. Melgar. Broiled chicken and beef tacos. A delicious experience.

$ - **My Javy's Hamburgers,** Blvd. Benito Juarez & Calle 20 Simon Morua next to the gas station. Map B29.

$ - **Pepos II,** Blvd. Juarez across from the high school as you enter town. Outdoor seating in parkside setting, casual and comfortable. Chicken with salad and potatoes, cheeseburgers, hot dogs, cheese, club, tuna and ham sandwiches. Ham and cheese tacos, fries and nachos, and rice pudding. Try the gelatin with rampope (a type of flan custard), milk shakes, ice crean and sodas. Map A2.

$ **Hansel Ice Cream,** next to Motel Senorial. Ices and ice cream. Map E9.

CHOLLA BAY
$ - **JJ's Cantina,** Cholla Bay, 011-52-638-32785. There aren't many restaurants in Cholla Bay, but JJ's does serve fast food tacos.

SONOYTA

$$ - Excelsior Cafe, Blvd. de Las Americas, next to the Restaurant Bar Cimarron. Map I12.

$$ - Mr. Blaynes Restaurant, Blvd. de Las Americas, next to Motel Sol Del Desierto, 011-52-638-21456. Mexican food, seafood and American favorites. Breakfast, lunch, dinner. Map I92.

$$ - Restaurant Bar Cimarron, in the center of town at the curve on the way to Puerto Peñasco. Breakfast, lunch, and dinner, steaks, seafood, chef specials. Mexican food includes guacamole, beans and topopos. Map I14.

$$ - Restaurant San Antonio, Blvd. de Las Americas, 011-52-638-21549. Mexican food, steaks, seafood. English spoken. Visit the bar, sing along with Karaoke music. Restaurant hours 7:00 a.m. to 11:00 p.m. Bar hours 3:00 p.m. to 2:00 a.m. Map I15.

$$ - Restaurant Tierra del Sol, at the Pemex gas station, 011-52-638-21433. Mexican, seafood and steaks. Open 24 hours, 7 days a week. Map I11.

Cantinas & Entertainment

*No, you never get any fun out of the things
you haven't done.*
-Ogden Nash

Of all the customs in Mexico, gringos have taken up the custom of drinking with more passion than any other. Thirsty travelers can purchase and consume local favorites such as *margaritas, mezcál, tequila,* rum and a wide variety of Mexican beer for a fraction of what it costs north of the border.

The early inhabitants of Mexico, the Aztec Indians, did not approve of drinking. Somehow they realized the evil that it possessed. Except for the old or those in a position of leadership, tribes were not allowed to partake in the consumption of alcohol. Drunks were brutally killed by strangulation or were clubbed to death. On the other hand, the *Conquistadores* indulged in the practice of drinking. The Spanish produced wine and liquors abundantly which prepared the way for new market potential.

Although Mexican custom permits and encourages ritual drinking, locals look upon public drunkenness with disfavor. Their drinking is usually done in bars, *cantinas* and at home. In Mexican society it is considered *macho* for Mexican men to tie one on, but if an unescorted Mexican woman does the same she is looked upon with scandal. Mexican *Fiestas* and public celebrations revolve around local alcohol refreshments. Custom dictates that guests of certain social and economic levels get totally drunk at religious and civil ceremonies such as deaths, births, and weddings. It is expected that everyone gets drunk to permit the union to have a successful start.

With the development of several new resorts in Puerto Peñasco, tourism in Puerto Peñasco is now being promoted internationally.

This world wide advertising is bringing in a new class of foreign visitors and continues to be a safe and fun place to enjoy food, drink, recreation and warm sunshine.

The drinking age in Mexico is 18. Most bars and nightclubs ask for picture identification. If you look younger than you are, you will be "carded," so bring your ID. Use your good judgment, never drink and drive. Local taxi's are abundant and cheap. Puerto Peñasco has a south of the border Alcoholics Anonymous group open to everyone. Check the Rocky Point Times for meeting dates and times.

Legal Prostitution

Prostitution is an accepted and legal institution in most of Mexico. Puerto Peñasco is no exception. The Crystal Palace has been catering to snorting studs for years. The first building that sheltered this bordello is Margaritavilla The Pirate Divers' Den, located on the road to Playa Marimar. In the early days, the Crystal Palace doubled as a nightclub with a bands and a dance floor. It was considered the "hottest spot in town." It was another place to meet friends and drink, and women were welcome. The current location is about a mile north of Cholla Bay Road, turn right at the large Tecate sign.

The Crystal Palace is positioned on a corner with the bar and dance hall located at the center. The doors open around 2:00 p.m. and stay open until 3:00 a.m. Closed holidays. A remarkable older lady named Lola graciously granted me several interviews so that I could include information for this chapter. Lola would be considered a "madam," as she has been working at the Crystal Palace for nineteen years, every other day year round.

The prostitutes (*putas*) live in the rooms next to the bar or live with their families at homes in town. Some come from Vera Cruz, San Luis, or Acapulco and travel throughout the country spending five or six months in one bordello. Nine to fourteen women work here year round, the longest being nine years. I interviewed a woman in her early 30's, she was from an area west of the Colorado

River in northern Mexico. She had been working the fields but ran into financial problems and needed to earn some fast money. She showed me a picture of her young son who was staying with her family until she returned.

> **Warning:** *The information on bordellos is included to educate you, not to encourage or condone risky sexual adventures. AIDS (called SIDA in Spanish) and other sexually-transmitted diseases are extremely serious and dangerous. Sex without latex condoms is like playing Russian roulette with a fully loaded pistol. Casual sex can be dangerous, especially for tourists who find themselves being charmed and courted by a local lover. Though it can be difficult to say no, the risk of AIDS is too great. If this warning doesn't cool you down, be sure to bring a good supply of latex condoms from home. The quality of Mexican condoms is uncertain. Remember, condoms are not 100% but certainly help reduce the risk of AIDS and other sexually transmitted diseases.*

Women sometimes approach the men themselves, but they usually wait for arrangements to be made through the bartender. The price for sex isn't much more than that for a round of drinks, which is about $40 for 20 minutes. Customers pay the girl, who keeps 10%. Tips are accepted. No condom, no sex.

The girls have check-ups every eight days at a clinic in town. They are tested once a month for sexually-transmitted diseases and AIDS but this is no guarantee they are disease free.

Beer

If you choose to partake in local hospitality, *"Uná Cerveza, por favor,"* (one beer, please), is a common phrase heard echoing throughout the point. Mexico is known for its excellent quality beer and measures up to many selected European beers in taste.

Bohemia is considered an American quality beer of simple character, a big favorite of beer drinkers.

Carta Blanca is a light bottled beer with a distinctive flavor.

Corona is well known and sold in the U. S. It is light, sold in bottles and labeled *Corona Clara*.

Negra Modelo is the dark version of *Corona,* while the light canned version is called *Modelo*.

Pacifico is similar to Corona in color and flavor.

Tecate is sold in bright red cans, darker in color, more expensive, and sometimes considered the *"macho"* beer.

Superior comes in tall brown bottles as a light beer, the counterpart is the well known dark *Dos Equis (XX)* which is sold in cans.

Liquor

Bacardí, Ron Rico and Castillo rum are the best quality while all others can give one a nasty headache with very little effort. Although, to the rum connoisseur, *Castillo* can have a strong and pungent taste rather than a smooth mellow taste.

You will find liquor stores in abundance in the area of Old Port and down main street on Blvd. Juárez. Supermarkets also have licenses to sell alcohol. Bars usually sell "to go" at much higher prices. You will get a better price in Puerto Peñasco than Sonoyta, so shop around if you are buying in volume or if you are with a group. Remember, you are only allowed to bring back 1 liter of alcohol per person every 30 days. See Chapter 1, Crossing The Border for more information.

Don Pedro Reserva Especial and Presidente are the best quality Mexican Brandies.

Mezcál is made from maguey which is any of a number of fleshy-leafed, fiber-yielding agaves. While it is not as strong as *Tequila,* a type of worm which lives in the maguey plant is added to each bottle to enhance flavor. It is sold as 76 proof, gold in color and claims to be aged, but for how long is any one's guess. Brands sold in local stores and bars are *Gusano Rojo* (Red Worm) and *Gusano de Oro* (Gold Worm).

Oso Negro and Kimberly are the favorite and best quality brands of gin and vodka.

Tequila is distilled from a mash made from the core of certain agaves. Plants from this family include the century plant and other species used in making rope and pulque. The two most popular brands of *Tequila* are *Sauza* and *Jose Cuervo* which are produced in the states of Jalisco, Nayarit and Tamaulipas under strict government regulations. These states grow the specific blue agave which is used to make these two brands. When the label boasts *especial, de reserva or conmemorativo,* it has been aged and claims to have a better flavor.

> *The true traveler, I believe, is the one who realizes*
> *how precious the passing moment is*
> *and how important the little fame of risk can be*
> *in the total travel experience.*
>
> *This kind of traveler lives on the edge and has*
> *no ambition to die in bed –*
> *not in his own bed, anyway.*
>
> -Caskie Stinnett

Liquor Stores

Beer Distributors: Corona Agency, Blvd. Juarez, Map B51. **Corona Sub-Agency,** Ave. Armanda Nacional, Map E16. Corona Agency distributes Corona Beer in cans, bottles or kegs. **Tecate Agency,** Blvd. Benito Juárez y Calle 18, 011-52-638-32444. Map B56. **Tecate Sub-Agency,** Blvd. Benito Juarez y Calle 22, 011-52-638-34411. Map A20. **Tecate Sub-Agency,** Calle 13, 011-52-638-32444. Tecate are distributors for Tecate, Tecate-Lite, Bohemia, and Dos Equis. In cans, bottles or kegs.

Kota's Liquor Store, Blvd. Juárez y G. Prieto. Cold beer to go, purified ice cubes, snacks, cigarettes, Tequila Sauza, Cuervo, and Budweiser. Map A14.

Licores Brisa, next to Baja 1000 on Blvd. Fremont on the road to Las Conchas. Ice, cold beer and a large variety of liquor available. Map D20.

Lisan, Armada Nacional & Pino Suárez, 011-52-638-32353. Wine, liquors, cigarettes, ice cubes, snacks, beer, Tequila, Cuervo, and Sauza. Map E13.

Tena Liquor Store, next to the Pemex Gas Station on Blvd. Benito Juarez and Nicholas Bravo, 011-52-638-36209, 32064. Coldest beer in town (what liquor store doesn't have cold beer?). Largest variety of liquor and wine. Ten brands of tequila and Mescal. Map B36.

Sonoyta
Ultramarinos Tito's, Sonoyta, Blvd. de Las Americas y Callejón, 011-52-638-21768. Liquor, beer, water, juice, ice, and snacks.

Lukeville
Gringo Pass, U.S. side of the border on highway 85 at Lukeville, 602-527-0887. Motel, 602-254-9284. Trailer park, pool, grocery store, drug store, coffee shop, post office, bonded warehouse complete with duty free wine and liquor. Souvenirs, magazines, postcards, beverages, notary public, Mexican insurance, tourist information hardware, ammunition, camp supplies. Laundromat, gas station with propane and white gas. New tax and duty free store, called Ueta, offers liquor, beer, cigarettes, perfumes, watches and sunglasses. Purchases must be taken into Mexico before being allowed back into the United States. Map G2.

Bars And Cocktails

ON THE BEACH
Las Glorias Bar, in the lobby of the Plaza Las Gloria Hotel, 011-52-638-36010. Map E26.

Manny's Beach Club, Calle 1, Primera & Coahuila, 011-52-638-33605, 34472. Enjoy dancing at the disco night club. "No shoes...No shirt...No problem." Outside and inside bar service. Located right on the beach. Map G11.

Pitahaya Bar, Calle 1 next to the Granada del Mar south of the Playa de Oro R.V. Park, 011-52-638-32742. Map G25.

Puesto Del Sol, Paseo Balboa, 011-52-638-32586. Located in the Playa Bonita Hotel. The best happy hour in town with a spectacular view of the sunset. Right on the beach. Map E20.

Rottweiler Bar and Grill, on the waterfront in Old Port. Come in and see the painted jungle and enjoy the sunset from our terrace. Burgers and hot-dogs cooked over an open grill. Map F50.

NEAR THE BEACH
Cocodrilos Bar & Grill, on Calle 13 on the left as you enter the Hotel Plaza Las Glorias complex, 011-52-638-36376. Terrace dining. International food, Mexican specialties, flavored margaritas, beer and wine. Map E23.

El Callejón, Calle 13 just east of the Plaza Las Glorias Hotel across from Villa Las Palmas Restaurant on the second floor. two for one national drink specials everyday. Ride the mechanical bull, 2 dance floors and pool tables. Map E10.

LF Caliente Racetrack, Race & Sports Books, Calle 13 in the Señorial Hotel, 011-52-638-33973, Fax 011-52-638-33910. Live horse and greyhound racing – satellite wagering. Mexico's newest sports books and betting parlors. Bet on tracks in New York, Florida, sports events, horses, dogs, international boxing, or the World Cup Soccer. Friendly service, fine liquors, and tasty food. Map E8.

Margaritavilla, The Pirate Diver's Den, Ave 10 Campeche toward Playa Miramar, 011-52-638-35344. Cheap drinks, classic rock, Reggae, darts, foozball, and Ping-Pong. Party at Puerto Peñasco's original Crystal Palace now a hot new party place. Map G1.

Pink Cadillac (Gringo Locos Cantina), Calle 1, 011-52-638-35880. Ocean view and bar service from upstairs patio. Watch sports on a satellite TV or choose your favorite CD's for listening or dancing. Map G22.

Playa Inn Suites Bar, Ave 18 Sinaloa, 011-52-638-35015. Located at the Playa Inn Suites International. Map G31.

Ranas Ranas, down from the Playa Inn Suites Hotel, 011-52-638-35095. Sports bar and disco, cover charge on weekends, pool tables, beach volleyball. Map G30.

Señorial, Calle 13, 011-52-638-32065. Piano bar lounge for your listening and dancing pleasure. Map E7.

Villa Las Palmas, Calle 13. Newly remodeled sports bar and adjoining restaurant with drink specials and friendly service. Map E12.

OLD PORT
Costa Brava Lounge, on the Malecón in Old Port, 011-52-638-34100. Full service bar and live entertainment. Map F55.

En Rocky 'O Discotheque, Viña de Mar Hotel in Old Port, 011-52-638-35911. Map F37.

El Delfin Amigable, Alcantar in Old Port, 011-52-638-32608. Full service bar with a beautiful terrace view of the Sea of Cortéz and the port. Map F9.

La Casa Del Captain, top of the hill in Old Port, 011-52-638-35698. Cocktails served 11 a.m. till 11 p.m. Enjoy the sunset atop the highest point in Puerto Peñasco. Map F61.

Latitude 31 Restaurant and Sports Bar, on the left side of the street as you enter Old Port across from the anchor, 011-52-638-34311. On the side of the hill with a beautiful view of the Marina and sunsets, indoor and outdoor seating. Daily lunch and dinner specials. Map D33.

Lily's, on the Malecón in Old Port, 011-52-638-32510. American and Mexican beer, including excellent Margaritas. Excellent sunset view over the Sea of Cortéz. Map F41.

La Curva, Blvd. Kino y Ave San Luis, 011-52-638-33470. The largest frozen mug of beer in town. Margaritas and the "Especial" are a must for thirsty travelers. Full service bar with friendly service. Map C22.

Marichi's, In the Fiesta de Cortéz Resort in Old Port, 011-52-638-33424. Live music on weekends and dancing. Map G3.

DOWNTOWN
Aztlan, Blvd. Kino north of La Curva restaurant, 011-52-638-32027, 33597. Bar is open from noon to 3:00 a.m. with live music, jazz and blues. Valet parking is available and includes a free car wash. Restaurant is open from 7:00 a.m. to 12 midnight serving sixteen different dishes, all you can eat, buffet style. Excellent service, clean restrooms. Map C26.

Mr. Amigo Bar, Blvd. Fremont. Music and dancing until 3:00 a.m. Map D16.

Grand Palace, Blvd. Fremont, 011-52-638-35415. Concerts and music events during the month. Map D17.

Mar Y Sol Sports Bar & Grille, located on the main highway above the Mar Y Sol Hotel, 011-52-638-35822. Half price drinks on Friday from 10:00 p.m. to 11:00 p.m. Saturday is ladies night, first drink free then half price from 10:00 p.m. to 11:00 p.m. All sports all the time, NFL, NBA, Hockey, Soccer Golf. Five satellites for complete coverage. Great food and snacks. Air conditioned.

Paraiso Del Desierto, Ave 12 Constitucion, 011-52-638-32175. Two bars, the "Paradise" with all your favorites, and a second bar with billiards by the pool. Map B8

Villa Granada, Ave 13, 011-52-63832775. Two bars, one inside and one poolside. Authentic Mexican atmosphere. Music six nights a week. Pool tables available. Map C7.

<u>Cholla Bay</u>
JJ's Cantina, Cholla Bay, 011-52-638-32785. Sports bar and eatery overlooking the bay. Satellite TV's, dancing and socializing. Arrangements can be made for private parties. Check the bulletin board for upcoming events.

The Reef, on Sandy Beach, take Cholla Bay Road, follow the sign, 011-52-638-32282.

JJ's Cantina in Cholla Bay is a favorite watering hole for thirsty fishermen and partying college students.

Emergency 9-1-1

Let the tourist be cushioned against misadventure,
but your true traveler will not feel that he has had his money's
worth unless he brings back a few scars.
-Lawrence Durrell

Emergency Telephone Numbers, Quick Reference

Airport	3-60-97
Ambulance Service	3-53-46
Bus Depot	3-41-29
Captain of Port	3-30-35
Chamber of Commerce	3-28-48
City Hall - Mayor	3-20-56
Clinic Santa Fe	3-24-47
Ecology Federal	3-42-75
Fire Department	3-28-28
Fisheries Department	3-21-10
Hospital	3-21-10
Hospital Admissions	3-27-77
Immigration Department	3-25-26
Navy	3-26-03
Police	3-26-26
Post Office	3-23-50
Railroad Office	3-26-10
Red Cross	3-22-66
Telegraph Office	3-22-88
Telephone Office	3-22-88
Tourism Office	3-41-29
Electric Company	3-26-84
Water Company	3-20-60

Cholla Bay Emergency Radio

These channels are assigned for emergency use only, please do not use them for other than their intended use.
VHF:
Monitor . . . CH 26   EMERGENCY . . . CH 16
CB radio:
Monitor . . . CH 3   EMERGENCY . . . CH 9
AM marine radio, ship to shore:
Safety & Calling   2182
Boat to Shore   2555
Boat to Boat   1638

Radio operators monitor CB Channel 3 and VHF Channel 26. At the same time CB Channel 9 and VHF Channel 16 are used as emergency channels. The operators of the Radio Room ask your assistance in using these airways for emergency use *only*. CB Channel 3 can be used for calling friends, ordering water, and all other non-emergency conversations. If you must hail someone on Channel 26, please go to an off simplex channel (12, 68, 70) as soon as your party responds.

<u>Puerto Peñasco</u>
Clinics and Hospitals

Central Clinic, 120 Juarez Blvd., 01152-638-32110.

Centro De Salvo Urbano Hospital, 12 Morua Avenue, 011-52-638-33310. Map B13.

Puerto Peñasco Municipal Hospital, 97 Barrera Avenue, Ave 15 & Calle 20, 011-52-638-32870, Fax: 011-52-638-32777. Map B102.

San Andres Clinic, Map C6.

Santa Fe General Hospital, 47 Morua Avenue, 011-52-638-32447, Fax: 011-52-638-35077. Map B13.

Santa Fe Clinic, Calle 20 Simon Morua & Ave 16. 011-52-638-32447. Map B14.

Santa Maria Clinic, 21 Heros Avenue, 011-52-638-32440.

Dentists

Dr. Rogelio Dicochea, 98 Juarez Blvd., 011-52-638-32778.

Dr. Ernesto Grijalva J., 81 Barrera Ave., 011-52-638-33242.

Dr. Eduardo Padilla Guiterrez-Family Dentistry, 138 Juarez Blvd., 011-52-638-32072.

Dr. J. Hernandez DDS., main street toward the fish market on your left, 011-52-638-34338. Graduate National University of Mexico City. No appointment necessary. Bonding, filling, and repairs. Office hours 9:00 a.m. to 1:00 p.m. and 3:00 p.m. to 7:00 p.m. Map D31.

Dr. Rolando Rojas DDS, Calle 13 & Ave. Guillermo Prieto, Office: 011-52-638-33923, Home: 011-52-638-33382. No appointment necessary. Fillings, repair, cleaning and dentures. Office hours 9:00 a.m. to 1:00 p.m. and 3:00 p.m. to 7:00 p.m. Map C19.

Doctors

Dr. Antonio Castro (General Medicine), 47 Morua Ave., 011-52-638-32442. Map B13.

Dr. Juan R. García M. D., Ave 10 Campeche & Calle 8. Map D29.

Dr. Jamie Rodriquez Gomez M. D., Blvd. Benito Juarez & Calle 22, 011-52-638-34252. General medicine, emergency transportation services. Map B2.

Dr. Theresa Hernandez R. (General Medicine), 47 Morua Ave., 011-52-638-32447. Map B13.

Dr. Eliel Lopez U. (General Medicine), 47 Morua Ave., 011-52-638-32447. Map B13.

Dr. Victor Villegas Lopez (General Medicine), 47 Morua Ave., 011-52-638-32447. Map B13.

Dr. Guadalupe Munoz (General Medicine), 47 Morua Ave., 011-52-638-32447. Map B13.

Doctor Luis R. Vazquez, M. D., 20 de Noviembre #2 in Old Port, 011-52-638-34040. 24 hour emergency service, English spoken. Map F23.

Dr. Jose Contreras Valle, 47 Morua Ave., P.O. Box 649, Lukeville, Arizona 85341, 011-52-638-32447. Map B13.

Fire Department

Fire Department, Blvd. Fremont, 011-52-638-32828. Map D23

Local Police

Police Station, Jail and City Hall, south of downtown past the overhead walkway, a modern white two story building on the corner, 011-52-638-32626. Map D24 & D25

Red Cross

Cruz Roja Mexicana (Mexican Red Cross), 24 hour Emergency Service, on Blvd. Fremont, turn east at the police station, the Caborca sign, 011-52-638-32266, Radio CB Channel 9, Radio 2 Channel 20. Instructors and technicians are available in case of a disaster. They do not receive funds from any government agency. You are invited to contribute when you see their ambulance parked along the highway as you enter or leave town. Map D15.

Sonoyta

Clinic

Caran Clinic, Drug Store & X-ray, Dr. Julio Alberto Vargas Alcala U.A.G., Blvd. de Las Americas, 011-52-638-21212. For all your medical needs, prescriptions and medicines. Also specializing in weight loss, gynecology, ultra sound and pediatrics. Available 24 hours.

Dentists

Clinica Dental, 131 Kino Ave., 011-52-638-21015.

Dr. Ruben Ortiz M., 16 September Ave., 011-52-638-21162.

Hospital

Sonoyta Hospital, Blvd. Fco E. Kino. Map I103

Federal Police

Federal Police, Blvd. Fco E. Kino, next to the Sonoyta Hospital. Map I102.

Local Police

Sonoyta Police Station, Ave. Altar and Blvd. Juarez, next to the Post Office. Map I24.

CPR Reminders

	Adluts	Children	Infants
If there is a pulse but no breathing, give 1 breath every:	5 seconds (12 /min.)	4 seconds (14 /min.)	3 seconds (20 /min.)
If there is no pulse, begin CPR by:	Tracing the ribs to the notch at the center of the chest. Place the heel of the other hand 2 finger-widths above the notch.	Same as adult	Placing 2 fingers one finger-width below the nipple line.
Push down on (compress) the chest with:	The heel of one hand on the breast-bone, with the other hand on top of it.	The heel of one hand only on the breastbone.	2 or 3 fingers on the breast-bone.
Compress the chest to a depth of:	1fi-2 inches	1-1fi inches	fi-1 inch
Number of compressions to breaths:	15:2	5:1	5:1

First Aid

In the time of your life - live!
-William Saroyan

First-aid treatment in the first few minutes of an emergency can often mean the difference between life and death. Knowing what to do, while reacting quickly and calmly before medical help arrives, will enable you to provide the best care for the victim, whether it is you or someone else. This chapter is designed to meet your immediate needs in emergency situations and to provide you with quick and easy access to basic information. It is not to be used in place of a doctor, but merely to guide you in helping the victim until professional help can be obtained. Our guidelines are based on what will happen with most victims in most situations; but there are always a few exceptions where the victim may not respond to your first aid as expected.

The Red Cross, located on Blvd. Fremont, Map D15, is open 24-hours and can handle any situation. There are Emergency Medical Technicians, nurses, doctors, and ambulances available.

Many over-the-counter and prescription medications found in the United States can be obtained from local pharmacies in Puerto Peñasco to treat common ailments.

Animal Bites - Animal bites that are not very deep and involve no puncture marks should be treated as a simple cut (see "Cuts, Scrapes, and Abrasions"). If the bite comes from a human or if it is very deep or has puncture marks, a doctor should be seen. A tetanus shot may be needed. If it is possible, the biting animal should be caught and checked for rabies. Dogs are not the only animals to carry rabies – cats, foxes, raccoon's, bats, skunks, and other animals can carry it as well. If rabies is suspected, immediate medical attention is needed.

Treatment:

1. Clean the wound thoroughly with soap and running water for 5 minutes or more to wash out contaminating organisms.
2. Put a sterile bandage or clean cloth over the wound.
3. Seek medical attention promptly, particularly for a bite on the face, neck or hands, which frequently can develop into serious infection.

Bleeding - Blood may flow from a vein or an artery or both. Venous bleeding is darker red in color and flows steadily. Arterial bleeding is bright red in color and usually spurts from the would. Arterial bleeding is more critical because blood is being pumped out at a faster rate, leading to greater blood loss.

Note: There is a concern among those who provide first aid, even on a onetime basis, that AIDS may be contracted from a victim's body fluids. It is extremely unlikely that you, as a first aider providing emergency care, will contract AIDS from a victim who is bleeding or from the saliva of a victim who may require mouth-to-mouth resuscitation or CPR. AIDS can be passed to others through an infected person's blood, vaginal secretions and semen (if there is an opening in the body for the AIDS virus to enter). The AIDS virus may be present in saliva, but cases in which AIDS has been transmitted through saliva are unknown at the present time.
Information provided by the American Medical Association

Treatment:

1. Direct pressure is the preferred treatment in bleeding injuries and, though it may cause some pain, constant pressure is usually all that is necessary to stop the bleeding.
2. Place a thick clean compress (sterile gauze or a soft clean cloth such as a handkerchief, towel, undershirt, or strips from a sheet)

directly over the entire wound and press firmly with the palm of your hand.

3. Continue to apply steady pressure.

4. *Do not* disturb any blood clots that form on the compress.

5. If blood soaks through the compress, *do not* remove the compress but apply another pad over it and continue with firmer hand pressure.

6. A limb that is bleeding severely should be raised above the level of the victim's heart and direct pressure continued.

7. If bleeding stops or slows, apply a pressure bandage to hold the compress snugly in place.

8. To apply a pressure bandage, place the center of the gauze, cloth strips, or necktie directly over the compress. Pull steadily while wrapping both ends around the injury. Tie a knot over the compress.

9. *Do not* wrap the bandage so tightly that it cuts off the arterial circulation.

10. Keep the limb elevated.

CPR (Cardiopulmonary Resuscitation) - CPR is a basic life-support technique used when the victim is not breathing and it is possible that the heart has stopped beating. CPR involves opening and clearing the victim's airway (by tilting the head backward and lifting the chin), restoring breathing (by resuscitation), and restoring blood circulation (by external chest compression's). CPR must be performed on a *bare* chest. Don't waste valuable time trying to undo buttons or looking for zippers. Tear or cut garments. Lift a woman's bra up to her neck. You must not delay. Time is critical.

Dehydration - Dehydration is lack of adequate water in the body and can be fatal. *Symptoms may include:* extreme thirst, tiredness, lightheadedness, abdominal or muscle cramping.
Treatment:
1. Move victim into the shade or a cool area.
2. To replace lost fluids and body chemicals, give the victim water, tea, carbonated beverages (shake to eliminate fizz), a commercial electrolyte-replacement fluid, flavored gelatin (in liquid form), or clear broth.

3. Seek medical attention if symptoms persist or if other complications arise.

Diarrhea - Diarrhea is frequent elimination or the passage of loose, watery stools. There are many causes of this condition. Among the most common are: food poisoning, dysentery, certain medications, emotional stress, excessive drinking of alcoholic beverages, viral and bacterial infections, and stomach flu. *Symptoms may include:* frequent loose and watery stools which may vary in color from light tan to green, stomach cramping, tiredness due to loss of potassium, thirst due to loss of fluid, blood streaks in or on stools.
Treatment:
1. Drink liquids to replace lost fluids.
2. If diarrhea persists longer than a day or two, or if urine decreases in both frequency and amount, seek medical attention because fatal dehydration may occur.
3. Avoid solid foods.

Drowning - In all emergencies involving a drowning person, remember first to be careful of your own safety. In deep water, a drowning person can drag a rescuer under water.
Treatment:
1. Start CPR at once.
2. If there is too much water in the lungs for resuscitation to be effective, turn the victim on their back and press down firmly on the back to force the water out before beginning again.

Fish Hook Injuries - A fishhook caught in the body is a common injury. If the fishhook goes deep enough so that the barb is embedded in the skin, it is best to have a doctor remove it. If a doctor is not readily available, the hook should be removed.
Treatment:
1. If only the point of the hook, and not the barb, entered the skin, remove the hook by backing it out.
2. If the hook is embedded in the skin, push the hook through the skin until the barb comes out.

3. Cut the hook with pliers or clippers at either the barb or the shank of the hook. Remove the part remaining.
4. Clean the wound with soap and water then cover with a bandage.
5. Seek medical attention as soon as possible. In such injuries there is always the possibility of infection, particularly tetanus.

Food Poisoning - Suspect food poisoning if several people become ill with similar symptoms at approximately the same time after eating the same food. Also suspect food poisoning if one person becomes ill after eating food no one else ate.

Salmonella

Salmonella poisoning usually occurs after eating fresh food that has been contaminated with salmonella bacteria. Foods most commonly affected include eggs, milk, raw meat, raw poultry, and raw fish. Salmonella poisoning can be very serious in infants, young children, and the elderly. *Symptoms may include:* abdominal cramps, diarrhea, fever, chills, headache, vomiting, weakness. Symptoms usually appear from 6 to 24 hours after eating contaminated food.

Treatment:

1. Keep the victim lying down.
2. Keep the victim comfortably warm.
3. After vomiting is over, give the victim warm mild fluids, such as tea, broth, or fruit juices.
4. Seek medical attention promptly.

Staphylococcus

Staphylococcus poisoning occurs most often by eating foods that have not been properly refrigerated. The most common foods affected include meats, poultry, eggs, milk, cream-filled bakery goods, tuna and potato salad. *Symptoms may include:* abdominal cramps, nausea, vomiting, diarrhea. Symptoms usually appear 2 to 6 hours after contaminated food has been eaten.

Treatment:

1. Keep the victim resting, preferably in bed.
2. After vomiting is over, give victim warm mild fluids – tea, broth or fruit juice.

3. It is best to seek medical attention, particularly if the symptoms are severe or persist.

Heart Attack - A heart attack is a life-threatening emergency. *Symptoms may include:* central chest pain that is severe, crushing, constant, and lasts for several minutes, pain may be mistaken for indigestion, chest discomfort moving through the chest to either arm, shoulder neck, jaw mid-back or pit of stomach, profuse sweating, nausea and vomiting, extreme weakness, victim is anxious and afraid, skin is pale, fingernails and lips may be blue, extreme shortness of breath.
Treatment:
1. If the victim is unconscious and not breathing, or is having difficulty breathing maintain an open airway and start CPR at once.
2. If the victim is conscious at the onset of the heart attack, make victim comfortable, loosen tight clothing, calm and reassure victim, get an ambulance or paramedics at once.

Heat Cramps - Heat cramps are muscle pains and spasms caused by a loss of salt from the body due to profuse sweating. Strenuous physical activity in hot temperatures can lead to heat cramps. Usually the muscles of the stomach and legs are affected first. Heat cramps may also be a symptom of heat exhaustion. *Symptoms may include:* painful muscle cramping and spasms, heavy sweating, possible convulsions.
Treatment:
1. Have victim sit quietly in a cool place.
2. Apply firm hand pressure to the affected area or gently massage the victim's cramped muscles.
3. If the victim is not vomiting, give clear juice or sips of cool salt water (1 teaspoon of salt per glass). Give victim 1/2 glass of liquid every 15 minutes for 1 hour. Stop fluids if vomiting occurs.
4. Medical attention is needed (if available) because of other possible complications.

Heat Exhaustion - Heat exhaustion can occur after prolonged exposure to high temperatures and high humidity. *Symptoms may*

include: body temperature normal or slightly above normal, pale and clammy skin, heavy sweating, tiredness, weakness, dizziness, headache, nausea, possible muscle cramps, vomiting and fainting.
Treatment:
1. Move the victim into the shade or cooler area. Have victim lie down.
2. Rise the victim's feet 8 to 12 inches.
3. Loosen clothing.
4. If the victim isn't vomiting, give clear juice or sips of cool salt water (1 teaspoon of salt per glass). Give the victim 1/2 glass of liquid every 15 minutes for 1 hour. Stop fluids if vomiting occurs.
5. Place cool wet cloths on the victim's forehead and body or use a fan to cool the victim.
6. If symptoms are severe, become worse, or last longer than an hour, seek medical attention promptly.

Heat Stroke (Sunstroke) - Heatstroke is a life-threatening emergency. It is a disturbance in the body's heat-regulating system caused by extremely high body temperature due to exposure to heat and from an inability of the body to cool itself. *Symptoms may include:* extremely high body temperature (often 106°F or higher), red, hot, and dry skin, sweating usually absent, rapid and strong pulse, possible unconsciousness or confusion.
Treatment:
1. Undress the victim and put them into a tub of cold water (not iced) if possible. Otherwise, spray the victim with a hose, sponge bare skin with cool water or rubbing alcohol, or apply cold packs.
2. Continue treatment until body temperature is lowered to 101° or 102°F.
3. Do not overchill. Check temperature constantly.
4. Dry off the victim once the temperature is lowered.
5. Seek medical attention promptly.
6. *Do not* give victim alcoholic beverages or stimulants such as coffee or tea.

Jellyfish - sting (Jellyfish have stinging cells located on the tentacle.) *Symptoms may include*: burning pain, swelling, rash, nausea, vomiting, cramps, shock or breathing problems.

Treatment:
1. If breathing difficulties occur, start CPR breathing techniques immediately. Treat for shock if necessary.
2. First wipe off tentacles with clean cloth, then wash affected area with salt water or ammonia diluted in water. Follow with hot Epsom salt soaks.
3. If glands begin to swell, apply an ice pack to sting site for 20 minutes each hour.
4. If severe symptoms appear, take to the Red Cross (Map D15) immediately.

Portuguese Man-of-War
Treatment:
1. Remove tentacles as soon as possible without leaving sucking discs.
2. See jellyfish stings for additional treatment.

Puffer Fish - consumption. **Eating Puffer, also known in the markets of Puerto Peñasco as "chicken fish" is not recommended.** *Symptoms may include*: itching sensation on the lips and tongue which gradually extends to the limbs and fingers, severe numbness, intense sweating, weakness, headache and low blood pressure, difficult and rapid breathing, and peeling of the skin. In the most severe cases, near total paralysis precedes death.

Scorpion Fish - prick. *Symptoms may include*: very intense pain, rapid swelling sometimes throughout the entire limb, nausea, restlessness, diarrhea, vomiting, and even fainting spells.
Treatment:
1. The same as for stingrays, immersion in hot water.

Scorpion Stings - The scorpion looks like a small lobster. It has a set of pincers and a stinger located in the tail, which arches over its back. Some species of scorpions are more poisonous than others. Scorpion stings are particularly harmful to very young children. *Symptoms may include:* severe burning pain at the site of the sting, nausea and vomiting, stomach pain, numbness and tingling in the affected areas, possible spasm of jaw muscles, making the opening of the mouth difficult, twitching and spasm of affected muscles, convulsions, possible shock and coma.

Treatment:

1. Maintain an open airway. Restore breathing and circulation, if necessary.

2. Keep the bitten area lower than the victim's heart.

3. Place ice wrapped in cloth or cold compresses on the bitten area.

4. Seek medical attention promptly, preferably at the nearest hospital emergency room.

Snakebites - When you are bitten by a snake, it is important to know whether or not it is poisonous. Poisonous snakes in this area include the rattlesnake, copperhead and coral snake. The rattlesnake has deep poison pits located between the nostrils and the eyes. It has slit like eyes and two long fangs. A unique feature of the rattlesnake is the set of rattles at the end of the tail. The rattlesnake and copperhead have a triangular shaped head and are pit vipers, recognized by deep pits (poison sacs) located between the nostrils and eyes. These snakes have long fangs that leave distinctive marks followed by a row of tooth marks. The coral snake has rounded eyes and fangs. Its markings consist of yellow, red and black rings with the narrow yellow rings always separating the red rings from the black. The coral snake always has a black nose. Nonpoisonous snakes have rounded eyes. They do not have pits between their eyes and nostrils and do not have fangs. Try to capture and kill the snake, if possible without deforming its head, and take it with you to the medical facility. *Symptoms of rattlesnake and copperhead bites may include:* severe pain, rapid swelling, discoloration of the skin around the bite, weakness, nausea and vomiting, difficulty breathing, blurring vision, convulsions and possible shock.

Treatment for rattlesnake and copperhead bites:
1. Maintain an open airway. Restore breathing and circulation if necessary.
2. Keep the victim quiet to slow circulation. Doing so will help stop the spread of the venom.
3. If the victim was bitten on the arm or leg, place a light constricting band such as a belt or elastic watchband 2 to 4 inches above the bite between the bite and the body. The band should not be so tight that it cuts off arterial circulation. You should feel a pulse below the band. You should be able to slip your finger under the band, although with some resistance. The wound should ooze.
4. If the area around the band should begin to swell, remove the band and place it 2 to 4 inches above the first site.
5. *Do not* remove the band or bands until medical assistance is obtained.
6. Wash the bite area thoroughly with soap and water.
7. Immobilize a bitten arm or leg with a splint or other suitable device.
8. *If a snakebite kit is available,* use the blade provided in the kit; otherwise, sterilize a knife blade over a flame. This must be done immediately after the victim has been bitten. Carefully make a 1/8 to 1/4 inch deep cut through each fang mark in the direction of the length of the arm or leg. The cut should not be more than 1/2 inch long. *Do not* make cross-mark cuts. Be very careful not to cut any deeper than the skin, as muscle, nerve or tendon damage may occur, particularly on the wrist, hand or foot.
9. If suction cups are available, place them over victim's wound and draw out body fluids containing venom; otherwise use your mouth if it is free of cuts and sores. *Do not* swallow the venom. Spit it out. Continue suction for 30 minutes or more. If the mouth method is used, rinse the mouth when finished.
Symptoms of coral snakes bites: some may not occur immediately. Any or all of the following may be present; slight pain and swelling at the site of the bite, blurred vision, drooping eyelids, difficulty in speaking, heavy drooling, drowsiness, heavy sweating, nausea and vomiting, difficulty in breathing, paralysis and possible shock.

Treatment for coral snake bites:
1. Quickly wash the affected area.
2. Immobilize a bitten arm or leg with a splint or other suitable device.
3. Keep the victim quiet.
4. Seek medical assistance promptly, preferably at the nearest hospital emergency room. If possible, have someone call ahead to notify the hospital of the poisonous snakebite and type of snake so that antivenin serum can be ready.
5. *Do not* tie off the bite area.
6. *Do not* apply cold or ice compresses.
7. *Do not* give the victim food or alcoholic beverages.

If bitten by a nonpoisonous snake:
1. Keep the affected area below the level of the victim's heart.
2. Clean the area thoroughly with soap and water.
3. Put a bandage or clean cloth over the wound.
4. Seek medical attention, as medication or tetanus shot may be necessary.

Stingray Fish - sting. Symptoms may include: extreme pain at sting site and swelling, decreased blood pressure, vomiting, diarrhea, irregular heartbeat, muscular paralysis, and even death.
Treatment:
1. Clean the wound of any remains of the stinger or its covering.
2. Place wound in hot water, as hot as the victim can stand without damaging the skin.
3. The wound should be kept in hot water for 30 to 90 minutes.
4. See a doctor if the stinger has broken off in the skin.

Sunburn - Sunburn is usually a first-degree burn of the skin resulting from overexposure to the sun. Prolonged exposure can lead to a second degree burn. Sunscreen of number 15 or higher is recommended if you are planning to spend time in the sun. Read and follow all manufactures instructions on sunscreen products. Limiting sun exposure is prudent. *Symptoms may include:* redness, pain, mild swelling, blisters and considerable swelling in severe cases.

Treatment:
1. Put cold water on the sunburn area.
2. If sunburn is severe, submerge the sunburned area under cold water until pain is relieved. It is also helpful to place cold wet cloths on the burned area. Do not rub the skin.
3. Elevate severely sunburned arms or legs.
4. If possible, put a dry sterile bandage on severely sunburned area.
5. Seek medical attention for severe sunburn. *Do not* break blisters or put ointments, sprays, antiseptic medications, or home remedies on severe sunburns.

The Red Cross, funded strictly by donations, provides 24-hour ambulance and paramedic services to the residents and guests of Rocky Point. If you see their van parked on the side of the road, drop a few coins in their can.

Business Services

Travel is one way of lengthening life.
-Benjamin Franklin

Air Conditioning

Sonora Solar Wind Charger & Gas Refrigeration, AP 180, Puerto Peñasco, 85440, P.O. Box 61, Lukeville, Arizona 85341, 011-52-638-36325. Authorized Carrier dealer. Kohler Power Systems, LP Gas gasoline. Servel Robur gas refrigeration, units use energy efficient gas and are compatible with solar systems. Authorized factory certified dealer, licensed in Mexico. Window units and heat pumps. Call Gary for information.

Attorneys

Attorneys at Law - Teachnor & McCrory S. C., Pescadores #7 in Old Port, 011-52-638-33182. Now open with a branch from Arizona to serve your legal needs, we are authorized to proceed legally in Mexico as well as in the U. S.

Brickner & Dariz Associates, S.A. de C.V., Blvd. Fremont #31, 011-52-638-36193. Law office, public accounting office, and title company. A public, civil, corporate experienced lawyer and official translation service. Map D32.

Castillo Montiel & Associates, Avenida Campeche y Calle Primera. Across from Rocky Garden Restaurant, 011-52-638-34137. English spoken, affiliated with Arizona attorneys. Map G14.

Lic. Lina Ma. Salazar N., Blvd. Kino y Ave. Sinaloa, 011-52-638-35675. Eleven years experience in civil law, contracts, leases, buying and selling. English spoken. Open every day.

Maria de la Luz Figueroa M., Ave Pino Suarez #122, just south of Villa Las Palmas Restaurant, 011-52-638-32992, 32534. English speaking.

Bakeries

Bakery, Calle 13 Miguel Hidalgo, two blocks from the light. Map C14.

Bakery, turn west at the covered walkway, one block after the railroad tracks, turn north, go about 1/4 mile, on the left across from the school. A small sign marks this in-home bakery. All items $.25. Items are baked in the morning in an old fashioned, hand made kiln. Around 2:00 p.m. everything goes on sale, by 4:00 p.m. almost everything is gone. Take a camera, this bakery is something to see.

Pan Bueno Bakery, Nicolás Bravo street & Cuauhtemoc. Bakes fresh daily, breads, cookies, cakes. Birote is 10 cents with bread. Map B61.

Cornejo Bakery, Old Port on Guillermo Munro across from the liquor store, 011-52-638-34121. English is spoken. Pastry and breads are baked fresh daily. Map F16.

Pastelería D'Irma, Calle 13 & Constitución Street, 011-52-638-32506. All your party needs, cakes and pastries. Map C14.

Banking Services
Banks

    Bancomer, Blvd. Benito Juárez & V. Estrella St., 011-52-638-32948. Hours 9-2 Monday through Friday. Map D10.

    Banamex, Blvd. Benito Juárez & Campeche St., 011-52-638-32053. Hours 9-2 Monday through Friday. Map D26.

Serfín, Blvd. Benito Juárez Blvd. & Calle 13, 011-52-638-34444. Hours 9-2 Monday through Friday. Map C8.

Ajo

BankOne, Ajo, Arizona, is the closest U.S. bank to Puerto Peñasco. Banking hours are Monday to Wednesday 10:00 a.m. to 3:00 p.m. Thursday 10:00 a.m. to 3:00 p.m. and 4:00 p.m. to 6:00 p.m. Friday 10:00 a.m. to 5:00 p.m. Closed Saturday and Sunday. In the U.S., 520-387-7616, Toll free from Mexico, 95-800-010-0068.

ATM Machines

Serfín Bank, lobby, Blvd. Benito Juárez Blvd. & Calle 13, 011-52-638-34444. Map C8.

Bancomer, Blvd. Benito Juárez & V. Estrella St., 011- 52-638-32948. Map D10.

Banamex, Blvd. Benito Juárez & Campeche St., 011-52-638-32053. Map D26.

Ajo

BankOne, Ajo, Arizona, on highway 85, across the street from ¡Si Como No!. In the U.S. 520-387-7616, Toll free from Mexico, 95-800-010-0068.

Money Exchange/Check Cashing

Bancomer Bank, Blvd. Benito Juárez & V. Estrella St., 011- 52-638-32909. Generally the best rates. Map D10.

Banamex, Blvd. Benito Juárez & Campeche St., 011-52-638-32053. Map D26.

Serfín, Blvd. Benito Juárez Blvd. & Calle 13, 011-52-638-34444. Map C8.

Casa de Servicios de California, Blvd. Benito Juárez, next to the Jim Bur Center. Drive through is open 7 days a week. Monday to Saturday 8:00 a.m. to 8:00 p.m. and Sunday 9:00 a.m. to 4:00 p.m., 011-52-638-33311, 36373. Map D8.

Irene Carrillo Angulo, Ave. Fco. Villa #65, the south side behind Motel Señorial. Open 24 hours, 011-52-638-32131. Map E31.

Money Exchange, Map A15.

Casa de Servicios Cimarron, between Bancomer Bank and Restaurant San Antonio on main street, 011-52-638-21372, and 21027). We give you more pesos for your dollar than any other place or we give you more dollars for your pesos. Map H16.

Barber And Beauty Shops

Barber Shop, Old Port next to Danny's Restaurant. Map F29.

D'Guille Unisex, Estilista Ave. Guillermo #33, 011-52-638-32441. Hair styling for men and women. Guillermo Salazar G. stylist. Map B91.

Glorias Beauty Shop, Ave. 12 Constitución #101, 011-52-638-32938. Unisex. Pamper yourself at affordable prices! Full service salon for men and women. Haircuts, styling, perms, frosts, tinting, manicures, pedicures, sculptured nails and facials. Check out the wide variety of beauty products and supplies at Arcticulos de Belleza de Peñasco.

Cookie Cutters, Old Port next to Victoria Originales, 011-52-638-33011. Full service salon for men and women. English spoken. Open Tuesday to Saturday 9:00 a.m. to 5:00 p.m. Map F6.

Heydi's Health & Beauty, across from La Fabula Pizza, 011-52-638-32878. A full service beauty salon. Unisex beauty shop offering permanents, dyes, cuts, manicures, pedicures, and shampoos. A corporal (body) therapy, massages for lymphatic drainage, sports, reductive and aroma therapy. Facial therapy including eyes, eyelashes and lips. We use Loreal and Aspid cosmetic products.

Rivera's Fashions & Beauty Shop, Boulevard de Las Americas, 011-52-638-21420. Fashion wear for men and women. Salon Unisex haircuts, hair styling, manicure, and pedicure. Map I88.

Boat and R.V. Storage

Peñasco Security Storage, 1fi mile north of the airport. In Arizona call 602-386-6800. Joe Dennis V. owner. Boat, R.V. and trailer storage.

David's Sea Side Storage Rentals, Blvd. Fremont on the road to Las Conchas, 011-52-638-33518, 35568. Reasonable rates based on monthly, semi-annual or annual rates. Full security. English spoken.

Builders

Design Maintenance and Construction, ask for Pedro Lasso or Inocencio Hernandez, 011-52-638-33761, Fax: 011-52-638-35087. English speaking, reliable, honest, reverences available, offering free estimates.

El Puerto de Oro S.A. de C.V. Design & Construction, Paseo Victor Estrella #23, 011-52-638-33537. We offer complete services in design and construction in the Puerto Peñasco area. Visit our model in Old Port. Your house is designed with you in mind. Remodels are our specialty. Special touches, court yards, fireplaces and entertainment centers. Map F34.

Francisco Pino, Calle Pescadores #7, in the Port District, 011-52-638-33182, Fax: 011-52-638-32165. Francisco (Pancho) Pino, designer and builder works closely with and recommends interior design consultant Vaughn E. Young of Scottsdale, for a special look that is uniquely yours. Free consultation and tour of homes. We work within your budget and help with site selection. Interior, exterior, and landscape design service. One year guarantee on all construction. English spoken.

Fausto Cesar Soto Arquitecto-Designer/Builder, APDO Postal #230, P. O. Box #312, Lukeville, AZ 85341, 011-52-638-32660. A touch of excellence in custom residential architecture.

Edilberto Velazquez M., Architect, Blvd. Fremont and Coahuila Street, 011-52-638-35614. Landscaping, Designer, Builder.

Churches

Catholic
Nuestra Señora de Guadalupe, Calle 20 Simon Morua. 7:00 a.m., 9:00 a.m., 6:00 p.m., 7:30 p.m.

Sagrado Corazón de Jesús, Old Port. 12 noon, 011-52-638-32959. Map F33.

San Martin de Porres, Ave Luis Encinas & Calle 27, by train station. 8:00 a.m. Phone 011-52-638-33364.

San Francisco, Blvd. J. Ortiz de Dominguez. 11:00 a.m.

San Judas Tadeo, near Cholla Road. 5:00 p.m.

Mormon
Cuauhtemoc Ave & 18th St.

Assembly of God
Luis Encinas Ave & 27th St., 011-52-638-33364.

Apostolic Church
Constitución Ave & 15th St. Map C25.

Family of God Christian Fellowship
Playa Elegante R.V. Park recreation room. Non-denominational. Sunday morning from 9:00 a.m. to 10:00 a.m.

World Light Church
Luis Encinas Ave & 16th St., 011-52-638-32765.

Clothing and Accessories
(See Chapter 13, Shopping)

Drug Stores
(See Chapter 13, Shopping)

Electrical

Lizola, Ave 12 south of Miguel Hidalgo. Electrical, plumbing, household and children's items, and miscellaneous hardware items. Map C15.

Peñasco Hardware & Plumbing, Ave 12 south of Miguel Hidalgo. Keys made, electrical, plumbing, construction, tools and miscellaneous hardware items. Map C16.

Veel Electrical Supply, Ave 13 Madero & Calle 17. Keys made, electrical, plumbing, construction, tools and miscellaneous hardware items. Map B55.

Florist

Florería Yeya, Comonfort & Justo Sierra Street, 011-52-638-32832. Plant decorations and flower arrangements, natural and artificial. Corsages and bouquets of roses, chrysanthemum, carnations, and orchids.

Gas Stations

PEMEX #1, Juarez Blvd., Map A6

PEMEX #2, 111 Juarez Blvd., 011-52-638-30739. Map B26.

PEMEX #3, 102 Juarez Blvd., 011-52-638-32281. Map B37.

PEMEX #4, 85 Estrella Avenue, 011-52-638-39000. Map F27.

PEMEX #6, near the airport as you enter Puerto Peñasco.

Cholla Bay
PEMEX #5, 340 Main Street.

Lukeville
Gringo Pass Chevron, Highway #85, Lukeville, Arizona 85341, 602-257-0887, Fax: 602-257-0887. Map G1.

Ajo
Holt Ajo Texaco, 429 2nd Avenue, Ajo, Arizona 85321, 520-387-6200.

Why Not Travel Store, 220 Hwy. #85, Why, Arizona, 85321, 520-387-7783, Fax: 520-387-6091.

Grocery Stores And Mercado's

California Produce, Blvd. Juarez. Fine selection of fresh fruits and vegetables grown in the agricultural center of Sonora. Map A19.

David's Super Value Market, Blvd. Fremont on the road to Las Conchas, 011-52-638-36393, and 33518. Puerto Peñasco's Circle K, beverages, snacks, candy, ice, cigarettes, grocery items and beer.

El Torito Carniceria Meat Market, on Blvd. Juarez across the street from Don Antonio Pharmacy, open Monday to Saturday 8:00 a.m. to 9:00 p.m. and Sunday from 9:00 a.m. to 4:00 p.m., 011-52-638-35533. We specialize in fine cuts of T-bone steaks, sirloin, rib-eyes, but we carry everything you need including pork, chicken, ground beef, roasts and *fajitas*. Map B32.

Mercado Del Pueblo, Constitución Ave, 011-52-638-32348. Daily specials, the great food market with everything you want; groceries, fruits, vegetables, meats. Other departments include hardware, electric and plumbing. José Ramón Infante León, owner. Map B45.

La Bellota, Blvd. Benito Juárez and Calle 18 Nicolás Bravo. Open 7 days from 8:00 a.m. to 10:00 p.m. with Saturday delivery. Largest selection of herbs, spices, groceries, fruits, vegetables, and packaged meats. Map B40.

La Huerta, Calle 21 & Prieto. Meat and vegetable market, can goods, beverages, dairy products, bulk foods, and paper products. Map B1.

La Merced, north of La Curva Restaurant about two blocks. The best selection of fresh fruits and vegetables. Paper products, household cleaning, meat market, and canned goods. Map C23.

La Tienda, Calle 1 at Playa Miramar next to Rocky Garden Restaurant, 011-52-638-32208. Open daily 8:00 a.m. to 10:00 p.m. Holidays until 12:00 p.m. Just like a small 7-11, good selection of snacks and beverages. Daily newspapers. Map G18.

Mercado Abarrotes El Texano, Calle 24 & Luis Encinas on the west side of town across the railroad tracks. Vegetables, meats, and fruits.

Pompano's, Old Port across from the marina boat launch, 011-52-638-34419. Beverages, snacks, and ice. Map F8.

Super Mercado Bonanza, Calle 20 & Ave. Jamie Nuno, 011-52-638-34400. Purified water, fruits, vegetables, groceries, ice and complete meat market.

Tienda La Michoacan, one block south of the Police Station toward the beach on Empresa de Solidaridad. On the corner. Map D27.

<u>Cholla Bay</u>
Licores la Cholla, Cholla Bay. A convenience store with all your essentials including groceries, bottled water, ice, beer and liquor.

Lukeville
Gringo Pass, U.S. side of the border on highway 85 at Lukeville, 602-527-0887. Motel, 602-254-9284. Bonded warehouse complete with duty free wine and liquor. Souvenirs, magazines, postcards, beverages, notary public, Mexican insurance, tourist information hardware, ammunition, camp supplies. Map G2.

Sonoyta
Mercado Bonanza, Blvd. de Las Americas, 011-52-638-21060. We have it all! Liquor, groceries, meat, fruits and vegetables. English spoken. Map I53.

Home Furnishings
(See Chapter 13, Shopping)

Home Improvement
(Hardware, Electrical, Paint, Tile)

Acabado's, 68 Prieto Ave.

Pueblo Supermarket, Constitución Ave, 011-52-638-32348. Hardware, electric and plumbing, plus much more. Map B45.

Del Puerto, Ave. Constitución #67, 011-52-638-33128. Del Puetto can make and install any type of window and door of aluminum and glass. Santana brothers, owners.

Distribuciones Ara, across from the Navy Hospital on Ave Luís Encinas. Hardware, caulk, paint, and thinners. Map D3.

Galo Badilla, Calle 21 #211, 011-52-638-32564. Refrigeration and heat installation and repair.

Implementos Marinos, Old Port, 011-52-638-32585, and 32733, Fax: 011-52-638-34020. Open Monday to Saturday 8:00 a.m. to 6:00 p.m. Closed Sunday. TruValue Hardware for all your construction needs. Caterpillar distributor and repair, Chevrolet distributor. Cement, re-bar, lumber, paint, sheet rock, and tools to do the job. Ask about delivery service. Map F1.

Lizola, Ave Constitution and Calle 13. Home furnishings, home improvement items, kitchen items and hardware. Map C15.

Maderreta De Peñasco S.A. de C.V., Ave. Altamirano #148, 011-52-638-32727, 33784. Chato Durán, Manager. Construction materials, wood, decorative mahogany and pine, plankwood in all measurements, electric and plumbing material.

Maderería San Manúel, Melchor Ocampo St. & Ave Iturbide, 011-52-638-33805, 33811, Fax: 011-52-638-33761. Construction materials, electrical, plumbing, wood, toilets, cement, paint, and hardware.

Mexican Tile Company, north of Cholla Bay road on Montes de Oca, 011-52-638-35839. Many handmade tile to choose from.

Osel Paints, Blvd. Benito Juárez across from the gas station. Map A9.

Peñasco Hardware, next to Lizola on Ave Constitution and Calle 13. A wide variety of home improvement items for plumbing, electrical, construction, tools, and tool supplies. Map C16.

Paint Store, Ave. Madero. Map B10.

Pinturas Y Acabado's Paints, Blvd. Benito Juárez & Calle 23, 011-52-638-32344. Map A11.

Rocky Tile, At the corner of Blvd. Benito Juarez & Blvd. Kino just north of the railroad tracks, 011-52-638-32200. Plumbing, floors, marble, gas/electric accessories, toilet accessories, compression pumps, mahogany doors. Tile has been tested in the U.S. and found to be of excellent quality but the grout tested poor. Map C12.

Veel Electrical Supply, Ave 13 Madero & Calle 17. Keys made, electrical, plumbing, construction, tools and miscellaneous hardware items. Map B64.

Insurance Agencies

Alejandro Portugal M. Insurance Agency, Blvd. Benito Juárez & Calle 20 Simon Morúa, across from the "Plaza" at the north end of town. Homeowners, cars, boats, and life insurance, 011-52-638-34070, Fax: 011-52-638-32390. Map B25.

YORA, Blvd. Benito Juárez #240, on the right as you enter Old Port, 011-52-638-36092, Fax: 011-52-638-36280. Yolanda Silva Guzmán. Automobile and personal property insurance coverage by the day, week, month or year. We provide translation services for your FM3 or real estate paperwork. English spoken. Map F3.

Mexico Bonito Realty, Cholla Road, 011-52-638-35737. Now offering insurance on your autos, homes and boats. We sell affordable policies from reliable Mexican companies and will give you a clear and concise explanation of the coverage and premiums. Thirty-five years of insurance experience expertise.

Pompano's, Old Port next to the marina boat launch, 011-52-638-34419. Automobile, boat, R.V., home and business insurance. Ask for Irma. Map F8.

Lukeville
Gringo Pass, U.S. side of the border on highway 85 at Lukeville, 602-527-0887. Motel, 602-254-9284. Grocery store, drug store, coffee shop, post office, bonded warehouse complete with duty free wine and liquor. Souvenirs, magazines, postcards, beverages, notary public, Mexican insurance, tourist information hardware, ammunition, camp supplies. Gas station with propane and white gas. Map H2.

Jewelry
(See Chapter 13, Shopping)

Key Shops & Locksmith
Locksmith, Map B22.

Teca's Key Shop, at the curve where Benito Juarez Blvd. and Ave. 12 meet, just north of the covered walkway, 011-52-638-30429. All kinds of keys made. Map B50.

Veel Hardware and Electrical Supply, Ave. 13 & Nicholas Bravo. Keys made, electrical, plumbing, construction, tools and miscellaneous hardware items. Map B64.

Zulema's, 97 Constitucíon Ave., 011-52-638-30527.

Laundry

Lavamatica Peñasco, Constitución & S. Morúa, 011-52-638-35785. Full service, fluff 'n fold, or washers and dryers available for your use. Open Monday to Saturday 8:30 a.m. to 7:30 p.m. Closed Sunday. Map B7.

Mail Services

Estafeta, Express Mail Service, Blvd. Benito Juárez and Calle 23. Map A13.

Rocky Point Times, Office is located on Blvd. Benito Juárez #121, at the corner of Calle 12, 011-52-638-36325. Mail service pick up and delivery, weekly trips to Lukeville. Map C10.

Movies, Records And Tapes

Buster Video, Ave Guillermo Prieto and Calle 17, downtown. Map B98.
Video Centro, Jim Bur Shopping Center. Map D9.

Video Genesis, Calle 24 & Barrera. Map A12.

Straus Records, Blvd. Juárez and Calle Simón Morúa, next to Javy's Hamburgers. Map B24.

Video Mundo, Calle 18 across from the gas station. Map B57.

Video Star, Calle Simón Morúa & Avenida de la Bandera, downtown. Map B23.

Video Store Max, toward Sonoyta, past La Estrellita Gas Station, 3rd block on the right, downtown. Map A16.

Newspapers

El Futuro, marketing office is located in Old Port on Calle Pescadores, 011-52-638-36099. Map F78. The printing office is located on Calle 16, 011-52-638-36099, Fax: 800-888-7785. Map B78. Arizona telephone: 520-888-7059/520-252-9231. E-MAIL: editor@hisp.com, WEB SITE: http://www.hisp.com.

Rocky Point Times, P. O. Box 887, Lukeville, AZ 85341, 011-52-638-36325. Office is located on Blvd. Benito Juárez #121, at the corner of Calle 12. Tom O'Hare is the Editor of the only newspaper written in English but his wife Sandy runs the show. Write to the address listed above for local information, letters to the editor or subscription requests. You may submit articles, photos, and letters to the editor. Map C10.

El Imparcial, Calle 18 next to Video Mundo. State of Sonora newspaper written in Spanish. Map B60.

Notary Public

Notary Public, Alcantar #34, 011-52-638-32006. Bank trust, certificates, contract and testimony. Lic. Osvaldo Rene Ortega Félix. Map F13.

Optometrist

Optica Crystal, Gilberto Pacheco, Optometrist. On Juan Aldama between Constitucion & Blvd. Benito Juarez. Available 24 hours. Laboratory on Premises. Complete eye exams. Glasses, repairs and frames. Open Monday to Saturday 9:00 a.m. to 1:00 p.m. and 3:00 p.m. to 7:00 p.m.

Optica Pau, located next to Dentista Hernandez in Old Port, 011-52-638-34338. Fashion frames, and contact lenses. Free eye exams. Map D30.

Pest Control

Pest Control, 011-52-638-33333. Complete services and termite control, for new residential construction and private homes.

Photography And Film Developing

Foto Estudio 2000, 53 Comonfort Ave., 011-52-638-33209. Video, portraits, film, and postcards. Map B71.

Michel's Importaciones, Avenida Constitucion, Sector Norte. Everything is imported from the U.S. Electronics, TV's, small appliances, film, film developing, batteries, perfume, baby clothing and accessories, kitchen gadgets and home furnishing accessories. Packaged foods including snacks, candy and gum. You can find everything you need! The "Wal Mart" of Rocky Point. Map B44.

Plumbing

Peñasco Hardware & Plumbing, Ave 12 south of Miguel Hidalgo. Keys made, electrical, plumbing, construction, tools and miscellaneous hardware items. Map C16.

Plumbing, call Eduardo García Hernandez, 011-52-638-36298. Repair and installation of water heaters, washing machines, toilets, sinks, showers and other plumbing problems.

Lizola, Ave 12 south of Miguel Hidalgo. Electrical, plumbing, household and children's items, and miscellaneous hardware items. Map C15.

Veel Electrical Supply, Ave 13 Madero & Calle 17. Keys made, electrical, plumbing, construction, tools and miscellaneous hardware items. Map B55.

Post Office

Post Office and Telegraph SCT Correos (Telegraph money). Behind the Jim Bur shopping center, open during business hours. Stamps can be purchased at some souvenir shops, just ask. Map D12 & D13.

Lukeville

Lukeville Post Office, Lukeville, Arizona, 85341-9998. From the U.S. call 520-387-6364, Fax: 520-387-5309. Postmaster Juanita Rose Arias. Lobby hours 8:00 a.m. to 5:00 p.m. Monday through Friday, 8:00 a.m. to 10:00 a.m. Saturdays. Window service 8:30 a.m. to 12 noon and 1:00 p.m. to 4:30 p.m. Map G2.

Property Management

Alberto's Reservations, P.O. Box 205, Lukeville, Arizona 85341, 011-52-638-35656. Condos, and beach front homes, at Playa Encanto, Peñasco Beach Club, Fiesta De Cortéz and Condominio Pinacate at the Marina Peñasco. Call or Fax. Map E18.

Brooks Real Estate and Property Management Rentals, P.O. Box 785, Lukeville, Arizona 85341, located on Ave Armanda Nacional down from the Marina Peñasco resort, 011-52-638-35080, Fax: 011-52-638-35080. Dee Brooks broker and owner. Condos, homes, commercial and private land available. Map E32.

Casa de Carolina Rentals, P.O. Box 589, Lukeville, Arizona 85341, 011-52-638-35482, Fax: 011-52-638-33144. In Arizona call,

602-248-0007. Ocean view apartments, beach front condos, and R.V. spaces.

Cindi's Sea of Cortéz Vacation Rentals and Property Management, located on the right as you enter town just north of the baseball stadium. P.O. Box 557, Lukeville, Arizona 85341, 011-52-638-35145. Rentals available every day of the week. A worry free vacation and worry free vacation property management.

Oceano Rentals and Property Management, located on the fork of Ruiz and Blvd. Juarez as you enter Old Port. Lupe Lopez office manager, 011-52-638-35413, Charlie & Sue Salem. In the U.S. call 602-935-3152, Fax: 602-935-3152. Map F5.

Rocky Point Reservations, established in 1987. Rocky Point specialists offering a large client base and reasonable rates. Cleaning and maintenance provided. In U.S. call 602-587-0345 or 1-800-42-ROCKY. In Mexico call 011-52-638-36092, or Alberto, 011-52-638-35656.

Servi Rents, Apdo. Postal #41, Puerto Peñasco, or P.O. Box 770, Lukeville, AZ 85341, 011-52-638-33225, Fax 011-52-638-33433. Servi Rents provides information on rentals and property which is for sale in the area. Many are located in the Las Conchas community. Most rentals do not provide sheets and towels and a deposit is required. A listing of their properties is printed monthly, stop by their office during business hours. Map B48.

Sylvia's Beach Condo's, 011-52-638-35249, Fax: 011-52-638-33144. Come to Rocky Point and relax on the beautiful Sea of Cortéz by the day, week or month.

Radio Station

XEQC Radio Station, 011-52-638-32201. The Queen of the sea, News, Sports, Music. 1390 Kcs. AM.

Souvenirs, Arts, Handicrafts
(See Chapter 13, Shopping)

Stationery And Printing

Bebo Imprenta, 89 Encias Ave., 011-52-638-33535.

El Estudiante Stationery, Calle 20 & Ave. Barrera. The "Office Max" of Puerto Peñasco. Map A21.

El Futuro, marketing office is located in Old Port on Calle Pescadores, 011-52-638-36099. Map F78. The printing office is located on Calle 16, 011-52-638-36099, Fax: 800-888-7785. Map B78. Arizona telephone: 520-888-7059/520-252-9231. E-MAIL: editor@hisp.com, WEB SITE: http://www.hisp.com.

Imprenta Y Papelera, 51 De Septiembre Ave., 011-52-638-21435.

Impresora Del Noroeste, Guillermo Prieto Ave. #25, 011-52-638-33550. For all your printing and copying needs, invitations, flyers, bills, publicity, and more.

Print Store Gary, Calle 17 & Ocampo. We can do a wide range of printing jobs on several new printing and copy machines. Bring your ideas or we can come up with some for you. Office supplies, paper, cards, pens, and gift items. English not spoken. Map B69.

Sistemas Grafico, 101 Bocanegra Ave., 011-52-638-33888.

Telephone And Fax Services

Telephone Service, to call direct to Mexico dial 011-52-638 + the number listed. 011 gets you to Mexico, 52 is the state of Sonora, 638 is the town of Puerto Peñasco. To dial out to the U.S. from Puerto Peñasco, dial 95, the rest is the same as in the U.S. Public telephones are located throughout town and in many of the larger hotels and restaurants.

- Telephone Office, downtown. Map B107.
- Manny's Beach Club recreation room. Map G10.
- La Curva Restaurant. Map C22.
- Servi-Rents Office, downtown. Map B48.
- Casetas Picos, long distance and Fax service.
  5 booths, open daily 7:00 a.m., to 11:00 p.m.
  Sundays 8:00 a.m. - 9:00 p.m. Map B68.
- Playa Bonita Hotel lobby. Map E19.
- Montiel Cellular Telephone. Map B34.
- Mr. Pancho long distance and Fax service. Map B72.

Aero Flash, experts in transport and fax service. Blvd. Juarez S/N Sucursal, 011-52-638-35181.

Tobacco
(See Chapter 13, Shopping)

Translation Services

Alberto's Reservations, P.O. Box 205, Lukeville, Arizona 85341, 011-52-638-35656. Office located in the Peñasco Beach Club, just ask for Alberto. Call or Fax. Map E18.

Brickner & Dariz Associates, S.A. de C.V., Blvd. Fremont #31, 011-52-638-36193. Law office, public accounting office, and title company. A public, civil, corporate experienced lawyer and official translation service. Map D32.

The Better Edge Vertical Blinds, 011-52-638-36209. We provide translation services for your FM3 paperwork. Map F32.

YORA, Blvd. Benito Juárez #240, on the right as you enter Old Port, 011-52-638-36092, Fax: 011-52-638-36280, Yolanda Silva Guzmán. Automobile and personal property insurance coverage by the day, week, month or year. We provide translation services, approximately $40, for your FM3 paperwork. English spoken. Map F3.

Transportation Services

Ajo Stage Lines, 1041 Solana, Ajo, Arizona 85321, for information call 1-800-242-9483, 1-800-942-1981, 95-800-942-1981, 520-387-6467, or Pathfinder Travel at 011-52-638-34420, 34032. Transportation provided from Phoenix, Tucson, or Ajo and Rocky Point and back. Ask about our package tours.

Travel Agencies

Pathfinder Travel, Blvd. Benito Juarez no. 154-4D, 011-52-638-34420, Fax: 011-52-638- 34032. Travel agency and real estate advisors, airline reservations, hotel reservations, rental houses, property management, tourist information. Map A16.

Bonel Travel Agency, Nicholás Bravo #12, 011-52-638-33555. We will arrange your pleasure or business trip in Mexico or any other part of the world. Airline ticket reservations, hotel and car reservations, organized excursions and tours. Map B38.

Upholstery

Tapiceria Munoz, 011-52-638-33471. Turn east off of Blvd. Juarez north of the railroad tracks at Rocky Tile, follow the road past La Curva and turn right at Merced market, 4 blocks on the left hand side.

Veterinarian

Cristobal Leon, 43 Morua Ave., 011-52-638-38100.

Posta Veterinaria María Teresa, Calle 20 & Ave. Prieto, 011-52-638-32574. Complete Veterinary service for dogs, cats, birds, and other animals. Map B18.

Sonoyta
The Old West Veterinarian, M.V.Z. Medico Guadalupe Díaz C., Lázaro Cárdenas, next to Mayra's Beauty Salon, center of town. We treat all types of animals. Vaccines, antibiotics, serums, surgeries and consultation. Map I79.

Water Distributors

Aqua Reyna, Calle 12 & Ave Sinaloa, 011-5-638-32161. Purified water in 1 or 5 gallon containers. Home delivery or buy direct at the plant. Purified by reverse osmosis.

Agua Solar, Blvd. Benito Juarez y Recleccion, on the main blvd. in front of the stadium, 011-52-638-32405. Purified water and ice cubes. Water sold by the gallon. Map A1.

Cielo Springs, next to La Tienda Market and Rocky Garden Restaurant. Open 8:00 a.m. to 10:00 p.m. Map G18.

Covadima, on Cholla Road across from the lumber yard. 011-52-638-33399. The best tasting water in town. A three gallon jug costs about $.40 to fill.

Oompas Water Company, 22 Juarez Blvd., 011-52-638-32060, 33507, Fax: 011-52-638-32626.

Welding Shops & Supplies

Gases Y Equipos Marinos (Air Products), 68-B Luis Ave., 011-52-638-32105, Fax: 011-52-638-32185.

Gases & Equipment Welding Supply (Atlas), 68 Luis Ave., 011-52-638-32105, 011-52-638-32008.

Pichirilo Welding, 114 Reelecion Ave., 011-52-638-33203.

Taller Para, near the harbor on Ave Luis Encinas across from the Caterpillar office, 011-52-638-34303. Map D2.

Window Coverings

The Better Edge Vertical Blinds, 011-52-638-36209. Small shop, but all work done at wholesale prices. Wood, mini, and pleated shades and window coverings. Call for free estimates. Map F32.

Cortinas Seaside Window Coverings, Nadero y Nicolás Bravo, located between Rocky Imports and Electrica Veel, 011-53-638-35191. Vertical blinds, custom draperies, pleated shades, horizontal blinds, mini blinds, roller shades made right here in Puerto Peñasco. Come in and ask for Benito or Marie. Map B63.

Real Estate

A man's feet should be planted in his country,
but his eyes should survey the world.
-George Santayana

A review of the rules on buying and owning real estate in the areas of interest to Americans are outlined in this chapter. New rules went into effect recently governing Americans and other foreign nationals buying and owning real estate in Mexico.

The acquisition of real estate in Mexico can be straight-forward, but common sense and the laws of Mexico must be considered if a buyer wants to obtain a good title and avoid problems. Failure to retain experts to assist in an acquisition can result in the same kind of problems encountered in the United States in acquiring real estate without proper advice from knowledgeable people. In order to avoid problems, it is advisable to obtain the advice of a qualified Mexico licensed attorney regarding legal and tax issues prior to depositing any money and prior to signing any form of agreement to purchase real estate.

The areas in which Americans cannot own property are within 100 kilometers (62 miles) along the border of Mexico and within 50 kilometers (about 31 miles) in from the coastline of Mexico. This area was formerly known as the "Prohibited Zone" and as of December 27, 1993, is known as the "Restricted Zone." Puerto Peñasco is considered part of the restricted zone.

In this restricted zone, under the former law, Americans and other foreign nationals could not acquire free title to real estate. However, they could acquire equitable title to real estate through a bank trust called a *"Fideicomiso."* Americans purchasing property outside of the prohibited zone can hold free title to the property.

The bank trust is a Mexican bank holding legal title to the real estate for the benefit of the American or other foreign national beneficiary. This American or foreign national is the equitable owner and possess the ownership (rights and duties) over the real estate. Under the old guidelines, a bank trust ownership ran for a period of 30 years. It could be renewed for an additional period of 30 years. This applies to both residential and commercial uses of real estate located within the restricted zone.

> *Note:* *It is very important to talk to a reputable agency before purchasing any property in Mexico. Get a second opinion. Do your homework and know the laws governing the purchase and sale. Do not give cash without obtaining a receipt, and do not act in haste.*

The new ownership rules under the December, 1993, legislation were changed to establish new guidelines. The first states that when real estate is to be used for residential purposes or activities, the bank trust system of beneficial ownership will remain in use. Bank trusts will run for a period of 50 years and can now be renewed for an additional 50 years.

Secondly, real estate to be used for non-residential purposes, such as commercial and/or industrial purposes, Americans or foreign nationals can establish Mexican corporations owning all of the stock in such a corporation. The corporation can acquire free title to the real estate as long as it is not being used for residential activities.

Corporations planning on acquiring real estate for commercial and/or industrial purposes must bear in mind that while no special permit will be required for such a purchase, each purchase will have to be recorded with the Ministry of Foreign Affairs.

Documents certifying the ownership of private land can be researched at the local Public Registry of Property in Puerto Peñasco. The Public Registry of Property is a government office in which documents are taken for registration so that third parties may research the ownership of land titles and liens on such titles. The Public Registry of Property is somewhat similar to a county recorder's office in the United States.

Title insurance is now available in Mexico. Lawyers Title Insurance, Latin Title, Stewart Title, and First American are providing title insurance for Mexico property.

The current bank trusts are being challenged in the courts. The Governor of Sonora and other Mexican officials are working to change the current laws to enable Americans and foreign nationals to acquire and hold the bank trusts for any and all properties they purchase for residential or commercial use.

Some American companies will finance loans for personal property and businesses investments in Puerto Peñasco. Check with a reputable real estate agency or your real estate office.

Notary Public

Notaries are authorized by the Mexican government in each state. The Notary Public works with buying and selling of property, foreign investments, inheritance, wills, mortgages, financial operations, credit titles and civil and commercial arbitration. He intervenes in civil and commercial business dealings working with the investors and businessmen. The Notary also works with the general public in giving judicial advisement. Every deal left in his hands will be a completely legal Mexican document.

The Mexican Notary Public is a highly specialized lawyer and must be consulted before investments are finalized in Puerto Peñasco. The authority of the Notary Public exceeds that of lawyers and is similar to that of an arbitrator in the United States. For over two hundred years the Notary Public has served the needs of the Mexican people and foreigners.

The Ejido System

The term "*ejido*" (pronounced â-heé-dô), refers to an agrarian community which has received and continues to hold land in accordance with the agrarian laws growing out of the Revolution of 1910. Simply, land owned in common by a peasant village. After the revolution of 1910 the *ejido* became the basis of land reform, whereby land was given to villages. Some property in and around Puerto Peñasco falls under the *ejido* system.

The ejido is organized according to highly democratic principles. The ultimate local authority rests with the general assembly wherein each member has one vote. The general assembly elects its executive committee by majority vote and the committee is responsible to the assembly. A safeguard is provided against possible human frailties by electing a vigilance committee to check on the activities of the executive committee as a guaranty that they will truly serve in the interests of the ejido and they will operate within the framework of the law. General supervision and guidance is provided for through the established agencies of the federal government who have representatives in every state. These include the Ministry of Agriculture, the Agrarian Department and the National Ejido Bank. The National Ejido Bank functions only among those ejidos to which it extends credit.

An *ejido* may vary from less than one hundred inhabitants to several thousand. According to the agrarian code, the code established by the Agrarian Department, land is not granted to a community unless there are at least twenty eligible individuals. Boys sixteen years of age and over are eligible to receive land. Each *ejido* is a legal entity. After the *ejido* is established, the principal function of the Agrarian Department is that of determining land boundaries and the settling of disputes which may arise.

Ultimate local authority is vested in the general assembly, with the administrative functions delegated to two local committees: (1) the *comisariado ejidal* (a type of executive committee) consisting of three elected members with three alternates, and (2) the vigilance committee, also consisting of three elected members and three alternates.

The general assembly, as the name implies, comprises all the *ejidatarios* in a given *ejido*. Meetings are held once a month at the call of the *comisariado ejidal* in which notice must be given at least one week in advance. A quorum at these meetings consists of one-half the total number of *ejidatarios* plus one. The members of the *comisariado ejidal* are elected for a term of three years by a majority vote of the general assembly. Unless the vote is unanimous, the minority elects the members of the vigilance committee. The principal functions of the general assembly are, (1) to elect and remove the members of the *comisariado ejidal* and the vigilance committee in accordance with the provisions of the code, (2) to authorize, modify or rectify the decisions of the *comisariado ejidal* according to the law, (3) to discuss and approve the reports rendered by the *comisariado ejidal* and make available the statements of account which they approve to be posted in a visible place for observance, (4) to request the intervention of the agrarian authorities on matters relating to the suspension or privation of rights of members of the *ejido*, (5) to issue rulings in which the ejido lands should be used.

The executive committee is in charge of the active management of the affairs of the *ejido*. The three members serve as chairman, secretary and treasurer. Once having been elected, a member of the executive committee may be removed from office for failure to comply with the decisions of the general assembly, violations of the provisions of the Agrarian Code, disobeying rulings, misappropriation of funds, being prosecuted for an offense punishable by imprisonment or for being absent from the *ejido* for more than three consecutive months without a justified reason. The general functions of the committee are as follows, (1) to represent the ejido with power of attorney before administrative and judicial authorities, (2) to administer such ejido property as is used collectively, (3) to exercise vigilance over the division of collective lands into plots, (4) to call a meeting of the general assembly at least once a month or when needed, (5) to acquaint the general assembly with the work carried out, the expenditure of funds, (6) to comply and enforce the rulings of the general assembly.

The vigilance committee is charged with the duty of checking up on the actives of the executive committee and to see that the mandates of the general assembly are carried out. This committee consists of three members, chairman, secretary and treasurer.

The *Ejido* Bank was organized in 1936 for the purpose of supplying credit to the ejidatarios. The central agency of the bank is located in Mexico City and thirty five are located throughout "convenient areas" of the country. An agency can overlap state boundaries. At present the bank is owned and controlled by the federal government.

Since *ejido* lands cannot be mortgaged or divided in any way, the main source of security to the bank lies in the crops and the accumulated equipment. Although the capital of the bank is controlled by the federal government, private funds are loaned through the bank with the latter guaranteeing them. The *Ejido* Bank is almost the only source through which the ejidatarios are able to secure credit. This is because their lands cannot be mortgaged and the only security they have to offer is their crops. The *Ejido* Bank does not extend any credit to private individuals.

> *Note: Frontier Travel Adventures and the author do not authenticate the business practices nor do we endorse any agencies listed in this chapter. Businesses are listed as reference information only. We recommend consulting more than one firm and doing your homework before making a selection.*

Real Estate Agencies

Brooks Real Estate and Property Management Rentals, P.O. Box 785, Lukeville, Arizona 85341, located on Calle 13 up from the Marina Peñasco Resort, 011-52-638-35080, Fax: 011-52-638-35080. Dee Brooks broker and owner. Condos, homes, commercial and private land available. Map E32.

Del Mar at Las Conchas, offices located across from Plaza Las Glorias Hotel. In the U.S. call 1-800-263-9563, 011-52-638-35712. A gated ocean village, brick paved streets, terraced home sites, underground utilities, waste water treatment, strict design control, club house, swimming pool, workout room, bar kitchen, barbecue areas, gated access to the beach. Map E24.

Mexico Bonito Realty, one block west of the highway on the south side of Cholla Road. P.O. Box 73, Puerto Peñasco, Sonora, 83550.

U.S. 1-800-727-6822, Tucson 502-294-0411, Mexico 011-52-638-35737, Fax: 011-52-638-35737. Commercial and private land real estate development. Property Management and information on all types of rentals.

Pathfinder Travel, Blvd. Benito Juarez No. 154-4D, 011-52-638-34420, Fax: 011-52-638- 34032. Travel agency and real estate advisors, airline reservations, hotel reservations, rental houses, property management, tourist information. Map A16.

Peñasco Beach Club, Paseo Balboa next to the Plaza Las Glorias Hotel, P.O. Box 245, Lukeville, Arizona, 85341, 011-52-638-34268, Fax: 011-52-638-33374. Exclusive beach front condominiums with two bedrooms and two baths, city utilities, appliances, ceiling fans, central air-heat systems, security parking, pool, Jacuzzi, tennis courts and more. Financing available. Map E18.

Playa Encanto, sales office is located on Blvd. Benito Juarez, 011-52-638-35790, Fax 011-52-638-33476. Fully approved subdivision located 15 miles east of Puerto Peñasco off Blvd. Fremont. Offering fifty year bank trusts, fifteen year financing with easy terms. Pristine beach front lots.

Proaset Realty, located on Ave 14 & Blvd. Fremont, P.O. Box 731, Lukeville, Arizona 85341, 011-52-638-34404, Fax: 011-52-638-33411. Lists only property that has a bank trust or that on which a bank trust can be obtained. Professional guidance throughout the bank trust procedure. Map D14.

Realty Network, located in Old Port across from the old Hotel Peñasco. In the U.S. call 602-569-1125. Mail address: 19848 N. Cave Creek Road, Phoenix, Arizona 85024. Map F24.

Servi-Rents, Blvd. Benito Juarez, 011-52-638-33225. A full range of real estate services, both residential and commercial. Property management available. English spoken. Map B48.

Vista Del Mar Realty, Cholla Bay, 011-52-638-33473, U.S. 602-838-3896. Specializing in Cholla Bay and Playa Encanto. Beach front lots, custom homes and resales. Bank trusts and financing available.

Watson Financial, Inc., 011-52-638-35852, in the U.S. call: 1-800-404-8000 or 602-569-9500. Financing available for your Mexico property, utilize 100% equity in your U.S. home. Contact Marilyn Watson, a Puerto Peñasco resident.

Rocky Point has come a long way since the 1940's. This picture was taken in the Old Port near the fish market. Photo courtesy of Guillermo Munro.

Shopping - Chic & Cheap

I will buy with you, sell with you, talk with you.
-William Shakespeare, *The Merchant of Venice*

Whether you are a weekend visitor or plan to live in Puerto Peñasco forever, you will find everything you need to make your stay a pleasant one. This small town provides everything from exceptional artwork to dime store knick-knacks, designer clothing to cheap tee shirts. Whether you are building a house or fixing a boat, there are plenty of businesses in the surrounding area to choose from and new ones are opening all the time.

The new Marina Peñasco Resort offers stores including liquor, travel agency, clothing boutiques, pizza restaurant, gift shops, boat rentals, candy and ice cream stores, mail boxes, copy center and stationery store, and many more services. Merchants are not listed individually because of unavailability at press time. Shops are clustered together in the area of the esplanade across from the Plaza Las Glorias Hotel. See Map E25.

Duty Free

Each visitor may bring back, duty free, articles not exceeding $400 in retail value. Duty must be paid on all items in excess of this amount. This exemption is allowed only once within a 30-day period. This applies to articles that are for you or your family's personal use, souvenirs of the trip. The articles must accompany you on your return to the U.S. The $400 exemption may include no more than 1 liter of spirits and no more than 200 cigarettes and 100 cigars. For complete information on restricted or prohibited articles, alcoholic beverages, gifts and duties see Chapter One, "Crossing the Border."

Bartering

Bartering is not an argument, it is a polite discussion of the price-and should be conducted calmly with respect for the other person. Haggling over the price, whether it being an ornament or a fine carving, is considered proper and is expected; that is why the price will come down if you work at it. By not bartering you will depress the elaborate pricing system and loose the opportunity to participate in friendly communication with the other person. Bartering is a way of shopping, in the marketplace and on the beach. Many shops in town and at the hotels have "set prices" which are not negotiable, they will let you know if this is the case.

People coming back from Mexico tell tales of fabulous deals they made by bartering with shopkeepers across the border. Acquiring and bringing back numerous souvenirs at bargain prices can be misleading to the average traveler. It may be a big disappointment, especially if you think you will be getting away with highway robbery. Although, you can earn a lot of respect from the people you deal with if you know how to barter, not to mention saving as much as 30% off the first asking price.

There is only one way to get a true bargain. The first rule of shopping is not accepting the first price you hear. Because you are a *gringo,* it is assumed you can afford it no matter what the cost. The merchant may quickly double or triple the price. When this happens, you can bet the quoted price is far above what the fair price should be.

The second rule is to never buy anything you feel is not a reasonable price for the item. Or, if you are not sure of the authenticity of the item. This is especially true when purchasing silver. There is nothing worse than the feeling you have been cheated, especially when you think you got a good deal from honest bartering. You may find that others purchased the same item for a lesser price, but as long as you feel you paid a fair price for the item, don't feel badly.

The most important thing to remember about bartering is that you are seen as willing and eager to communicate and to acknowledge local customs. Merchants have little respect for *gringos* who throw their money away and are marked as fools.

What To Pay?

Start with a greeting. In many foreign countries this is expected before talking to anyone. Otherwise, you might be ignored. Squeezing, smelling, lifting, and tasting are all considered acceptable, followed by the word *"¿Cuánto?"* (How much?), or *"¿Cuánto cuesta?"* (How much does it cost?), or try *"¿Cuánto es?"* (How much is it?), each followed by *"por favor,"* (please). When you are quoted a price, ponder on the thought, examine the merchandise and think about your counter offer. This can be the amount you are willing to pay or less than what you want to settle on so you have room for negotiation. You can say something like: *"Lo llevo en ...dolares,"* (I'll take it for...dollars), *"¿No me da en...$$$?"* (Won't you give it to me for...?) or *"¿No sale en...$$$?"* (Won't it go for...?). By the shopkeeper's reaction and counter offer, you can judge the proper offer and selling price. Bartering can be addicting. Once you have made your first "deal" you won't be able to stop.

Never act like the merchandise is inferior or unappetizing. The locals are proud people and no matter how much you think the item is stained, faded or soiled, they still think it is top quality. Once you have degraded them or their merchandise the sale is over. It is best to move on and not make the same mistake again. You can question whether there is another item available because there is a problem with the one you are looking at. With honest communication you can get exactly what you want and merchants will be eager to comply with your requests.

Walking away after the last rock bottom offer has been made is not always the best technique. This may be effective, but sometimes it is best to hang around waiting for the vendor to make a decision. On small purchases, if you leave too soon, they may not bother. As you leave always say *"Gracias, adiós"* (Thank you, good-by), which brings attention to your departure.

Businesses

Attorneys
(See Chapter 11, Business Services)

Automotive Parts and Service/Boat Repair
(See Chapter 4, Behind The Wheel)

Banking
(See Chapter 11, Business Services)

Barber and Beauty Shops
(See Chapter 11, Business Services)

Boat and Boat Storage
(See Chapter 11, Business Services)

Builders
(See Chapter 11, Business Services)

Candy Stores

Dulces Lupita Candy, Ave 15 & Melchor Ocampo. Map B81.

Lupita Candy, Blvd. Juarez. Map A18.

Dulces Paty Candy, Ave 15 & Melchor Ocampo. Map B82.

Churches
(See Chapter 11, Business Services)

Clothing And Accessories

Almacenes El Rey, Avenida Constitución. Women's clothing, stockings, under garments, dresses and jeans. Children's clothing. Luggage and beach towels. Men's suits. Map B42.

Bazaar, turn east on I. Aldama, 6 blocks, Casa Dorothy is located on right side of the street, a two story, burnt orange, stucco building is on the left, turn left. This two block area is filled with small stores catering to locals. You will find everything from appliances to home furnishings, household items, clothing, jewelry, shoes, children's clothing and school supplies. The Bazaar is worth an afternoon stroll.

Boulevard One Men's & Women's Clothing, Mini Mall on Blvd. Benito Juarez & Calle 22. Jeans, tee shirts, shorts, tops, hats, jewelry for men and women. Map A24.

De Deveras, Cuauhtémoc Ave. & 17 Street. Shoe store, large selection for the whole family.

Exclusive Brenda Women's Clothing, Calle 19 & Ave 12 Constitución. Map B30.

Gutycor Perfumería, Juan de la Barrera & 17. Gifts, cosmetics and imported perfumes. Map B108.

Krirval Children's Clothing, Mini Mall on Blvd. Benito Juarez & Calle 22, (011-52-638-34492). Swimwear, costume jewelry, hose, belts, tops, blouses, shorts, and slacks. Map A23.

Michel's Importaciones, Avenida Constitucion, Sector Norte. Everything is imported from the U.S. Electronics, TV's, small appliances, film, batteries, perfume, baby clothing and accessories, kitchen gadgets and home furnishing accessories. Packaged foods including snacks, candy and gum. You can find everything you need! The "Wal Mart" of Rocky Point. Map B44.

Miscelanea Betzy, #237 & Ave Luis Encinas, west side of town beyond the railroad tracks. Clothes for every occasion. Fran Palomino Torres, owner.

Puerto Peñasco T-shirt & Clothing Co. since 1994, Paseo Victor Estrella, one block from the fish market in Old Port, 011-52-638-35286. Open 7 days from 9 a.m. to 6 p.m. T-shirts and clothing designed and made here, wearable fit, sweatshirts, swimwear, children's clothing and Hanes Beefy-T/Oneita. Map F26.

Ropa y Novedades, Avenida de la Bandera. Women's, children's and men's clothing. Cosmetics, lotions, and perfume. Map B105.

Zapatería Pinacate Hills, Blvd., Juarez and Calle Simón Morúa. Men's, Women's and children's shoes, boots and casual shoes. Map B31.

Drug Stores And Farmacias

In the main areas of town they are modern, clean and well organized stores with large selections. It is best to compare prices.

Botica Don Antonio, Blvd. Juárez & Cuauhtémoc, 011-52-638-32170, Fax: 011-52-638-35018. Open Monday through Saturday 9:00 a.m. to 9:00 p.m., Sunday 9:00 a.m. to 3:00 p.m. Drug store, money exchange, film, hair color, lotions, Retin-A, Premarin, Motrin, Ampicilin, Penicillin. Map B39.

Botica Lux, Calle Melchor Ocampo #146, 011-52-638-32881. Open 8:00 a.m. to 11:00 p.m. Film, Coppertone solar filters to protect the skin, Retin "A" and powdered milk. Map B111.

Botica San Francisco, Cholla Bay Road.

Botica San Jorge, S. Morúay & San Luis, 011-52-638-32856.

Drug Store Silvia, Cholla Bay Road, 011-52-638-33643. English spoken, offers a discount on all medication. Good selection including Tagamet, Azantal, Pen V. K., Retin-A, Naproxen, Ventolin, Ampicilin, Nicorete and Nizoral.

Farmacia Hegar, Ave 10, past the Police Station, one block off main street on the road to Playa Miramar. Dr. Juan R. García, General Medicine is next door. Open 7 days. Monday through Saturday 9:00 a.m. to 8:00 p.m., Sunday 9:00 a.m. to 2:00 p.m. Complete drug store including health and beauty supplies, Retin-A, film, camera accessories and more. Prescriptions filled. Map D28.

Farmacia San Andres, Constitucíon Street & 14 Ave in back of the electric building, 011-52-638-34453, 32902. Open daily 9:00 a.m. to 9:00 p.m. English spoken, prescriptions filled, perfumes, gifts, toys, Retin "A." Map C5.

Farmacia Santa Fe, S. Morúa & Blvd., next to the hospital, 011-52-638-33431. Map B15.

Farmacia Santa Rosa, L. Encinas & Calle 15, the west side of the railroad tracks, at the light, turn north, one block, 011-52-638-32906.

Farmacia Zygle, S. Morúa & J. de la Barrera, 011-52-638-32211. Prescriptions filled, cosmetics, lotions, women's clothing and undergarments, hose, purses, baby toys, diapers, and accessories. Map B20.

P. H. Pharmacy, Blvd. Kino and Calle 12. Perfumes, baby items, shampoo, lotion, hair color, film, cigarettes, jewelry, purses and prescriptions filled. Map C18.

San Martín, Cholla Bay Road and San Luis Ave. Prescription medicine, perfumes, gifts, film, ice, bottled water and Retin "A," with special attention given to tourists if requested.

<u>Sonoyta</u>
Botica San Marcelo, Blvd. de Las Americas. 011-52-638-21024. Prescription medicine, perfumes, gifts, film, ice, bottled water and Retin "A". Special attention given to tourists, if requested.

Botica San Luis, Francisco E. Kino Street & 16 de September #51, 011-52-638-21068. Drug store, prescription medicine, perfumes, gifts, film, purified ice cubes and water, toys and copies made. Map 15.

Farmacia Moderna, Blvd. de Las Americas. Map I71.

Electrical
(See Chapter 11, Business Services)

Grocery Stores and Markets
(See Chapter 11, Business Services)

Home Furnishings

Casa Bonita, 20 de Noviembre across from Hotel Peñasco in Old Port, 011-52-638-35372. A nice selection of hand-crafted furniture, gifts, home accessories, glassware, linens, and wall decorations. Design service and custom orders available. Map F22.

El Tanichee, across from the gas station next to Cheiky's Pizza in Old Port, open 7 days a week from 9:00 a.m. to 5:00 p.m., 011-52-638-35421. Fine Mexican art decor and antiques. The largest and rarest sea shell selection in town, beach toys, inflatable rafts, beach mats, and swimming suits. Unique contemporary southwest fashions, home of the Mayo & Yaqui willow, saguaro, pig skin and wrought iron furniture. Map F42.

Jim Bur Plaza, Blvd. Benito Juarez. A variety of stores which sell home furnishings and curios. Map D9.

Originales Victoria, Alcantar in Old Port, 011-52-638-33707. Beautiful hand-painted furniture. Attended by Owner Victoria Priego. Special orders, your design or theirs. Curios, accessories and gifts. You must see this shop for one of a kind items! Map F7.

Pueblo Viejo De Peñasco Fine Furniture, Old Port, 011-52-638-35248, 36363, Tucson 520-791-2149. The largest selection of home furnishings, rattan & wicker, southwestern, iron pieces and stone work, pots, lamps, fabric selections, bath and linen accessories. Very unique and different items hand-crafted in Mexico. Complete design service. Map F21.

Paloma Blanca, up the hill from the fish market in Old Port. Open from 9:00 a.m. to 6:00 p.m. daily. Furniture, Mexican curios, purses, hand made saguaro furniture, handicrafts from Jalisco, Mexico. Map F57.

Home Improvement
(See Chapter 11, Business Services)

Ice Cream
(See Chapter 7, Eateries)

Insurance Agencies
(See Chapter 11, Business Services)

Jewelry Stores

Joyería Brillante, Calle 20 Simón Morúa and Blvd. Juarez. Discover a world of magnificence: diamonds, jewelry and semi-precious stones. Rings, earrings, clocks, translators, watches by Venrus, Bulova, and Citizen. Map B24.

Joyería La Perla, Ave Constitución & Calle 17. Magnificent quality and affordable prices, jewelry and watches. Map B43.

Pablo's Casa de Amatista, Old Port, 011-52-638-33545. Fine jewelry, mineral specimens, semi-precious stones, gifts. Closed during the summer months. Map F60.

Joyería Reyna Jewelers, Blvd. Benito Juárez & Calle 23 across from the gas station. Map A10.

Shops And Locksmith
(See Chapter 11, Business Services)

Laundry
(See Chapter 11, Business Services)

Liquor Stores
(See Chapter 8 Cantinas & Entertainment)

Mail Services
(See Chapter 11, Business Services)

Movies, Records & Tapes
(See Chapter 11, Business Services)

Newspapers
(See Chapter 11, Business Services)

Optometrist
(See Chapter 11, Business Services)

Pest Control
(See Chapter 11, Business Services)

Photography
(See Chapter 11, Business Services)

Plumbing
(See Chapter 11, Business Services)

Post Office
(See Chapter 11, Business Services)

Property Management
(See Chapter 11, Business Services)

Souvenir, Arts, Handicrafts

Amigas, Old Port on the waterfront. Unique one-of-a-kind, moderately priced gift items, occasional furniture, unusual artist pieces, interesting objects d' art, hand made in Guanajuato and Guadalajara. Don't miss this experience. Map F49.

Bubbles and Things, Paseo U Estrella #23, across from Puerto Peñasco Investments in Old Port, 011-52-638-33537. Fine Mexican arts, gifts and furniture. Map F35.

Como Tu, on the waterfront in Old Port. Indian style clothing, jewelry, hats, and accessories from the heart of Mexico. Map F48.

Cholla Mall, located on the road to Cholla Bay, also known as "Rodeo Drive." Many stores selling local handicrafts, clothing, home furnishings and accessories, tee-shirts and hand made creations. Use bartering here!

David Hoyos, located on the side street off of the road to Old Port, turn near the oil tanks. Stain glass designs, gulf artistry in copper and brass.

La Artesiana Mexicana, Jim Bur Shopping Center. Souvenirs, Mexican handicrafts, sandals, swimwear, shorts, dresses, tee-shirts, artwork, holiday decorations, and vanilla. Casual clothes for men, women, and children. Map D9.

Local Bazaar, downtown, go east on I. Aldama at Blvd. Juarez, six blocks, Casa Dorothy is located on the right, a two story stucco building painted burnt orange is on the left. Turn left. The whole block is filled with shops chock-full of adult clothing, shoes, children's clothing and household items. Across the street you will find new and used furniture, home appliances and tools. Adventuresome travelers will find this Bazaar worth a visit.

Luis & Company, in the Jim Bur shopping center, 011-52-638-33011. Kites, beach clothing, beach toys, sport kites, diving supplies, film, and cameras. Map D9.

Mercado de Artesanias Las Palmas, Old Port before reaching the boat dock on the right side of the street. Independently owned shops selling local handicrafts, clothing, blankets, bags, wall hangings, lotions, jewelry, accessories, knick-knacks, ponchos, hammocks, etc. Use bartering here! Map F2.

Old Port Galleria, on the Malecón next to Lily's, 011-52-638-36321. Paintings, sculptures, art objects, designer jewelry and distinctive clothing. Map F59.

Old Port Curios, on the waterfront in Old Port. Variety of shops that offer clothing, blankets, tee-shirts, lotions, vanilla, shell decorations, footwear, hair accessories. Map F17.

Go Fly A Kite, Old Port. 011-52-638-33545. Open 7 days a week from 10:00 a.m. to 5:00 p.m. Kites, windsocks, banners, toys and flags. Map F19.

Victoria's Hormiga, Old Port, Calle: Alcántar #52. Victoria Priego, owner. Original hand painted furniture can be special ordered, home accessories, glassware, jewelry. Map F7.

Wendy's Curios, 16 de Septiembre y Zaragoza across from Pueblo Viejo in Old Port. 011-52-638-34249. Clothing, Talavera, glassware, ceramics and clay items made in Mexico. Map F14.

Sonoyta
Vázquez, Blvd. de Las Americas. 011-52-638-21189. Thousands of square feet packed with unique merchandise. Beer, wine, liquor, gifts, souvenirs, curios, glassware, bird cages, handmade furniture, tables and chairs. Map I91.

Stationery & Printing
(See Chapter 11, Business Services)

Telephone & Fax Services
(See Chapter 11, Business Services)

Tobacco

Tobacco Shop Tabaqueria Malecón, Old Port, on the sidewalk of the Viña del Mar Hotel on the Malecón, 011-52-638-35493. Cuban cigars. Open seven days a week. Map F58.

Transportation Services
(See Chapter 11, Business Services)

Travel Agency
(See Chapter 11, Business Services)

Upholstery
(See Chapter 11, Business Services)

Veterinary
(See chapter 11, Business Services)

Water Distributors
(See Chapter 11, Business Services)

Welding
(See Chapter 11, Business Services)

Window Coverings
(See Chapter 11, Business Services)

Winter visitors will find everything from letter openers to poncho's at Cholla Mall, which is also known as Puerto Peñasco's "Rodeo Drive."

Mexican Handicrafts

Blankets And Sarapes

If you are looking for a blanket or *sarape* to be used for decoration, the selection is endless. A coarse, uncleaned wool mixed with a stiff *burro* hair is widely used in most weaves. They will not get softer, but rather, scratchier after a few washings. The finest blankets and *sarapes* are made of an acrylic blend, which are warm and wash beautifully. Mostly are multi-colored, with each side showing a dominant color.

Price is determined by pattern, size, wool content, weight, color and tightness of the weave. Wool is more expensive than cotton or acrylic. The price range of *sarapes* is wide. It takes diligent shopping to find a really good one that isn't targeted to the tourist dollar.

Clay

Clay is one of Mexico's most distinctive tools in creating popular art. Pottery clay is simply earth of a pliable consistency. It is abundant in many areas of the country and inexpensive to use.

After pots and other objects are formed, they may be left plain or they are decorated by adding small pieces of soft clay to the surface. Surfaces are carved, pierced, or incised with a tool. Color is applied either before or after the piece is fired in a kiln. Colored slip or glaze is painted on with a brush or the whole piece is dipped into a colored liquid glaze. Slips add color to clay pieces, glazes add both color and a protective glossy finish. Cooking pots, dishes and glassware are glazed inside to make them "wet proof."

Mexican pottery can be described as low-fired in kilns built directly on the ground or in underground chambers lined with brick and fired from a pit underneath. Fuel for the kiln is wood, reed, grass, corncobs, dried dung and any available material that will burn. Many Mexican pots, sculptures, and toys are left in their plain earth color: buff, red, brown, or black. The color is determined by the chemicals in the clay and sometimes by the way it is fired.

Tempra paints are inexpensive. Opaque colors are made with an albuminous base and are water soluble. They are used to paint most of the hand-crafted objects or toys in Mexico. They are not colored with ceramic colors or aniline dyes.

Copper

The craft of soldering and hand hammering *cobre* to make decorative containers, candlesticks, etc. is said to have been taught to the natives by a Spanish bishop in the sixteenth century. The *tarascan* Indians living in the high mountains carry on the craft almost exclusively in one small village called *Villa Escalante*. Skilled metal workers hammer out handsome copper plates, trays, urns, vases, pots, cups, mugs, pitchers and bells which are sold throughout Mexico. All have the characteristics of subtle hammer marks in the metal, achieved only by hand forming. The styles have another-century look. Craftsmen specialize in making tiny copper miniatures of all the same objects. The work of making a very small copper vase or pitcher is in some ways even more difficult than producing the larger pieces. They can be found in enough shapes and small sizes to gratify the most discriminating collector.

Fireworks

Fireworks may be called a favorite toy of Mexico and there is a calendar full of occasions on which they are used during the year. The *pirotécnicos* and *coheteros* who make these fireworks are considered

---

important artists with highly specialized skills, not to mention a bit of daring. They must be licensed to handle explosives, but in Mexico there are no laws against their products. Most fireworks are outlawed in Arizona and many other states. Trying to smuggle them across the border could result in fines or imprisonment.

Hammocks

Shops offer a wide variety of *hamacas,* from cheap nylon to wonderfully comfortable linen models edged with finished wooden frames. The best hammocks come from Merida in the Yucatan.

The largest hammocks can hold two people. The size is about 16 feet long, weigh 4-1/2 to 5-1/2 pounds, stretch out to 10-16 feet in width without pulling too hard. It will have about 100 or more pairs of strings at each end.

A medium sized hammock, for an adult or two children, should weigh 2-1/2 to 3-1/2 pounds, with slightly smaller measurements and string count than the large size.

The best hammocks are pure cotton. Nylon end strings are becoming common but they are inferior to natural fibers. The thinner the thread the better. Thin thread is longer fibered, wears better and is more comfortable than thick threads. Cotton resists stretching, is more color fast and feels better than synthetics.

Along the edges there should be 10 to 16 strings that are tightly secured to the rest of the hammock. This is important to prevent sagging and to maintain the shape of the hammock.

The tighter the weave the more comfortable and resilient the hammock will be. The best are double or triple woven with the holes between being very small. With one person in a large size hammock, the weave looks almost like a solid cloth. It is said that 5 miles of thread is used in a large size and 3 miles in a medium size hammock. The fewer splices, or knots, the better.

The end loops should be thick and very tightly wrapped. Hammocks should be washed in cold water, by hand. Store in a moth and mouse-proof container when not in use.

Piñatas

The origin of the *Piñata* is uncertain but the idea may have been brought first to Italy from the Orient by Marco Polo. The Spanish copied the diversion from the Italians who played their game with a clay pot called a *pigñatta*, hence the name. It was then an entertainment for nobles and ladies of the sixteenth or seventeenth century who hoped to gather up some of the jewels and baubles with which their host had filled the breakable pot. The game is now played in Mexico in exactly the same way as in Italy and later in Spain, where it became a Lenten custom. *Piñatas* can be seen hanging in the curio shops and markets. They are made of pots covered in tissue paper in shapes of animals, birds, cartoon characters, and Christmas ornaments.

The *piñata* is hung overhead from a rope, one participant in the game is blindfolded and given a long stick with which he or she tries to hit the pot. Children take turns at being blindfolded and swinging the stick. Finally, when someone hits the pot hard enough to break it, the other players scramble on the ground for the scattered prizes. The game goes on for quite a few minutes since a controlling cord is used to swing the pot out of reach of the batters. It is a kind of noisy and happy version of grab bags.

Those who seek Christian symbolism and connect the *piñata* with the Christmas season say the decorated pot represents the spirit of evil. The goodies are symbolic of temptation and the blindfolded player is the child's blind faith that destroys evil. Light-hearted youngsters taking a swing at the *piñata* are surely not aware of this ponderous interpretation.

Sandals

Huaraches (sandals) will last for years if you follow a few basic rules while shopping. They vary in price depending on the detail work of the leather and the sole that is used.

A non-adjustable should fit snugly when they are new. If you plan on wearing socks with your sandals, then wear them when you try a pair of *haraches* on the first time. Sandals will stretch with use, the thinner the leather, the more they will stretch.

Salt rots leather, so soak them in fresh water and wear them until they dry. Do this several times or more until the sandals shape themselves to your feet.

Thick tire tread soles are heavy and not very flexible. You may want to purchase a pair with average or thin soles.

Carefully check the straps and fasteners. Straps wired to the sole will rub and wear through faster than a looped or sewn-on strap. Cheap plastic or metal buckles will break quickly and cut through the leather. The longest lasting sandals are the basket weave, semi-shoe type or the variety which have two or three wide leather straps. The latter type is open and cool.

Straw

Long ago *artesanos* discovered the properties of wheat straw for weaving and ornamental objects. Hollow straws of wheat are softened in water, they become very flexible for weaving and braiding. The wet straw can easily be pinched flat or tied in a knot and will not break or split. These wheat straw ornaments are hung as Christmas decorations taking the shape of birds, angels, or stars. Other miniatures are shaped into airplanes, baskets, doll hats, and little animals.

Broom straw is the wiry end branches of a plant called broomcorn or *popote*. Broom straw folk art requires painstaking work and the ornaments are designed for collectors of miniatures, not for children to use as a plaything. The broom straw star is woven together and fastened near the center with a few flexible strands of thin straw. The heavier broom straws that form the points of the star are carefully matched in weight and length. The ends are secured with a fine copper wire. The airy, little hanging ornament is cleverly and skillfully made. This interesting and artistic craft is also used to cover small items. The miniature guitar is carefully carved of wood and strung with six pieces of fine nylon cord, each wound into its own tiny peg. The entire surface of the guitar, except the neck, is covered with designs of broom straw dyed in five colors, cut and applied to the wood with glue. It is then decorated with an abstract pattern or a Mexican street scene in sunset colors.

Toys

Bright-hued plastics are seen everywhere and since they are cheap and attractive to people who love color, they are slowly replacing many of the charming indigenous wood, clay, reed and straw objects of the country. The latter are beginning to be regarded as old fashioned by the natives. The modernization of Mexican cities is a looming threat to the artesian traders, now that plastic toys, synthetic yarns, and dyes are commonly available.

The playthings of Mexico are not designed under the guidance of a child psychologist nor are they made in factories by the thousands so they will not break, chip, fade, or hurt anyone. They never include instructions, and are not made to last forever. Most Mexican toys are handmade by artesians at their own whim, at their own pace. Children in the past have been responsive to them and many can still be found in the shops and markets. They add character and atmosphere when used as gifts, party themes, and decorations.

Recreation

*The car has become the carpace, the protective and
aggressive shell, of urban and suburban man.*
-Marshall McLuhan

Whether you visit for a short time or stay for the winter, you
will find Puerto Peñasco fun, relaxing, and enjoyable. Water sports
and fishing are the primary lure for tourists to this area. The waters
of the Gulf of California are fairly calm and offer sailors a chance to
relax under the power of the wind. Swimming, snorkeling or such
beach-bound activities as volleyball, Frisbee and relaxing on the sand
are favorite pastimes.

Tourists and foreign residents have been attracted by the natural
beauty of Puerto Peñasco for more than 50 years. Part-time inhabitants
get together for annual club and association meetings to plan
recreational activities. The activities provide a way for residents to
give their valuable help and selfless generosity to the community in
which they live and frequent. The North American Clubs and
Associations seated in Puerto Peñasco are: The Cholla Bay
Sportsmen's Club with 1500 members, Old Boy's Social Club with
160 members, Singles Club with 30 members, The Cholla Bay
Home Owner Association with 600 members, Las Conchas Home
Owner Association with 550 members, the Cornucopia Yacht Club
with 300 members and the American Desert Racing Association
with 3,200 members.

Sportfishing Regulations

All persons who wish to sportfish in Mexican waters must have
an individual permit as well as a permit for their boat. These permits

are not transferable. Children 12 years and younger are not required to have a permit providing they fish in the company of an adult who has a valid and current permit. Each person aboard a sportfishing boat must have a valid permit even if he or she is not fishing. Charter fishing boats in Puerto Peñasco have boat permits and will help you obtain an individual permit. Permits average $7 per day, $17 per week, $26 per month, $34 per year, per person. Permits are not required if you are fishing from the shore.

All boats in National waters, whether it be for sportfishing or aquatic activities, are required to pay permit costs. Charter boat owners who take passengers and fishermen out for sportfishing must also carry a valid permit. It is prohibited for charter boat services that rent boats for sportfishing, to rent to people who do not have a valid permit. Businesses who provide sport fishing services must keep waste products disposed of properly within their area of jurisdiction, including their boats.

By law only 5 kilos of fish per person may leave the country. Fish caught by means of sportfishing is for purposes of consumption or to be given to scientific investigation. It is not to be sold or exchanged for other goods.

The Cholla Bay Sportsmen's Club

The Sportsmen's Club was founded by Al Scott in 1955. The purpose was to organize sportsmen, promote fellowship, and to help one another enjoy Cholla Bay. The annual Fishing Derby was started in 1956 as a fund raiser and helped provide polio immunizations for many school children of Puerto Peñasco. By 1957 membership had grown to 170 members. By 1960 over 800 anglers and guests attended the Fishing Derby.

Over the years, donations and volunteers have built a children's play ground, organized clothing drives, provided desks for the school and helped purchase medical equipment and an ambulance for the city. The club plan's activities throughout the year including a fishing derby and a Christmas party for the children and families living in Cholla Bay. In 1972, a lot in the center of town was donated and named for Gus Brown, Sr. and a permanent structure was built to hold the annual fish fry and serve as a social gathering place for local events.

The Cholla Bay Sportsmen's Club Radio Room operates as a safety network for boaters in case of an emergency. In 1960 a Mexican permit was issued to Bob Taylor of the CBSC for a radio transmitting station to assist boaters in the Puerto Peñasco area. Mexican officials from Hermosillo met with six club officials and dedicated the new station while a 55 foot tall pole for the antenna was put into place. Thousands of dollars in new and upgraded equipment have been added since then. VHF uplinks, a repeater on top of the mountain in Puerto Peñasco and ground to air radios for search and rescue have also been added. This radio room is one of the finest facilities of the northern Sea of Cortéz and can reach up to 100 miles of VHF and even further on SSB Marine radios.

Donations and annual dues from the Cholla Bay Sportsmen's Club have financed this valuable project. For the past 20 years full time employees answer calls. Annual salaries are paid by the CBSC membership fund. This safety network, benefiting all parties in the Northern part of the Sea of Cortéz, is the direct result of the members of this organization. Membership is open to all residents and visitors. Applications are available at the CBSC Radio Room in Cholla Bay or write to Cholla Bay Sportsmen's Club, P. O. Box 7171, Phoenix, AZ 85011, for more information.

CHOLLA BAY EMERGENCY RADIO

These channels are assigned for emergency use only, please do not use them for other than their intended use.

VHF:

Monitor . . . CH 26   EMERGENCY . . . CH 16

CB RADIO:

Monitor . . . CH 3   EMERGENCY . . . CH 9

AM MARINE RADIO, SHIP TO SHORE:

Safety and calling	2182
Boat to shore	2555
Boat to boat	1638

Radio operators monitor CB Channel 3 and VHF Channel 26. At the same time CB Channel 9 and VHF Channel 16 are used as emergency channels. The operators of the Radio Room ask your assistance in using these airways for emergency use *only*. CB Channel 3 can be used for calling friends, ordering water, and all other non-emergency conversations. If you must hail someone on Channel 26, please go to an off simplex channel (12, 68, 70) as soon as your party responds.

Fishing For All Seasons

Spring	**Fall**
Mar - Apr - May	*Sept - Oct - Nov*
Grouper	Dolphin
Pinto Bass	Marlin
Snapper	Sailfish
Yellowtail	Sierra
	Skipjack
Summer	**Winter**
Jun - Jul - Aug	*Dec - Jan - Feb*
Dolphin	Grouper
Marlin	Pinto Bass
Sailfish	Snapper
Sierra	Yellowtail
Skipjack	

Always fish with the incoming tide, that is, when the fish are coming in to feed near shore. Most fishermen use a plain hook baited with shrimp or a small chunk of fish and cast without any sinker. Fishing from shore at Sandy Beach with a spin outfit is unpredictable – sometimes you can go for a day without a strike and then again you may land thirty or forty sea trout in a couple of hours. These good eating fish run about twenty inches long. Many fishermen like to use small (three inches or less) chrome spoons like the "kastmaster" with one treble hook. Others use feathered jigs, but small off-shore reefs play havoc with lures and you can lose a small fortune in a day or two. In addition to sea trout you may catch a pompano or two from shore.

Aquatic Boat Regulations

Protecting the environment comes naturally to most boaters and others who practice being a good neighbor, on land or water. Especially on the water every action or sound affects others sharing the waterway. It also impacts the water itself, the marine life living in it and the ecosystem inhabitants near and on the shoreline.

If you have not been fishing or boating in Rocky Point before, it is advisable to check with the Cholla Bay Sportsmen's Club Radio Room before going out on the water. It is advisable to carry a VHF radio when venturing out for a day on the water.

You can rent a boat in Cholla Bay for approximately $60 a day per person for up to five people. If you have a boat, it should be at least 16 foot long with a broad beam and good depth. If you're going out into the blue water you must have at least a 25 HP motor in addition to an auxiliary motor. The auxiliary motor is a back up in case of engine failure. Once you are away from the protection of the little bays, fierce waves can engulf you with awesome swiftness. Be prepared for the unexpected especially when you notice the weather changing.

A common sense approach while boating will help protect the aquatic environment. The following suggestions will help protect the environment.

1. Observe local and federal marine toilet rules.
2. Know and use legal bottom paints.
3. Take special precautions when sanding your boat hull.
4. Do not drop trash and litter into the water.
5. Avoid spills on the water.
6. Keep your engine well-tuned.

Totoaba And Vaquita Fish

In the 1920's, the totoaba was the first fish caught and sold for profit in Puerto Peñasco. Today, the National Oceanic & Atmospheric Administration under the U.S. Department of Commerce have listed the marine fish totoaba and the harbor porpoise, commonly referred to as vaquita as endangered species under the U.S. Endangered Species Act.

Due to severe depletion from over fishing, habitat alteration and the lack of fresh water through the Colorado Delta River to the Gulf of California, Mexico enacted laws to protect totoaba in 1975. Despite these protections, totoaba continues to be caught with gill-nets in the northern Sea of Cortéz. If you are fishing in the northern Sea of Cortéz, and you accidentally catch a totoaba, release it immediately. Please be aware that Mexico and the U.S. have laws that protect the totoaba and violators are subject to civil and criminal provisions.

Most tourists vacationing near the Sea of Cortéz, Mexico, have a deep appreciation for protecting the living marine resources found here. But some may be unintentionally contributing to a problem

---

Pez or Pescado?

Have you wondered when a Pez (fish) becomes a Pescado? Well, according to an old man from the sea, a fish is a "Pez" while in the water. But once on board a boat, or the beach, it becomes a "Pescado."

---

that could threaten the existence of two species, one of which is among the world's most endangered marine mammals.

The totoaba is a large, bottom-dwelling marine fish, renowned for its large size of up to 300 pounds and 6 feet in length. Totoaba, a type of "corvina," closely resembles white seabass and orange mouth corvina. It may be distinguished from all the other corvinas by the presence of three pairs of chin pores. At one time, totoaba supported an important commercial and sport fishery, based primarily on its annual spring breeding migration (January to June) to the shallow, brackish waters near the mouth of the Colorado River. Today there are no longer enough of these fish to support a fishery.

Found exclusively in the shallow waters of the extreme northern Sea of Cortéz, the vaquita has the most limited geographic range of any marine cetacean (a group that includes whale, dolphin, and porpoise). The vaquita has black eye patches, a large curved dorsal fin, and is one of the world's smallest cetaceans measuring no more than 4.5 feet in length.

The Gulf of California Harbor porpoise is a rare and seriously endangered species and only an estimated 300-500 remain.

Reduction in the consumption of totoaba may reduce the amount of gillnet fishing and save the vaquita from entanglement. An estimated 30 to 40 vaquita drown in gillnets in the northern Sea of Cortéz each year. Although the primary source of this incidental mortality is the illegal totoaba gillnet fishery.

The National Marine Fisheries Service (NMFS), in cooperation with U.S. Customs officials, has increased enforcement operations at the U.S./Mexico border to detect the illegal entry of totoaba. Also, the NMFS has established a new forensic method to identify totoaba. Whole or processed fish (e.g. fillets) that is suspected to be totoaba, may be seized for analysis.

Game Fish

Black Skipjack *(Barrilete)*
Their body color is dark on top, silvery on the bottom with stripes running down the back and three to five black spots on the abdomen just below the pectoral fin. They migrate to the upper Gulf in late May or early June. They may weigh up to 12 pounds. The meat is very strong in flavor. Skipjack makes excellent bait.

Cortéz Halibut *(Lenguado)*
A flat fish with both eyes on one side. Found throughout the Sea of Cortéz both inshore and offshore. Dark brown above with 8-10 dark spots and a white underside. Prefers sandy bottoms. Takes drifted live or dead baits and small feathers. The mouth has a large single row of sharp teeth in each jaw. They average 3-5 lbs. but can get up to 25 lbs. and are excellent eating fish.

Dolphin Fish *(Dorado)*
The body is a brilliant golden-green in color. The snout profile of older males is blunt and high forheaded, whereas the females head is more tapered. The *Dorado* likes warm blue waters and migrates to

the upper Gulf in late May or early June. They are an excellent food fish and can grow up to 6 feet in length and weigh up to 90 pounds.

Giant Black Sea Bass *(Mero Prieto)*
Body dark gray to black and has numerous fine teeth. They feed on Mackerel, Lobster, Tuna, Shark and large chunk baits and can grow to over 500 lbs. Giant Black Sea Bass prefer deep rocky bottoms. Strong fighters, they make excellent table fair.

Paloma Pompano *(Palometa Pompanito)*
Pompano are common throughout the Gulf. They are usually taken from shore or in shallow water on shiny spoons and lures. The body of the Pompano is dark on top with bright silvery sides and black tips on the dorsal fins. An excellent eating fish that grows to 20 inches and up to 50 pounds.

Red Snapper *(Hauchinango)*
The body and fins are bright red with a pink to white belly. They prefer deep water around 250 ft. and feed mainly at night. The average weight is 2-5 lbs. but do get up to 15 lbs. Excellent eating.

Sailfish *(Pez Vela)*
The Sailfish's body is dark blue on its back with a bright silver stomach and a very large dorsal fin. They may be seen basking on the surface following the warm waters to the upper Gulf in late May or early June. One hundred pound Sailfish are common but fish up to 182 pounds have been recorded. Sailfish are very poor food value, so please release.

Spotted Sand Bass *(Cabrilla De Roca)*
Body is spotted and barred, third dorsal spine is the longest. Lives at shallow to moderate depths over sand or rock bottom. They can grow up to 22 inches. The fillets are good eating. Makes excellent bait for larger fish.

Scuba Diving And Snorkeling

In the late 1940s the scuba system was first introduced to the United States by Captain Jacques Cousteau. Records show that as early as 3000 B.C., man attempted to penetrate the sea for food, but he was often frustrated by his physical limitations. Divers dating back to 900 B.C. breathed from air bladders carried underwater. Stone carvings of this period show these people underwater with the bladder devices strapped to their chests and extending down to their hips.

Diving and snorkeling brings you freedom, thrills, a challenge, and maybe another chance to find out something more about yourself. Diving teaches you much about self-reliance and using acquired skills to your own advantage. Ultimately, it makes you more confident in many other areas of life as well as diving.

If you are trying diving and snorkeling for the first time, it is advisable to visit your public library and do some preliminary research. Books on these topics provide information on fitness, skills, using and purchasing equipment, water safety, scuba requirements, diving physics, the environment of the sea and hazardous marine life. The next step is to visit the dive shop in Old Port for equipment rental and information on certification.

If you are snorkeling around the Puerto Peñasco area it is advisable to visit the dive shop for important information on tides, seasons for hazardous fish, and the times and best places to see marine and sea life. The dive shop also offers sunset cruises, dive and snorkel trips to Bird Island and areas around Puerto Peñasco.

Windsurfing

No other water sport has developed so far, in such a short period of time, as windsurfing. In just under 15 years it has grown from a somewhat bizarre variation of surfing, to an international sport with more than a million participants all over the world. Research and development in equipment and manufacturing techniques is highly advanced and sophisticated, and goes some way towards justifying the sport's inclusion in the 1984 Olympics.

Unless you happen to be a natural windsurfer, by far the quickest way to learn is to enroll at an International Windsurfer School before you plan to visit Puerto Peñasco. Courses usually last one or two days, and could save you a lot of time later trying to shake off bad habits.

Boat Repairs & Servicing
(See Chapter 4, Behind The Wheel)

Boat Storage
(See Chapter 11, Business Services)

Water Sports & Fishing Operators

Excursiones Paraiso, located on the beach of Playa Bonita Hotel and Blvd. Benito Juarez #104-C, on the right side of Tena Liquor Store and Union Gas Station, 011-52-638-36209. Offering beach rentals by the hour, half day or full day, Wave Runners, Quads, sail boats, kayaks, Boogie Boards, umbrellas. A small deposit is required, credit cards, drivers license or personal check accepted. Excursions to the Pinacate Mountains, La Pinta & Morua Estuary's. Fishing trips, full or half day, sightseeing, whale watching, boat tours and trips to Bird Island. Trips arranged at the Old Port Information Center on Ira de Junio, one block north of the Catholic Church.

JJ's Cantina, Cholla Bay, 011-52-638-32785. Sports and other fun events such as bathtub, sailboat, and motorcycle races. We sponsor a fishing derby and chili cookoff every year, come and watch or join in the fun!

Pompano's Fishing Charters, on the main road into Old Port, 011-52-638-34419. Catching fish is our business! Fishing charters, full tackle, fishing licenses and boat launching. Open year round. Snacks, ice and bait available. We have fishing permits. Map F8.

Rojo's, 011-52-638-35824. Now located in the Marina Peñasco. Home of Cholla Bay Divers. We do fishing and diving and sightseeing trips.

Sand and Sea Rentals, Calle 13, 011-52-638-35824. ATC, wave runner, paddle boats and dune buggy rentals. Tune-up and maintenance available. Charter fishing trips, full and half day group rates. Map E15.

Santiago's Ocean Services, boarding at the Marina Peñasco boat slips. See Rocky Point like never before, from a birds eye view. Safety equipped, U.S.C.G. approved, no age limit or skills required. American owned and operated. Map E30.

Seaside Treasures, Paseo Victor Estrella, next to La Cita Cafe in Old Port. Everything you need to spend a comfortable day playing on the beach, swimwear, sunglasses, hats, umbrellas, water toys and much more. Map F44.

Secretary Charter Boat, ask for Johnny at the Señorial Trailer Park in Miramar, 011-52-638-33530, 32876. Boat charters for what you want to do. Map G21.

Sun N' Fun Rentals & Sales, at the entrance to Old Port where the road divides, 011-52-638-35450, U.S. 602-566-7614. Full service dive shop and water sport rentals. Offering snorkeling, scuba instruction, modern equipment rentals and sales, quality air. All day dive trip from 8:00 a.m. to 6:00 p.m. includes breakfast, lunch, drinks, two tank dive, and weight belt. Half day, full day, overnight and two or three day trips. Dive mastered charters and water sport rentals. We book fishing trips on a 46' boat. Four hour introductory scuba - NAUI PRO facility. Map F4.

Suprema, Kino Blvd. & G. Prieto St., 011-52-638-33700. Fishing supplies and everything else you need to catch that big one. Map C20.

Irma Brown with a sailfish she caught in the Sea of Cortez at the Cholla Bay Sportsmen's Club Annual Fishing Derby. Photo courtesy of The Cholla Bay Sportsmen's Club.

Day Trips

He travels the fastest who travels alone.
-Rudyard Kipling

If you happen to be on the curious side there are several day trips out of Puerto Peñasco that will satisfy the adventuresome side in you. If you prefer taking a guided tour instead of venturing on your own, contact one of the tour companies listed at the end of this chapter. Many tours require a minimum number of passengers and vans fill up very quickly during the spring and winter months, so make reservations in advance.

There are three day trips you can make from Puerto Peñasco. The Sierra Pinta Gold Mine is about forty miles from downtown and offers some nice views of La Pinta Estuary, Bird Island, Morua Estuary and La Pinta Mountains. Caborca offers an excursion through hills scattered with cactus shrubs and wild flowers, agricultural areas, small *ejidos* and the Church of La Concepcion del Caborca that Father Kino built on the outskirts of town. The Pinacate Mountain is mysterious, mystical and one of the richest archeological areas in the southwest.

Making some advance preparations and precautions will provide the means to enjoy your experience and ensure a safe trip:

1. Always take a friend or go in a group. It is a lot more fun and you have help if you need it.
2. Tell someone about your planned route or let the front desk know where you are going and what time you will return.
3. Get an early start and allow enough time to return back to town-well before dark.
4. Use common sense. When traveling in the desert during the summer months the temperatures can reach 120º. It is wise

to travel with a competent guide to the Pinacate Mountains and The Sierra Pinta Mine only during cool weather from November to March. Rattlesnakes are common during the summer months, give them a wide berth.

5. Take a marine radio if you will be traveling into the desert. See chapter 911 for channel and frequency. Advise the Radio Room of your plans. They have volunteers working 24 hours a day should you need their assistance in an emergency.

6. Take the first eleven items listed on page 15, "Survival Checklist."

7. Bring your own drinking water, one gallon per person per day is recommended for visits in the fall. Three times that amount is recommended for summer trips.

8. You will need to exchange dollars for pesos if you are going to Caborca. It is wise to do this the day before departing. The banks in Rocky Point, open from 9:00 a.m. to 3:00 p.m., are very busy, lines can be long, and the service slow.

9. Driving in the Pinacate is somewhat more difficult than in other areas of similar terrain. The roads are not signed, maintained, or patrolled. Keep to the established roadways.

The Sierra Pinta Gold Mine

Exerts from the book *The Legend of Gillespie's Gold, The Saga Of The Southwest's Most Incredible Millionaire*, documented in a book by Earl MacPherson, are used in this section.

Bernard A. Gillespie, born January 1894, owned the 12,000 acre Sierra Pinta Gold Mine approximately fifty miles south of Puerto Peñasco.

The Indians were the first to find gold in the Sierra Pinta Mine. They made the mistake of showing it to the Spaniards who killed most of them after making them dig out all they could. The Spaniards held onto the mine during the Mexican revolution then escaped, and President Díaz took it over. Then the mine was leased to an English syndicate who built the railroad, the mill, and improved the old loading wharf on the bay at Bahía San Jorge. After the English left, the Mexican prospectors came in and staked out their claims with white monuments which were deposited on almost every corner of each claim.

Bernard describes in his own words how he acquired the Sierra Pinta Mine, "I stole it from a Gringo named Richards. Course he was a crook, too, and never paid his workers, or I never could have got it."

In 1945 Bernard had gone into partnership with Richards who was operating the mine. They both agreed to put up $100,000 each for the expansion that had already produced millions of dollars in gold for the British syndicate. When Bernard's partner could not come up with his half, Bernard bribed the Mexican politicians and took over the Sierra Pinta.

The mine is located behind the Gillespie ranch which backed up to the foothills of the rugged Sierra Pinta Mountains. The ranch stretched from the mine to the sea, the hacienda was located near the ocean about 25 miles from Puerto Peñasco. It took Bernard about five years to get the property and five years to build the house.

The large stone residence, named "La Pinta", was built high on the beach above the deep blue water of Baja San Jorge and still stands. The stone came from an old ore pump on the beach where they used to load quartz onto the boats. The heavy timbers ended up on the beach after a barge washed ashore in a storm. Bernard found this idyllic spot after a storm blew him in one night after sailing all the way around the cape from California. When he awoke in the morning he saw a herd of antelope on the beach and thought it was the most beautiful place he had ever seen.

Bernard discovered water at the base of an old palm tree and turned the area around the hacienda into an oasis. Near a sharp ridge the road follows a deserted, long cook-shack, and a rock house that Bernard built on a cliff. Beyond the rock house was a large crusher, a machine shop with a tin roof, and several small adobe and rock buildings. At one time about a dozen Mexican families lived in the area and helped operate the mine. The ruins of La Pinta still stand. A major resort is in the planning stages for development on this spot.

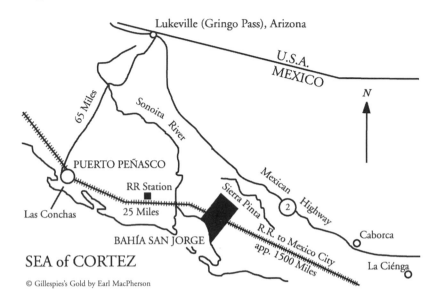

© Gillespie's Gold by Earl MacPherson

Bernard also built a 20 mile access road to the mine. During the operation of the mine, a rocky road lead up to an old, weather-beaten mill hoist. It originally had a gallus frame attached to a small rusted ore cart and was poised to descend about seven hundred feet with several laterals. There was electricity, a gasoline generator and an air compressor. Near there are tailings of more than a century of man's conquest over this isolated area of earth.

Millions of dollars of gold have been taken out of the Sierra Pinta mine. About the same amount was removed by the Spaniards who worked higher on the hill behind the deep hole. In addition, Bernard admitted he had also found a small fortune in gold dust by taking up the floor of one of the original buildings next to the mine. With the help of two loyal Mexicans he made his own gold bricks which he exchanged for Mexican currency at the Banco National in Hermosillo.

Bernard's interesting story starts with his father Frank A. Gillespie. Frank moved his wife and three sons from Ohio to Kansas around the turn of the century. From a series of small land leases and producing wells he parlayed his luck into the Gypsey Oil Company with his partner, a half breed named Jackson Barnett. They brought in some of Oklahoma City's first big oil gushers. Frank was netting $20,000 per day. These were the days before controlled drilling and excess profit taxes.

By the time Bernard graduated from high school he was the oldest son of Oklahoma's newest millionaire. Bernard was a prolific boxer, played on the University of Kansas football team, pledged with a fraternity and became a star halfback in his sophomore and junior years. Bernard gave it all up to return home and marry his pretty blond neighbor Katherine Kerr. They had one son named Bernard Jr.

While Bernard was in college, adventurous Frank A. Gillespie discovered a new state, Arizona. In order to have his newly married son with him he gave the newlyweds a honeymoon package to the Adams Hotel in Phoenix. Bernard and his new wife remained and set up permanent residence.

Frank Gillespie, with the help of Bernard, put together the Gillespie Land and Irrigation Company which totaled over 80,000 acres in the Gila Valley. In 1920 Frank put Bernard in charge of the company and moved to the very fashionable Beverly Hills, California. Between 1920 and 1925 Bernard built a spacious ranch for himself and his family and directed construction of the Gillespie dam on the Gila River.

Bernard made frequent cattle buying trips into Mexico. During this time Bernard washed ashore at Bahía San Jorge and started building his spacious beach hide-out and acquired the Sierra Pinta Gold Mine. In 1935 Katherine passed away. At fifty, Bernard was perhaps the most eligible bachelor in Phoenix. He was a fine adventurous-looking gringo.

In 1945 near Cananea, Mexico, Bernard met Grace Cooly Castle, a beautiful daughter of an American mining engineer. He built a beautiful new adobe home on the Gila Bend Ranch for his Mexican bride and settled down to the normal life of an adventurous millionaire. They had two children, James Alpine born in 1947 and Bernadette Ann in 1949.

For reasons unknown the idylic home life at Gila Bend ended, maybe because of Bernards love of the colorful and mysterious land and people of Northern Sonora. Or it may have been the taste Grace had for the glamorous social whirl of Phoenix that caused them to drift apart. In 1957 Bernard sold the Gila Bend Ranch and holdings for $8,000,000 and bought Grace and the children a beautiful home in the Phoenix Country Club area.

Bernard spent more of his time in Mexico with a million or so that came from the sale of the Gillespie Ranch and Irrigation Company. He established residence in Nogales and started the paperwork to become a citizen of Mexico to try and secure a better legal right to his holdings there.

In time Bernard wanted to sell the Baja Jorge Ranch for $1,000,000 but was unable to because Grace's name was on the title and she refused to let Bernard take the ranch for himself. He found a way under the Mexican Agrarian Land Reform Law. Bernard's caretaker, Guerrera planted a small vegetable garden next to the house. It was protected with elaborate screening to keep the birds and desert varmints out. Guerrera became a farmer and could claim the land because Bernard and Grace were not farming it. Bernard got power of attorney over Guerrera so he had to do everything Bernard said. A year later Grace brought a lawsuit against Bernard in Hermosillo for the return of her interest in Bahía San Jorge.

A sales brochure was prepared offering one of "America's last unspoiled beach properties." The unique property with two and one half miles of virgin beach frontage offers an excellent frost and pollution free climate. The resort and recreational potential is endless because of its location on St. George Bay, which is sheltered by an offshore reef. The property has the finest yacht anchorage in the northern end of the Gulf of California. An airstrip could be built near the beach at nominal cost, so that owners of this rare piece of resort and recreational land could arrive by rail, sea or air. The water table in this area lies at about 130-foot depth and doubtless is from an underground accumulation of good water from the nearby Sonoita River. Additional small wells could produce enough water for the needs of a small community. While the asking price of $750,000 is firm, the owner is willing to retain a 20% interest in the property so that his knowledge of it can be of value to the buyer or developers. No buyer was ever found.

Bernard also owned and operated a mill in La Ciénega about forty miles from Caborca. Near the crest of a pass in the mountains at the headwaters of the Rio Magdalena the view opens up like the pages of a book. Waving palm trees and the incredible green of a natural oasis was hidden here in the desert before recorded time.

For thousands of years the primitive Seri Indians lived around the large, natural pond fed by springs that never went dry. To them, this little island in the desert must have been a paradise until a Spaniard discovered it. As the story goes, the Spaniard was chasing wild horses and unexpectedly came upon the oasis and the Seri's. He camped with them, while washing his dishes in the pond, discovered gold dust in the bottom of the pan. The gold may have been brought in on the hoofs of herds of wild horses as they came to drink, or washed in by rains from the arroyos, but it spelled doom for the Seri's. Soon more Spaniards came with gifts of colorful clothing for the Indians and date palms to plant in the moist soil surrounding the oasis. The palms lived, but the Indians died. The Spaniards had inoculated their gifts with smallpox.

Bernard hired a loyal Mexican family to run the mills. Señor C. Alfredo Badilla Martinez. Their spotlessly clean house could not have contained over 200 square feet.

The biggest problem with being a millionaire, especially in Mexico, is that everyone wants some of it. Bernard's $100,000 La Ciénega Mill was shut down twice by lawsuits. The mill was enclosed in a high wire fence and surrounded by piles of high grade gold ore. Net income was about one thousand dollars a day and probably was the biggest placer deposit of gold on the North American continent. Señor Badilla was the mayor at a time when over a thousand people lived in the area, all panning gold. Bernard states "I bought the biggest nugget I've ever seen from a Mexican who panned it outta that wash down there, for $500.00 I sold it to a museum for $3,500."

Bernard Jr. returned from the war a hero, but could not adjust to civilian life. He died in 1962 a the age of 44. Bernard was in his early seventies.

On Bernard's 78th birthday he inherited three million dollars from the estate of Frank. A Gillespie, one item on the list of three long pages of stocks and bonds was 3,850 shares of Standard Oil of New Jersey. Most of the inheritance was put into a trust for the future Gillespie's.

The Road To Caborca

If you plan to make a trip to Caborca it does require advance planning and a car permit is needed. Caborca is outside of the designated "free zone," about 110 miles from Rocky Point. The journey will take about two hours, more if you stop for sightseeing and photographs.

Violence has marked the history of Caborca. Its first resident priest was the martyr Francisco Xavier Saeta, who was installed by Father Kino at Caborca in October 1694. Father Saeta immediately set about constructing a church which was finished the following April. Shortly after, the priest and his servants were murdered by rebellious Pimas from Tubutama, Oquitoa, and Pitiquitol. The Saeta chapel was burned almost completely in June of the same year.

In June 1698, Father Kino took Gaspar Barrillas to be the resident missionary at Caborca, but because of the threat of further uprisings he left the following month. Father Satea's chapel was reconstructed and the building was again usable. In 1701, Father Barrillas came back once more but he fled once more before Father Kino began the large church of La Concepción del Caborca near the small chapel.

What happened to Father Kino's church after 1706 is not clear, but by 1708, Father Luis Velarde took over after Kino's death. There is no way of being certain who built or rebuilt Caborca's last Jesuit church. It was standing, by no means in good condition, when the *cabecera* was taken over in 1768 by the Yuma martyr, Juan Díaz. Díaz described the church as being located on dangerously low and level ground, and suggested it be moved to avoid the threat of floods. In later years, the flood danger was more than just a menace. There is very little high ground around Caborca, and all of the churches have apparently been at or near the west margin of the river where the town is. Had Father Dial suggestion been followed, it would have resulted in the church being placed across the river to the east at a considerable distance from the community and inconveniently separated by the river. But had anyone paid any attention, the 20th Century flood which tore out the entire sanctuary and half the dome of the last Franciscan church would have passed harmlessly by.

Today, Caborca is a modern and bustling community, with U.S. style motels and swimming pools, good restaurants, and all the advantages which an active Chamber of Commerce can encourage. The town has moved toward the west.

The Mysterious And Mystical
Pinacate Mountain

The best word to describe the area known as the Sierra del Pinacate is "unique." In this corner of western Sonora, beneath the earth's crust, a magma factory has been melting rock for four million years. When pressure was great enough to force magma up through the surface, volcanoes erupted, including the volcanoes that created the giant craters which have made the area famous. No other place has the same moon-like landscape of craters, black soil, cinder cones and extinct volcanoes, plus a large volcanic mountain, all overlain by Sonoran Desert plants and animals. In addition, the Pinacate is one of the richest archeological records in the southwest, relatively untouched by erosion or man.

In 1979 the Pinacate Protected Zone was established by Presidential decree to preserve this astonishing area. The name "Pinacate" probably comes from the local pronunciation of "pinacat!" an Aztec word for a certain black beetle which roams the desert. In 1983 the Mexican federal agency in charge of urban development and ecology (SEDUE) incorporated the zone in order to propose it as a "biosphere preserve," under the Man And The

Biosphere Program. Currently the zone is administered by the Federal Department of Agriculture and Water Resources (SARA).

Access

The Pinacate area is accessible from three different entrances. The mileage calculations listed from Sonoyta are measured from the Rio Sonoita Bridge in the center of town.

NORTHEAST ENTRANCE - From Route 2 near KM post 51, 32 miles west of Sonoyta, 2 wheel drive.

NORTHWEST ENTRANCE - From Route 2, near KM post 71, 44 miles west of Sonoyta, 4 wheel drive.

SOUTHEAST ENTRANCE - From Route 8, near KM post 51, 32 miles southwest of Sonoyta, 2 wheel drive, with some sandy spots.

Regulations

PERMITS - Permits are not required; however, for safety and information reasons you should check in with the rangers at the headquarters of the park at KM 51 on Route 8, 32 miles southwest of Sonoyta on the road to Rocky Point.

DRIVING - Please keep your vehicle on established roadways. Off-road driving damages desert vegetation and can destroy surface archeological resources such as intaglios and ancient foot trails.

WILDLIFE - No hunting, collecting, or disturbing wildlife is permitted.

PLANTS - Plants are protected. No plant collecting, firewood gathering or wood cutting allowed.

FIRES - Ground fires are permitted if wood is brought in, but burning of native wood is prohibited.

ARCHEOLOGICAL RESOURCES - Archeological resources are protected; leave artifacts where you find them and don't let your vehicle destroy surface resources.

TRASH - Carry out your trash; do not bury it.

FIREARMS - It is prohibited to possess or use firearms in the Pinacate Protected Zone.

COMMERCIAL OPERATIONS - Commercial operations such as mining and wood cutting are prohibited.

Safety

ON YOUR OWN - The Pinacate area is a remote and undeveloped area with few visitors. You are on your own if breakdowns occur or problems arise. Extra water, ample gasoline, food, shovels, tools and basic auto parts are recommended.

WHEN TO VISIT - The ideal time of year to visit is November through March, when daytime high temperatures range from 60 to 90 degrees F. If you make a trip in the summer, be prepared for temperatures which may exceed 120 degrees F.

DRINKING WATER - There is no drinking water in the area; you must bring in your own. One gallon per person per day is recommended for visits in the fall, winter or spring and three times that amount for summer trips.

ROADS - Driving in the Pinacate is somewhat more difficult than in other areas of similar terrain. The roads are not signed, maintained, or patrolled, and more roads exist than are shown on the map. Drivers should be prepared for occasional wrong turns, and some difficulty in knowing which way to go. Many of the roads are suited for four-wheel drive only, requiring high clearance and low gears for rough or sandy spots, but some can be driven in two-wheel drive, high clearance vehicles most of the time. However, even the "better" roads can become impassable when flooding deposits sand waves or deep mud. Information on current road conditions can be obtained at the ranger office. A caution: don't make 'new' roads – keep your tracks on established roadways.

Pinacate People

The Pinacate has been a place that people have known and occupied for thousands of years. The earliest inhabitants were part of a large southwest group of hunters and gatherers, the San Dieguito culture. They were probably living in the area at least 12,000 years ago. Julian Hayden, the authority on Pinacate archeology, has suggested they may have been in the area as early as 40,000 years ago. This early date was derived through a variety of dating techniques, including measuring desert varnish, calculating calcite build-up, correlating desert pavement formation with climatic periods and dating shell artifacts.

The San Dieguitans abandoned the area when the climate changed and a major drought lasting several thousand years, set in. When the rains returned, new generations of San Dieguito people came back. But their descendants, too, were forced to move out when a second dry period began. At the end of this second drought, 5,000 years ago, a different group of people moved into the area and developed a lifestyle very similar to their predecessors. The were Amargosans, possible ancestors of the Pima and Tohono O'odham Indians. The Pinacate was to be their home for the next 4,900 years.

Prehistoric Pinacate people centered their lives around the Tinajas. They made trails from waterhole to waterhole as well as trails to the gulf and elsewhere. They had campsites, but built no houses; the desert pavement was their home. They left behind trail shrines, sleeping circles (cleared areas in the desert pavement, often ringed with stones), stone tools, and giant geometric figures on the ground, called intaglios. A concentration of all these traces can be found at nearly every Pinacate Tinaja.

The Pinacate archeological record is clearly defined and beautifully preserved on the erosion-resistant lava rock. This volcanic chaos holds one of the finest archeological laboratories in North America, but also one of the most fragile. Unlike most southwestern archeological sites, the Pinacate prehistoric record is all on the surface. The slightest disturbance of an artifact, even just turning it over, can ruin its value.

If the most recent volcanic eruption in the Pinacate occurred only 2,000 years ago, there probably were people living here when the volcanoes were still active. This fact brings up interesting questions. One wonders how the volcanoes affected the religion, the daily lives, the security, the world view, the legends, and maybe even the language of these people.

"Pinacateño" is the name for the small band of Amargosans who made their home in the volcanic chaos of the Pinacate. By late A.D. 700, they had become an isolated and distinct group, losing touch with the lifestyles of their Amargosan cousins in other parts of the Southwest. For instance, they deliberately cremated skeletons of game animals such as bighorn, antelope and deer, a habit not shared by other Amargosans. They also invented a unique tool, which archeologists call a "gyratory crusher," used for crushing mesquite pods.

The Pinacateños had been living in the Pinacate country for over 4,000 years when the first Spaniard, Melchoir Díaz, saw the area in 1540. Other Spaniards followed. The Jesuit priest, Eusebio Francisco Kino, climbed Pinacate Peak in 1698 and 1706, and Juan Bautista de Anza's expedition traveled just north of the Pinacate in 1744, headed to the west coast, over a route that came to be known as the *Camino del Diablo* (the Devil's Highway).

The Amargosan Pinacateños lived in the area into the late 1800's, narrowly surviving an 1850 epidemic of yellow fever. About 1890, a posse from Sonoyta was organized to put an end to their reported attacks on travelers along the *Camino del Diablo*. Almost all were killed.

Vegetation

The Pinacate is part of one of the hottest and driest sections of the Sonoran Desert, the Lower Colorado Valley division. Rainfall is under five inches annually and very unpredictable.

During the hottest part of the year, high temperatures range from 100 to 120 degrees F. Winter lows occasionally dip below 32 degrees F. The plants and animals living here must cope with prolonged excessive heat as well as occasional freezing.

The distribution of plants in the Pinacate is vitally linked to its geology. For instance, rocky slopes support richer and denser perennial vegetation than flat sandy plains, because they provide increased soil moisture. You can see an example of this if you hike to Pinacate Peak, through several species-rich communities, where additional rainfall, cooler temperatures and porous soil all translate into more water in the ground for plants.

Some of the plant communities in the Pinacate area are distinctive and easily recognized. The water poor creosote bush community is one. Almost pure stands of creosote bush sparsely cover the sandy plains surrounding the lava field, creating a sea of low shrubs around a volcanic island. Although individual creosote bushes may be seen elsewhere, the creosote bush community stops quite abruptly when the soil changes from sand to lava rock.

The cinder soil community is another, with its serenely smooth, windswept lapilli soil interrupted by an occasional Palo Verde, ocotillo, senita, burro bush or saguaro. Teddybear chollas appear here and there, usually in dense clusters. Cinder soil tends to hold moisture well, but rainfall here is intermediate, so this community is neither particularly sparse nor dense. Fine examples of the community can be seen north of Crater Elegante.

The rocky, upper slope of the hills is the exact opposite of serenity. It has a disorganized, cluttered appearance due to a busy mixture of rock, creosote bush, timber-bush, ocotillo, brittle bush, barrel cactus and saguaro.

Two eye-catching plants stand out, however, an evergreen shrub called pygmy cedar, which looks like a little conifer, but in fact, is a member of the sunflower family. A striking cactus known as the many headed barrel, a huge mound shaped cluster of stems. Here, on the bajadas, soil moisture is fairly high and so is plant diversity.

A distinctive community of plants found on the younger lava flows results from the most unusual combination of geology and flora anywhere in the Pinacate. If you walk across a recent lava flow, you will see small gardens in the fine brown clay which collects in pockets in the lava, as does moisture.

Blue flowering solarium, desert lavender, bright yellow brittle bush and orange mallow makes these gardens spring showcases for desert plants. Elephant trees, with thick trunks and peeling, papery bark, add an almost tropical look.

Volcanic Craters

Scattered across the volcanic field are the nine giant craters that have made the Pinacate region famous: Elegante, MacDougal, Sykes, Molina, Badillo, Celaya, Moon, Kino, and Cerro Colorado. They were formed at the same time as the cinder cones, but they are structurally different from both the cones and the shield volcano. Their origin is not fully understood. They appear to be "maar" volcanoes, which are formed when hot magma contacts underground water and steam explosion blasts material skyward, excavating the crater. But there are some questions about the source of the ground water and present location of all the excavated material. There is plenty of evidence that steam explosions did indeed initiate the creation of these craters, with the explosions blasting throughout older rock and depositing materials such as "tuff," compressed volcanic ash, on the crater rims.

But there is also evidence that the craters resulted from the collapse of rock back down into a void created by the eruption. On the edge of Crater Elegante, for example, looking across the one mile diameter of the abyss, one can readily see a light colored rim of tuff (result of steam explosions) above sheer cliff walls (evidence of collapse). This construction, a tuff ring with sheer cliff walls of older rocks below, is typical of most of the giant Pinacate craters. Cerro Colorado is unique because its crater is very shallow and it lacks the old rock basalt typical of other Pinacate craters. It is composed almost entirely of soft tuff, which has been extensively eroded. Pathways of thunderstorm rivulets have etched its south side and carved wavy sculptures on its rim.

While it is unlikely that any individual volcano (or any one volcanic feature) in the Pinacate field will erupt again, the field itself is far from inactive. Magma still rolls deep down, the factory continues to melt rock. But for the time being, none of this activity is surfacing. The individual eruptive points may be extinct, but the field itself is simply "resting" dormant. It seems certain that the magma will someday rise again.

The Shield Volcano

Volcan Santa Clara is the central feature of the Pinacate, a shield volcano locally known as Sierra del Pinacate, with long gently sloping sides formed when lava quickly flowed out and away from the central vent (in typical volcanoes a cone is built up around the vent). Father Eusebio Kino named the mountain Santa Clara, but his name seems now to be almost forgotten.

The highest of the three Santa Clara peaks in Pinacate, at 3,904 feet, a favorite target for summit-seekers who are willing to make the 2,500 foot cross-country climb.

These cinder cone peaks were created by volcanic eruptions that occurred long after Volcan Santa Clara was formed. Lava flowed from their fissures and vents, down the slopes, filling canyons with molten rock that today looks as if it cooled and hardened just yesterday.

Cinder Cones

Scattered throughout the 600 square miles of the Pinacate volcanic field are over 400 cinder cones. These cones were built by volcanic eruptions two thousand to one million years ago, about the time Volcan Santa Clara was in its last throes of eruption. A cinder cone fits the popular conception of a volcano. It is constructed of loose, pyroclastic (fire-broken), airborne materials of ash and cinders ejected in a fire fountain eruption and then piled up around the vent, creating a steep-sided cone.

Lava Flows

When the gas activity in the magma of a volcanic eruption is not intense enough to break the magma into pyroclastic fragments, liquid rock (lava) will flow out of the volcano.

Most of the Pinacate lava is old, weathered and not particularly noticeable, but the younger flows are spectacular wonderlands of rock. Two types of recent lava flows can be seen in the Pinacate, with names borrowed from Hawaii: the billowy "pahoehoe" lava which is smooth, ropy and looks like chocolate icing; and the "aa" lava which is crusty, jumbled rubble of rough, jagged rocks.

On both kinds of lava, hundreds of bizarre forms squeeze up bubbles, spatter cones and lava tubes can be found on the Pinacate flows. One of the largest lava tubes, near the base of Camegie Peak, is a sacred place to the Tohono O'odham Indians (Papago).

A walk on hardened lava may chew up a pair of hiking boots, but it will reveal a fantastic display of unusual forms and textures. The Pinacate lava flows are known for having some of the most diverse shapes and structures anywhere in North America.

Note: Information about the Pinacate Mountains has been published previously by the Sonoran Department of Tourism, some of which is included here.

A Brief History

Travel: A childish delight in being somewhere else.
-Sigmund Freud

The area located in the heart of the Gran Desierto de Altar between Yuma and Puerto Peñasco is the driest desert in all of North America and contains a fascinating history. Historians and archaeologists theorize that the Gran Desierto region may have been inhabited as early as 37,000 years ago. If these theories are correct, there is no other known geographical area which so completely covers such a time span of human occupation.

The prehistory of man in this area of the desert is largely shrouded in mystery. One of the great heritage's of this desert is the story of human occupation that began centuries before the coming of white men. Indians were the first human inhabitants who settled and made the desert their home in the area we now know as the Sonoran Desert. During this time, the climate was more humid, and the wet lands, rivers, plants, and animals offered many more advantages for existence. These Indians knew the problems of the desert and solved them.

Over thousands of years these early inhabitants of the desert region increased in numbers, separated into family groups, bands and tribes, and established a variety of cultures suitable to their different localities. While living in this area they became a part of nature and adapted themselves to whatever resources could be harvested whether it be plants, fish, or mammals. They found all the materials they needed to provide food, clothing, and shelter in the desert, lakes, or slopes. They traveled according to the seasons. They made use of the desert waters, developed elaborate rituals, spiritual traits, and crafts. Permanent villages did not exist. Some of the history of these people can be partially reconstructed. Most of it has been lost to us forever because their existence was precarious and their culture was not advanced.

In time the Hohokam people from northern Mexico migrated into this area. They brought with them stone-etching techniques, pottery construction methods, and the practice of trading with other tribes as far west as California.

"El Camino del Diablo"
The Devil's Road

Crossing the Camino del Diablo was never easy. It was, and still is, known as the deadliest immigrant trail in North America. This area in the southwest corner of Arizona contains a 4,100 square mile no-man's land. This desert region proved hostile even for the native Sand Papago. The Sand Papago claimed this area as their ancestral land and ultimately marched into cultural extinction.

Bordered on the north by the Gila River, on the west by the Mojave Desert, on the east by the ancestral Sonoran desert lands of the Papago, and on the south by Sonora's *Gran Desierto*. One of the only trails that traversed this forbidden domain was the 130-mile-long Camino that tied each distant water hole to the next.

Historic routes in this area of Southern Arizona include the Hohokam shell trail to the Gulf of Mexico, circa A.D. 1000; Sand Papago route to Dome, pre A.D. 1540; The expedition of Padre Eusebio Francisco Kino, around 1699; The Yuma Wagon Road, 1854; El Camino del Diablo, (Sand Papago route first used by Spaniard Melchoir Díaz in 1540), 1850s; Gila Trail, (immigrant trail first used by the Maricopa-Halchidoma Indians, pre-1700s), 1850s.

Expeditions by foot and on horseback started some one thousand years ago by the Sand Papago who first used the route to travel between water holes. The first of six principal wells is Bates Well. The caretaker has long made a practice of leaving a 5-gallon jug of water for travelers striking out from Sonoyta to Ajo. Papago Well is a mere 31 miles east of Tule Well. Tule well was dug sometime before the 1893 boundary survey. The foul-tasting, sulfur-laden water is legendary; one enterprising Mexican reportedly sold water here until he was shot to death by a thirsty customer. Tinajas Atlas known as High Tanks was one of the Sand Papago's main encampments; while camped here in 1699, Padre Kino described them; "Here Majne counted 30 naked and poverty-stricken Indians who lived solely on roots, lizards and other wild foods." Through the years, desperate men and women struggled on hand and knee to reach this ancient water hole, a series of ten rock tanks. The lowest pools are always the first to evaporate. At one time, 150 graves were counted on the Little Mesa of Death, below the Tinajas Altas.

Spaniard Melchoir Díaz is the first European to cross the Camino and the first well-known European to die on it in 1540. Jesuit missionary and explorer Padre Eusebio Francisco Kino and Lt. Juan Manje make the second crossing of the Camino and provide the first eye witness account of the Sand Papago's desperate existence in 1699. Padre Francisco Tomás Garcés is the first to traverse the Camino in the summer of 1771. Juan Bautista de Anza pioneers a new leg of the Camino along the west slope of the Gila Mountains in 1774. Ensign Santiago de Islas leads families across the Camino in 1781. Lt. Col. Pedro Fages returns along the Camino with the bodies of Padre Garcés and three murdered missionaries in 1782. During the 1850s to the 1900s, thousands of Mexican immigrants travel the Camino to reach the California gold fields. During this period, historians estimate between 400 and 2,000 people died of thirst, making the Camino the deadliest immigrant trail in North America.

Andrew Gray and a Texas Western Railroad crew surveyed the Devil's Road in June, 1854. Army Lt. Nathaniel Michler and José Salazar surveyed the new international boundary for the Gadsen Purchase in 1855. Henry Crabb's 93-man expedition followed the Camino to Caborca. In 1857 all but one are massacred by irate locals. Harvard Professor Raphael Pumpbelly crosses the Camino in July 1861. He barely escapes death when it rains. Capt. D. Gaillard and the International Boundary Commission surveys and marks the

U.S.-Mexico Border from 1891 to 1896. W.J. McGee camps at Tinajas Altas throughout the summer of 1905, and recounts the incredible ordeal of Pablo Valencia in his paper *Desert Thirst as a Disease.* William Hornaday and D.T. McDougal explore Sierra del Pinacate. In 1907, Hornaday documents his journey in *Campfires on Desert and Lava.* Norwegian Carl Lumholtz explores the region in 1910, and produces one of its best maps and an ethnographic account in *New Trails in Mexico.* Hunter and naturalist Charles Sheldon climbs the region's rugged peaks. In 1913 his diary is published in *The Wilderness of The Southwest.* Geologist Kirk Bryan explores much of the region in 1917, in a vintage Ford touring car. Bryan produces a landmark survey, *Routes to Desert Watering Places in Papago Country.* Sonoran desert historian and writer Bill Broyles retraces the route of prospector Pablo Valencia during a solo mid-August trek in 1980. The Annerino-Lohman-Robertson party make an unsupported, mid-august, 1988, trek along the Camino, linking the Yuma Wagon Road, the ancient Camino and de Anza's historic route.

Unsolved Mysteries In Puerto Peñasco

In 1960, Mr. Armando López Macías, his wife Chelito Reyna and Mr. José López Rojas, among others, were building a septic system three meters below ground when they found a brick wall cemented together with mud. Construction apparently ceased when the wall was scarcely one and one half meters high and about three blocks long. It extends from 13th (Miguel Hidalgo) Street to 15th (León de la Barra) Street.

Questions still remain. What was the structure? A small fort? The beginning of a mission, built in an effort to convert this area of Old Port into a port of entry for the Franciscan priests living in Sonoyta? Where did the bricks come from in this land of endless dunes? Who built that brick wall which remained buried for such a long time? How many years are necessary to bury a construction three meters deep in the desert? Could this be the legendary Mission of the Four Evangelists which to this day remains lost in the desert?

The State Line

The Pimeria Alta included what is now southern Sonora and southern Arizona. It extended from the Altar River in Sonora, to the Gila River, and from the San Pedro River to the Gulf of California and Colorado in the west. During that time it was all included in the province of *Nueva Vizcayrnas*.

There was no Arizona during the years prior to 1831. Under the constitution of 1824 there was one Mexican state in the Northwest called El Estado Libre de Occidente (The Free State of the West), which included the present Mexican states of Sonora and Sinaloa along with what is now Arizona. By 1831, however, the Sonoran's had become so unhappy that their state and Arizona was separated from Sinaloa and given separate statehood. The officer who commanded was the military commander and the chief civil and judicial official. He functioned as a lieutenant governor for the region.

A war between the United States and Mexico resulted in the entry of the Americans in 1846. The causes of this conflict were far removed from the Southwest. They can be traced to a clash of cultures, to the debts owned by Mexico to American citizens which Mexican officials refused to pay, the boundary of Texas and the unwillingness of Mexican politicians to seek a peaceful solution to the issues separating the two nations. In fact, some Mexican politicians were seeking the war to gain power at home.

Odie B. Faulk writes, in his book *Destiny Road,* the story of the Arizona and Mexico boundary. A glance at a map of the present United States shows that the boundary between this country and Mexico takes peculiar turns and twists for no known geographical, social or economic reason. Colorful stories have been told to explain such meaningless jags as that just west of Nogales, Arizona, where the boundary turns to the northwest to run in a straight line to the Colorado River just south of Yuma. One version has it that the surveyors working on the boundary were drunk on tequila and thought they were still going due west, while another says that these men were hot and thirsty and simply decided to survey in a direct line to Yuma, the nearest place where they could get cold beer. However, it was not drunkenness or the desire for beer that explains the final course of the boundary. Rather than in large measure it was the location of Cooke's Wagon Road that figures prominently in the setting of this dividing line.

James A. Crutchfield writes in his book, *It Happened in Arizona:* In July 15, 1853, James Gadsen, a sixty five year old native of Charleston, South Carolina, was called to the office of the Secretary of State, William L. March. James Gadsen, a Yale graduate, former army colonel and head of a marginally successful railroad company, had been selected by President Franklin Pierce to go to Mexico and resolve the discord that had been growing between the two countries in five years since the end of the Mexican War.

A six thousand square mile area was being claimed by both countries. The primary point of contention was that after years of meetings, negotiations, and surveys the two countries could not agree on the boundary line between the Mexican states of Sonora and Chihuahua and what are now New Mexico and Arizona.

It was not so much the size of the territory that bothered American authorities. Rather, it was the fact that Colonel Philip St. George Cooke's popular wagon road traversed part of it. If the United Stated did not own the entire route of the wagon road, future American immigrants might have trouble getting to California. In addition, plans were under way for a transcontinental railroad, and one of the proposed routes ran through the contested area.

No one in the United states, Democrat or Wig, was in any mood to go to war with Mexico again. March made it clear that Gadsen was expected to steer the dangerous boundary talks back on course. Gadsen had been highly recommended by the secretary of war, Jefferson Davis, a fellow southerner who made no secret of his desire to route the transcontinental railroad across the southern part of the country. When Gadsen left Marcy's office, he carried the authority to "pay liberally" for the borderlands required to accommodate the railroad.

Gadsen was in a good position to negotiate when he arrived in Mexico City a year later. General Antonio Lopez de Santa Anna, of Texas Independence and Mexican War fame, had recently returned to power in Mexico and was in the midst of a financial crisis. Mexico needed money far more than it needed land.

After weeks of meetings, Gadsen signed a treaty that he hoped would end the international boundary dispute once and for all. The treaty called for the United States to pay Mexico fifteen million dollars to yield most of the contested area. The boundary was now located from just north of El Paso, Texas, southwest to the 111th meridian. From there, the border was to turn northwest to the head of the Gulf of California.

The U.S. Senate narrowly failed to ratify the treaty. Instead, it set the boundary where it is today—allowing Mexico to keep more territory—and it cut the payment to Mexico to ten million dollars. Gadsen was so angry that his advice was ignored that he actually lobbied against the revised treaty's passage. However, both countries finally approved it, and on June 29, 1854, the document was signed by President Franklin Pierce.

A new boundary commission was established, with Major William H. Emory, a well-qualified topographical engineer who had ridden with the Army of the West in the Mexican War, serving as the U.S. Commissioner. Emory split his survey team into two sections, one to begin its work at El Paso and move westward, and the other to start at Yuma and work eastward. On august 16, 1855, both parties met in the middle, and the long, complicated mission of establishing the international boundary was finally completed.

Hotel Peñasco Marine Club

The most colorful history of this area came around the late 1920's. During the days of prohibition in the United States and the famous "Dry Law," a visionary by the name of John Stone and an associate of the famous gangster Al Capone, built the Hotel Peñasco Marine Club with a partner named Charlie Ren.

The book *Historia del Municipio de Puerto Peñasco*, by historian Maria Eisabel Verdugo, describes an official paper signed by Stone, named "Official Document of June 12, 1929." Engraved with an official seal, it was sent to Governor Francisco S. Elias. Stone asked permission for airplanes of Scenic Airways to land in a place which was already prepared as a landing strip near Old Town Puerto Peñasco. It was almost impossible to come down from the border across the desert because much water was needed. Travel was difficult in many areas due to soft, deep sand.

Stone also owned the Cornella Hotel in Ajo, Arizona and the Cactus Club in Sonoyta with his partner, Ren. But legend has it that the Marine Club was really owned by Al Capone. This location on a desolate outcropping near the Sea of Cortéz was not a problem. Blocks used to build the hotel came from a nearby hill called "La Ballena." A well was dug, 18 feet deep, and a water generating station was built close by. It was the only well in town.

Locals described the Marine Club as "a beautiful cantina, the most elegant you can imagine with oak beams and ceiling fans." At night, the player piano could be heard all the way to the fishing camp. Jazz music including the "Charleston" would be playing long into the night. Every year, more fisherman arrived in Puerto Peñasco and the most daring demanded to be taken care of at the bar. When they arrived, Stone threatened them with guns and refused them entrance.

Charlie Ren took hunters to Kino Bay and Puerto Libertad. They traveled all over in airplanes and specially equipped cars with horses, guns, drinks, and often brought women. Visitors staying at the hotel sometimes came from as far away as Alaska.

Townspeople thought Ren was a liquor smuggler. There were two boats; a modern yacht named "Scandia Pacific," and another unregistered boat called "El Blanco." It was said that El Blanco was used to transport liquor from Guaymas to El Mayor, the uppermost city of the Colorado River in Baja California. They would take refuge from "running" in Puerto Peñasco.

Years later, Stone sold a boat to a local named Nick Corona and one of his partners by the name of Benjamín Bustamante and his wife Tecla. The authorities did not approve of the sale and sued them. But others say that local officials demanded some of Stone's profits from the gambling and bootlegging that discreetly took place. When Stone refused to pay the authorities money, his liquor license was revoked. As the story goes, a disagreement ensued and Stone burned the hotel and dynamited the water well. Stone never came back again.

For five years after this happened, fresh water was trucked to town over 60 miles of unpaved roads. Bustamante and Tecla took over the Marine Club, made repairs and renamed it the Hotel Peñasco.

The locals of Puerto Peñasco have inherited the legend, be it myth or reality. Today the Marine Club or Hotel Peñasco is abandoned and in ruin. It has a lot of history as one of the first historical sights in Old Town. It sits as a link to the past, waiting to be born again. It stands as the oldest original building in Old Town.

Fishing Camp

The first fishermen from Guaymas, Kino Bay, Puerto Libertad, and other locations in the state of Sonora arrived in 1920. Victor and Benjamin Bustamante were the first settlers to call the place "Punta Peñasco" or Rocky Point. They distilled sea water in homemade stills and lived in caves and tents surviving on fish. Totoaba and shrimp were abundant in the waters of the Gulf of California and totoaba was the only fish caught for profit. Risking the hot desert and roads of deep sand, trucks made the trip to the border to sell their "catch." When the season was over many went back to their own homes and waited for the next season.

In 1932, the Police Department was formed under the jurisdiction of the Sheriff's Department in Sonoyta under the protection of the City of Caborca. The Hotel Cortéz, named by Ricardo Hussong, was built in 1948 from brick brought from the United States to accommodate President Roosevelt of the U.S. and President Cárdenas of Mexico. They planned a meeting to discuss the measures that were to be taken in case of a Japanese invasion through the Sea of Cortéz. Puerto Peñasco formed its own Sheriff's Department in December 1941. In July 1952, the Sheriff's Department separated itself from the jurisdiction of the City of Caborca and the Sheriff's Department of Sonoyta.

Early travel to Rocky Point was by team and wagon. Even after cars came into use, they would bog down in the sand and had to be dug out. The road from Sonoyta to Rocky Point was paved with wartime emergency funds. Mexico Highway 2 was completed from Mexicali Baja, California to Sonoyta, Sonora, Mexico in 1953.

Mexican Customs

Most of Mexican Fiestas are the products of boredom
-Herbert Cerwin
These are the Mexicans, 1947

People And Traditions

Tact is the essence of social interaction. Arrogant or inconsiderate behavior is poorly received in Mexico. Impatience is an emotion Mexicans do not seem to feel themselves or appreciate in others. Mexicans appreciate it when visitors approach them on equal terms and are careful to avoid the appearance of patronizing them. If respect and appreciation for the beliefs of others is not shown, establishing a rapport will be very difficult.

Punctuality is not a Mexican habit as the term is understood in North America or Europe. Visitors should allow at least an extra half hour in relation to appointments and starting times. Mexicans are very ready with invitations and offers of hospitality. If an engagement is arranged, more than likely the meeting will be in a restaurant or public place. An invitation to the host's home is proof of enormous confidence and a sincere acknowledgment of friendship.

The midday siesta between 2 p.m. and 5 p.m. is a sacred institution. Although it may not be religiously observed in Puerto Peñasco, it is a custom that dates back to the early history of Mexico.

On the other hand, requests for help are rarely refused. The helpfulness of local drivers to other motorists in difficulty is very genuine so look at it that way. In certain circumstances an offer of money can work wonders. Public officials, who tend to be poorly paid, will expect some recognition even for services that are a part of their official duties. To Mexicans this seems perfectly in order. They do not see it as implying bribery and corruption.

Society And Values

Mexico was born out of conquest. Its people are the offspring of neither the conqueror nor the conquered, but rather the relationship between the two. The Mexican cannot take pride in the thrilling victories of his Spanish ancestors. Neither does the Mexican feel the solidarity and dignity that comes from sharing past oppression. This sounds foreign to the North American because they have never questioned who they are. North Americans have identified themselves not as who they are, but in *what* they have done. They believe that accomplishments are more important than roots.

On the surface they can seem a lot alike but Mexico's values and behavior are at odds with those of the United States. Mexican society is unique blend of Indian, Spanish, pagan and Catholic. The vast majority of the population is *mestizo,* a combination of Indian and Spanish. This term originally was used to denote the offspring of Europeans and Indians. Mexicans use terms that designate social status, not describe a person's genetic roots like in the United States. Although, Mexicans are conscious of a person's complexion and show a preference toward a lighter skin color. Race in Mexico is a relative concept, not an absolute one.

Spaniards and Indians had concepts toward race which are different from the United States. Both recognized the differences of race and of society. They were hierarchical societies that not only accepted formal inequality but recognized distinct orders of people with its own set of privileges and obligations. These included, but were not limited to, nobility, clergy, peasants, and slaves. As a result of intermarriage over time, they began to think in cultural terms and designated race as to how a person lived. One can identify with an individual's social class by the way he or she speaks and dresses.

Mexico has focused inward, it does not seek to play a leadership role in world affairs. Throughout most of its recent history, Mexico has endeavored to establish an independent role for itself rather than to try to influence events on a wider scale. In matters of culture Mexicans have traditionally looked to Europe, emulating their art forms and sending their sons and daughters to study there.

As a Third World nation, Mexico is unique in its common border with the United States. Easily one-fifth of living Mexicans currently reside in the United States, have lived in the United States or know someone who has. Mexicans admire our economic opportunity. Desperation, not desire, drives most illegal immigrants. Balance of trade produces the momentum to increase tourism.

Step one foot across the border and you will see that Mexico is a poor country. Its per capita income is less than $2,000, only one-tenth that of the United States. The wealthiest 10% of the population receives close to 50% of the nation's national income, while the poorest 10% receives slightly more than 1% of the national income. During the 1980's the proportion of the urban population living in poverty has increased. The poor comprise between 25% and 40% of Mexico's population. They include peasants who own barely enough land on which to support their families, and the hundreds of thousands of migrants who flock to Mexico City, the border towns and to the United States, most have no regular employment. The government estimates that almost 40% of its population is under employed.

Religion

Mexicans have always been a religious people and are so today. North Americans will find contradiction in the Mexican Catholic religion. The church as an institution has been as responsible for violence as any single issue in the nation's history.

In pre-Colombian Mexico, the world was a fearsome place. Human beings had little control over their destinies and were at the mercy of forces more powerful than themselves. Human sacrifice was a very important part of pre-Columbian religion, not just simple killing, it was surrounded with much ritual.

Spain brought Roman Catholicism to the new world. It was rich in ceremony and grandeur. Priests dominated great civilizations and temples dominated their cities. Early Catholicism reflected a world in which saints, angels, and devils actively intervened in the daily lives of the faithful.

The conquest of Mexico was a war between the gods in which the Christian God defeated the Aztecs Gods. It took two hundred years for Spain to defeat the Aztec empire and bring Christianity to the natives of the new world.

The church soon became an equal partner in government. The church came to possess huge amounts of wealth in land and mines and became a giant bureaucracy. The "New Spain" as it was called, became a catholic society because of its power not by the piety or virtue of its members. Grand cathedrals, altars covered in gold and silver, statues and shrines were seen everywhere.

A prestigious career with a secure income were guaranteed if young men joined the priesthood. In addition, the convent was one of the few places in which women could achieve power and wealth.

The Indians accepted Christianity but did not give up old beliefs. The appearance of Our Lady of Guadalupe in 1531 was the single most dramatic event in the conversion of the Indians to Christianity. Michael Burke writes in *Hippocrene Companion Guide to Mexico:*

> Juan Diego was a humble, devout Indian recently converted to Catholicism. While crossing a barren hill, Tepeyac, on his way to Mass, the Virgin suddenly appeared before him. She told him to go to the bishop, Juan Zumárraga, and tell him that she wanted a church built atop the hill. Two days later Juan Diego was granted an audience, and gave Zumárraga the message. The bishop was sympathetic, but demanded proof, which Juan Diego relayed back to the Virgin. The Virgin then told Juan to gather the roses growing on top of the hill, where roses had never grown before, and take them to the bishop. Juan complied, gathering them in the blanket he carried, and returned to show the bishop, however, the roses had disappeared. Instead, an image of the Virgin, modestly adorned in Indian garb, appeared on his blanket. Zumárraga accepted the evidence, and ordered a church built where the Virgin had requested.
>
> The Symbolism of the Virgin image was powerful. It was not the image of a European woman, but rather a dark-complexioned

Indian woman with notably Indian features. The message was clear: Christianity was a religion not only for white Europeans, but for all. To the Indians, the Virgin of Guadalupe was one of them, welcoming them into the new faith. To the Spaniards, the Virgin of Guadalupe denied the second-class membership of Indians within Christianity. And to the Mexicans of the future, the Virgin of Guadalupe became a national patron.

The location of the apparition was even more compelling. Tepeyac had previously been a site where Indians went to worship Tonantzin, a mother figure in indigenous religious belief that predated the Aztecs. Whether or not by design, the location further promoted the transition from traditional belief to Christianity.

The garment bearing the image was hung above the altar on a small chapel built the following year. The chapel, in disrepair and closed to the public, still stands near Mexico City atop the hill of Tepeyac.

With all of its grandeur and influence, the church also had its enemies. Anticlericalism is opposition to the power, wealth, and autonomy of the church and its clergy. Anticlericalism continues to be a significant force in Mexican history almost to present day.

For over 100 years Mexico fought over the position the church should have in Mexican society. The 19th century brought a war of independence. There was a continuing struggle between the liberals and conservatives. Liberals were generally middle class and advocated the destruction of the Church whom they considered as a wealthy, powerful institution immune from government control. Conservatives were generally wealthy land owners who supported the churches monopoly over religion as essential to keeping public morality. The clergy supported conservatives to protect their own interests.

The church became an issue in 1917. Anticlericalism was included into the constitutional convention and guidelines were set stating its future position. The constitution deprived the church of its traditional role in education, political participation, and the number of clergy and churches were limited. Marriage became a civil ceremony, divorce became legal and religious processions were banned.

Since 1940 the Church and State have come to terms with each other to coexist. As long as the Church maintained a low profile, government looks the other way. The government now maintains the status quo. Religion still remains a crucial part of the Mexican experience and provides valuable insight into the Mexican soul.

Religious Customs

Customs are traditional practices, modes of behavior, or social habits. When they are associated with holidays they become calendar customs and when such events are celebrated annually by a community, they become festivals. A working definition might simply say that a custom is what folks do "just because they have always done something that way" or because they grew up among relatives who did the same. The Mexican has a gift for finding his own way of expressing his feelings on important occasions – and his expressions are apt to be demonstrative.

Mexico's Catholics are devoutly religious and so are Mexico's Indians – in their own way. Each have great reverence for their religious occasions and celebrate them faithfully. But fiestas, with the excitement of their color, dancing, music, toys, and decorations, are for everyone. They are truly a Mexican expression and an essential part of life.

Epiphany - January 6th is Epiphany, a feast of the Catholic church which commemorates the coming of the Magi, as the first manifestation of Christ to the Gentiles. It is the day of the year that children anticipate with great excitement, the day they receive their annual gifts. Christmas is not a time for giving and receiving gifts, but a holy day reserved for worship honoring the birth of Christ. On Epiphany, it is customary to serve a fancy cake decorated with fruit *Rosca de Reyes* – "twisted cake of the Kings." It contains a tiny porcelain figure of the Christ child. Whoever receives this has to give a party on February second–*día de la Candelaria.*

St. Anthony's Day - January 17th is St. Anthony's Day, when children take their pets or farm animals to the church to be blessed by the priest. This is a charming ceremony to see.

Lent - The period of Lent, culminating on Easter Sunday, is celebrated throughout Catholic Mexico to commemorate the crucifixion and resurrection of Christ. Until Palm Sunday, there is an impressive medley of sound from solemn church bells everywhere to announce services and holy days.

Palm Sunday - Palm Sunday is a very important occasion. The use of palm leaves is a custom based on the story of when Jesus arrived in Jerusalem. His followers waved palm leaves and olive branches to greet him and to express their devotion. Native artisans weave their intricate and decorative designs made of the soft green palm leaves. Before the first mass begins, people come to look at their array of palm ornaments and carry the prettiest ones into church on this holy day. Each member of the family carries a palm leaf of some kind, and each is blessed by the priest with holy water and a prayer. The leaves are held in the hands of the members of the congregation during the service. Afterward they are taken home and placed on the wall or over a doorway as a holy symbol and remain there until the next year.

All Souls Day - For Mexicans, neither birth nor death is seen to interrupt the continuity of life and neither is considered overtly important. The concept of death as a celebration is unfamiliar to Gringos. In Mexico, however, the most important festival of the year is during the first couple of days of November (All Souls Day, a national holiday) when the dead are brought back to life through memory and honored with flowers, food, and drink. There is nothing macabre about this celebration with death. It is brought out into the open, celebrated, and laughed with and not hidden behind veils of secrecy.

Mexicans believe the life hereafter is a luxury worth waiting for. This dates from long before the arrival of the Catholic Spanish. Pre-Hispanic cultures also saw death as a great honor, particularly on the battlefield or in childbirth and warriors or ball-game players who died in action were often deified. Even today, the pragmatic Mexicans have a furious energy to live for the moment.

A death-related aspect of folk art exists in many parts of the Southwest in the form of *descansos* (resting places) that relate to ancient custom. The *descansos* along the roadsides were hallowed by custom and small shrines are sometimes built. They mark the spot where someone died in an automobile or other accident, or just a memorial marker where flowers were brought on Memorial day.

Some of the *descansos* are ornate, some are simple. They are not only reminders of a journey never completed, they are a work of art and perhaps one of the few authentic non commercial folk arts of Mexico's Hispanics. They are created out of love in a time of pain and wonderment. These *descants* are sculptures, in a sense earth works, that occupy a unique relation to the land and the environment. Though most are carved, some are assembled out of parts from the wrecked auto, built out of rocks or poured cement, and others incorporate photos. Only out of true love does a work of art evolve.

Christmas Festivals - Celebrations in honor of the Virgin of Guadeloupe are customary throughout Mexico. As the "brown virgin," she represents an ethnic model for Hispanics. The Christmas season traditionally begins on December 12th, the feast day of the Virgin of Guadeloupe and does not end until January 6th, *El día de los Reyes Magos,* Day of the Kings or Maji.

Among the most colorful and enduring of the customs are the drama like *posadas.* A series of night journeys when the Holy Family goes from house to house seeking shelter, being turned down repeatedly until finally one family opens its doors. After the pilgrims enter the home that is opened to them, a piñata is hung up for children to break.

Today, these are called *luminarias* and are part of a custom that was very common during the Spanish Colonial days, with the appearance of paper sacks brought by the traders on the Santa Fe trail in the 1820's. The custom of bonfires was converted into using candles set in sand in the bottom of sacks, a variation which is the current form of the custom. People illuminate their homes, churches, driveways, and sidewalks with the sacks for several nights preceding Christmas.

Weddings

Courting and wedding customs are very important with elaborate church ceremonies planned months or years in advance.

An official courtship takes place, but in earlier times the couple was seldom seen together without chaperones. Invitations to the wedding are delivered personally. The groom is expected to pay for all the expenses but the bridesmaids and groomsmen pay for their own attire plus other expenses associated with their part of the wedding.

Quinceañera

The *quinceañera,* a celebration of girls turning fifteen, is a continuing custom honoring hundreds of years of tradition. Early Mayans and Toltecas believed "a woman did not become a human being until she was fifteen." It is not something just the wealthy can afford. Some families spend almost as much on a *quinceañera* celebration as on a wedding. The purpose is to mark the entrance of a young woman into adulthood in a social sense, and into adulthood in the church. Successful events are planned months in advance.

I arrived at church on a Saturday evening to find a quinceañera celebration ready to begin. Eight girlfriends and their escorts made up the girls "court" while a congregation of about 60 friends and relatives gathered to watch. The girl, escorted by her parents, grandparents, and godparents, filed into the church behind the "court." Prayers were said that she would grow up virtuous. Scriptures were read by the godparents and a renewal of her baptismal vows was made by the girl. Then, there was picture taking galore. After a lengthy mass, the group went to a dinner, reception, and a dance for about 300.

Government

Mexico is a federal system. Its powers are divided between thirty one states and a central government. The formal title is the United States of Mexico. Mexico City serves as the Federal District and is self governing. The power in both the federal government and in the states is divided among a legislature, an executive branch and a judiciary. The president of Mexico serves a six year term and cannot be re-elected.

The president is all powerful, his role as head of the single party that has governed Mexico for sixty years, the Party of the Institutional Revolution, (PRI). The PRI was an escape from Mexico's history of anarchy, dictatorship, and revolution.

The PRI is observed by some outsiders as Marxist (based on economic class), and Fascist (based on corporate interests rather than individual ones). The PRI has created a power structure that makes it possible for persons from humble beginnings to rise to considerate wealth and power within the system. Organized labor usually negotiates with the government before striking against private interests. Peasants, labor and business are not interest groups but rather active players in the internal decisions of the party.

The PRI had a long record of providing social programs to help the poor and establishing economic policy that brought prosperity to many. Then it proved incapable of dealing with economic downturns and began to lose its political legitimacy and become the target of abuse for electoral fraud and repression.

Since the mid 1970's the presidency has been given to professionals without first-hand political experience. For example, Carlos Salinas de Gortari, Mexico's president in the early 1990's, was educated at Harvard University where he earned a doctorate in economics.

The PRI supports its own with profitable government posts. Joining the PRI will successfully lead to an established political career in Mexico. Each president single handily names his successor after consulting with the PRI before making a final decision.

Corruption in Mexico has been a part of government administration since Spanish Colonialism. Today the *mordida,* or bite, is a part of the system. It aids in avoiding prosecution for an infraction of the law or by having official forms processed for which one has no legal right. For a citizen of Mexico, it is a cost of doing business. From a government view the *mordida* threatens implementation of policy. For years, the government in Mexico City has not been successful in getting rid of corruption on the United States border to encourage tourism.

The *camarilla* is an involved network of political loyalties. Their first obligation is to their patron, not to the agency in which they work. Thus, a successful leader must constantly earn the loyalty of others to make things work.

Mexico has a very impressive political life. Unlike other countries, the results are known before the campaigning begins. Opposition parties are highly visible before elections and provide an outlet for those who have competing interests. The largest party is the National Action Party (PAN). Started in 1939 it brought together those who opposed the fundamental principles of the revolution. PAN opposes state intervention in the economy, organizations such as the *ejido,* (see the chapter on real estate), and the anticlerical stance of the PRI. Supporters come from the middle class in Mexico City and from the northern states that border the United States. Recent campaign issues have been opposition to corruption and fraudulent elections.

Opposing parties on the left are the Popular Socialist Party (PPS), which follows a Soviet path; the Mexican Workers Party (PMT), a socialist party advocating democracy and anti-foreign relations; the Mexican Socialist Party (PSM), and in 1988 was renamed the Party of the Democratic Revolution. Also on the left is the Party of the Authentic Mexican Revolution (PARM), formed by opponents of the governments interest in big business.

In Mexico individuals count more than rules. Officials exercise discretion in choosing what rule to enforce, what client to serve, or what fee to charge. Lawyers are very good at navigating the bureaucracy. The laws are filled with strict regulations of conducting business. Permits are required for every venture. Yet it is universally known that many regulations are almost never enforced. Business in Mexico is far less regulated on a day to day basis than in the United States, although the rules are there for government to enforce as it so chooses. When there is an outbreak of anti-Americanism there is more observance in following the letter of the law than for locally owned corporations.

For the North American residing in Mexico, or doing business there, this can be very disturbing. There are no rules; no one ever knows exactly where he or she stands. At the same time, those who are sophisticated in manipulating the system or hire someone who is, there is far more freedom to operate on the edge of the law than in the United States. In criminal cases, no presumption is made on either side. The defendant has the obligation to respond to evidence presented by the prosecution. Judges are inclined to adhere to official policy, guidelines of a advocate or the incentives of a gratuity.

The government owns a majority share of utilities, transportation, and banking. In addition, the government owns significant shares in heavy industry, from automobiles to railway cars, and competes with private enterprise at the retail level. During the past few years the government has auctioned off its shares of major enterprises from the national telephone company to the banking industry. The government tells private industry what it can produce, but it also mandates an array of fringe benefits, from restrictions on layoffs to compulsory compensatory education of workers, seldom found in free economies. Many enterprises are a joint public-private venture. Much of the Mexican steel industry is owned by such joint ventures.

Mexican banks were nationalized in 1982 so that the government could better direct capital to where it was needed most.

PEMEX, the national oil monopoly, came into existence as a result of the expropriation of the oil industry under President Lázaro Cárdenas in 1938. Since 1976 PEMEX has also been a major source of funds for government to invest in less profitable enterprises. Ironically, PEMEX itself is capital-poor since its profits are immediately confiscated by government for use elsewhere. PEMEX prices its products according to policy considerations, not market prices. Thus high octane gasoline is expensive, and diesel is cheap.

Sea of Cortéz

The sea: A highway between the doorways of the nations.
-Francis K. Lane

The Sea of Cortéz is a place rich with marine life, saltwater marshes, and isolated sandy beaches. It is a place that is cherished by many because of its superb fishing, mild winter climate, and relaxed atmosphere.

This great body of water is bounded by Mexico on three sides and opens at the bottom into the Pacific ocean. In geologic years, it is considered one of the youngest seas, having been created some 10 to 15 million years ago as a result of major earthquake activity along the San Andrea's fault.

At this time the earth was torn apart and a large chunk of the west side of Mexico lifted and wrenched free forming the peninsula of Baja California and the Pacific came gushing in producing a new sea.

Nearly 500 years ago, while Hernando Cortéz was loading up on pearls at La Paz, he sent three ships to explore further up the channel. The commander of this expedition named the waters *El Mar de Cortéz,* the Sea of Cortéz. Called the Gulf of California on most U.S. maps, it is said there is no other sea like it in the world. And just think, it is only 60 miles from the U.S. border.

Intercultural Center For The Study Of Deserts And Oceans

Natural forces that shape Puerto Peñasco's unique environment attract scientists from around the world to study with The Intercultural Center for the Study of Deserts and Oceans (CEDO). Started in 1987, CEDO is a non-profit educational and conservation foundation dedicated to preserving the Sonoran Desert and the Gulf of California. CEDO's goals are to learn about the natural resources of the northern gulf and the surrounding Sonoran Desert. CEDO shares this knowledge with the public and uses this information to direct the wise use and conservation efforts of the gulf's overexploited resources.

CEDO, a joint Mexican-U.S. venture, investigates such ecological problems as the steady decline in the shrimp harvest over the years and the death of much of the pelican population at Rocky Point in 1991. The Agustin Cortéz Building in Las Conchas, the home of CEDO, is named in honor of a Puerto Peñasco pioneer. It operates as an education center and field station. Classes and researchers from everywhere use the laboratories and dormitory. A small natural history museum, library, and bookstore are open to the public. One hour tours are free on Tuesdays at 2:00 p.m. and Saturdays at 4:00 p.m. A staff of two full-time and two part-time workers lead the tours and take students out to explore the unique plant and animal life. A skeleton of a 66 foot whale that was beached in 1982 is on display next to the center. It is an interesting tourist attraction and a remarkable backdrop for photographs.

The Intercultural Center For The Study Of Deserts And Oceans (CEDO), pictured here, is a non-profit educational and conservation foundation dedicated to preserving the Sonoran Desert and the Gulf of California.

CEDO is a U. S. non-profit organization. Donations are tax deductible. For more information on projects or to subscribe to the bilingual natural history newsletter, write: CEDO, Inc., P. O. Box 249, Lukeville, AZ 85381.

Center of Technological Scientific Investigation

Three kilometers on the road to Las Conchas, you will find the Center of Technological and Scientific Investigation of the University of Sonora (CICTUS). Here, experiments are performed by biologists on the life and reproduction of shrimp. A specific process is followed. Shrimp are picked from the deep sea, their larva is placed in a special water pond until a juvenile age is reached. At this stage they are transferred to a pond where they are fed and monitored. The shrimp are considered market ready upon reaching 23 weeks of age. Currently, agreements between CICTUS and local fishing associations may lead to the commercial growth of shrimp.

Tides

The edge of the sea has been a region of fascination for scientists, students, children, and adults throughout history. The area around Rocky Point has attracted marine biologists from all over the United States and Mexico for many years. The tides here are among the most extreme on earth, varying vertically as much as 24 feet (7.4 meters). The shallow enclosed shape of the northern Gulf of California is probably the most important factor in determining the extent of the tides in this region. The monthly timing of tidal extremes is dictated by the alignment of the earth, moon and sun at full and new moons.

The highest tides come when the sun and moon are aligned and the gravitational pull of both causes "spring tides" on an average of every fortnight. Under these conditions the gravitational pull of the sun and the moon are working together to produce extreme tides. There are two high and two low tides per day, which bring food or exposure to sea animals. During an eclipse, the alignment of the sun, moon and earth is even more precise. On July 11, 1991, a total eclipse of the sun produced tides that were spectacularly low in this area.

The shores around Playa Bonita and Playa El Mirador beaches slope gently and large areas are uncovered during the early morning. This is the time to explore and view some of the most interesting and unique sea life. Tidal maps are printed on calendars and can also be found in the *Rocky Point Times* newspaper.

Intertidal Etiquette

Collecting sea life is discouraged. Look at it, smell it, but leave it there. Seemingly innocent activities such as collecting shells contribute to the environmental degradation of the area. Critters such as hermit crabs inhabit some shells which die when removed from the water.

Flatworms, porcelain crabs, sponges and brittle stars all live under boulders and in the tide pools. Discovering them and exploring their world is exciting. Two simple rules of intertidal etiquette will enable these delicate creatures to survive your explorations. If you turn over a rock, be sure to put it back in the original position. All animals and plants living under and on the rocks will appreciate your consideration. Do not take living animals and plants from their seashore home. Remember even apparently empty shells may have a hermit crab inside.

Sea Conditions

Keeping records of the sea conditions is important because turbulent seas can affect the behavior of many marine animals in this area. In heavy seas, pelicans and other diving birds have difficulty feeding and are often injured when attempting to dive. In 1806 a man named Sir Francis Beaufort devised a system to measure wind and sea conditions. His calculations were based on the amount of sail that a fully rigged warship of his day could carry in a wind of a given strength. This form of measurement is still used today.

CEDO has maintained a small weather station near its facility in Las Conchas since 1980. Readings of air temperature, humidity, wind, evaporation, cloud cover, sea surface temperature and sea conditions are taken daily. The highest sea conditions recorded by the CEDO weather station were in August of 1983 and November 1985. The 1985 storm did considerable damage to houses in the Las Conchas community, east of Puerto Peñasco, and to the waterfront in Old Port. Small palm trees along the *Malecón* were planted to replace the large trees carried away when the storm waves broke along the walkway. These waves measured as high as 25 feet.

Isla San Jorge

Often referred to as Bird Island, Isla San Jorge lies approximately 25 miles offshore southeast of Puerto Peñasco. Day trips are offered to Isla San Jorge for fishing and snorkeling, see the chapter on Recreation. On clear days, it is visible as three, or four, small pyramids on the horizon. It is home to thousands of California sea lions and tens of thousands of sea birds such as brown pelicans, boobies, cormorants and gulls. In the afternoon the island appears white, a result of the presence of so many birds.

Occasionally temperature inversions in the lower atmosphere produce a mirage effect around these islands. The most common mirage is the appearance of two images of the island, one above the other. Sometimes the upper and lower images merge to form a cylindrical shaped image of the island.

This image is a result of light rays which bend as they travel at different speeds in different densities of air – colder air is denser than warmer air, for example. This bending or refracting of light rays as they travel from a distant object through a "lens" of different temperature air produces the effect called a mirage. People associate mirages with the desert, but the changing image of Isla San Jorge is a frequent reminder that mirages can and do occur over the sea.

Stingrays

Stingrays are the most notorious of the vertebrates for disrupting tranquillity at the sea's edge in Puerto Peñasco. Stingrays are close relatives of sharks and, like them, have a skeleton made completely of cartilage. Stingrays have one or more spines on their tails, which are made of a rigid material coated with enamel called vasodentine. The spine, which looks like a tail, is serrated and covered with a layer of skin containing glandular cells that produce toxins.

Stingray are the most dangerous of the venomous fishes. The most common species in Puerto Peñasco, however, are small, and the stings rarely produce anything more than a painful scare. It produces a wound that is almost always a result of someone inadvertently stepping on it while wading at the water's edge. When the stingray feels pressure on its body, it swings its tail, like a whip, stabbing the spine into one's foot or lower leg. As the spine is removed, its serrated edge tears the victim's skin, often leaving behind fragments of poisonous mucus and tissues wedged in the wound. Almost immediately, a searing pain develops within 10 cm of the wound, radiating to the entire limb and reaching a maximum intensity in less than 90 minutes. The pain gradually diminishes, disappearing anywhere from 6 to 48 hours later. The intensity of the reaction depends on the type and size of the stingray, as well as the location of the wound and the victim's size and susceptibility to the toxin.

There are about twenty five species in seven families of rays in the Sea of Cortéz. A few you might see in the waters around Puerto Peñasco are: *Shovelnose Guitar Fish,* the snout is sharply pointed, having two dorsal fins, it is brownish gray in color. This type of stingray is abundant in Cholla Bay and Puerto Peñasco. The *Round Stingray,* is shaped like a circular disc with a short rounded tail. A venomous sting is closer to the end of the tail than the body. A sting can cause a painful wound. Favorite hangouts are on the sandy shores throughout the upper Gulf. *Longtail Diamond Ray* has a tail almost twice the length of the body. The stinger is located closer to the base of the tail than to the tip and the body is diamond shaped. It can be found on sandy beaches at moderate depths. *Bat Ray* has a distinct head protruding beyond origin of the pectoral fins. These rays are good jumpers. A small stinger is preceded by a small dorsal fin. It is very common in the Gulf.

Stingrays bury into the sand and blend in so well it is difficult to see them. That is why, at low tide, it is advisable to be extremely cautious if entering the water on foot, so you can avoid being stung by one. At low tide, when entering the water wear tennis shoes or water socks and shuffle your feet. This way you will frighten them away without stepping on them. Information about first aid for fish bites and stings can be found in Chapter 9-1-1, Emergencies.

There are two ways to treat a stingray sting: soak the foot in ammonia or apply meat tenderizer. Get to a doctor immediately to check if the stinger has been left behind. Rays have a flattened body, pectoral fins fused to the head, ventral gill slits and the absence of a transparent eyelid.

Scorpion Fish

Another venomous fish is the Rock or Scorpion Fish, *Scorpaena mystes,* which has small venom producing glands on its dorsal spines. As its name indicates, this fish resembles a rock and tends to remain immobile for long periods of time on the rocky reefs on which it lives. This makes it very easy for divers and swimmers to touch, pricking themselves with the dorsal spine if they are not careful. A very intense pain immediately invades the puncture area, causing rapid swelling which sometimes involves the entire limb.

Puffers

There are several species of puffers in the Sea of Cortéz. The Bull's Eye Puffer, *Sphoeroides annulatus,* being the most common. These fish possess an extremely strong poison, called tetraodotoxin, which is found mainly in the vital organs (especially the liver), gonads and skin, with concentrations possibly varying according to geographical location or season. There is a wide range of reactions to puffer poisoning from consumption, depending on the quantity of ingested toxin and on an individual's sensitivity.

In most cases, near total paralysis precedes death. There is no antidote to tetraodotoxin, thus medical efforts must focus on respiratory complications and the drop in blood pressure.

Although puffer meat is delicious and considered a delicacy in Japan, the risk of contamination by the toxin while filleting the fish is very high if not done with great care. In Japan, chefs who prepare puffer, or *fugu*, must be licensed by the government. Tetraodotoxin, a chemical produced by the puffer fish, does not break down after frying or boiling the meat. There are reports of deaths caused by eating the liver of puffer in the Gulf of California. Eating puffer is not recommended.

Fin Whales

The fin whale is found all over the world but it prefers cold temperature waters. Within the Gulf of California it is the most abundant of the baleen whales, especially during winter and spring months. There are fin whale sightings in all seasons and most months, however, scientists believe that there may be a year-round population living in the Gulf. The sightings of fin whale calves and studies comparing the vocalizations produced by whales in and outside the Gulf seem to support this hypothesis, but further studies are being done by CEDO.

There are several areas where fin whales concentrate inside the Sea of Cortéz: the Canal de Ballenas and Canal de Salsipuedes, off Puerto Peñasco and Puerto Libertad, San Pedro Mártir Island, El Dátil, south of Tiburón Island, and between La Paz Bay and Cármen Island. During winter months, when fin whales are more abundant, it is possible to see them feeding at the surface, rolling their massive bodies to the right side and swallowing huge amounts of water from which they filter small shrimp-like animals and young fishes.

To appreciate the massive size of these creatures, you are invited to CEDO, the Intercultural Center of the Study of Deserts and Oceans to see the skeleton of a small, juvenile fin whale, only 16.7 meters or 55 feet long. Adults can reach greater than 80 feet or 25 meters in length – second only to the mighty blue whale. At 2:00 p.m. on Tuesday or 4:00 p.m. on Saturday you can enjoy a full explanation of the lives of these great whales.

Bird Watching

The conditions of a solitary bird are five:
The first, that it flies to the highest point;
The second, that it does not suffer for company,
not even of its own kind;
The third, that it aims its beak to the skies;
The fourth, that it does not have a definite color;
The fifth, that it sings very softly.
-San Juan de la Cruz, Dichos de luz y Amor

Each year thousands of people take up the absorbing hobby of bird watching and Puerto Peñasco is becoming a bird watchers haven. The area around the northern tip of the Sea of Cortéz serves as a nesting ground for hundreds of species of birds.

This chapter has been added to help you identify the species in this area. It is not all-inclusive of the southwestern birds, but presents the most common birds of the desert and grasslands of the Southwest area around Sonoyta and Puerto Peñasco. There are no "real" Mexican birds in Puerto Peñasco because it is a bonanza for northern migrants that barely make it over the Mexico frontera, but you will see enough varieties to make your trip worthwhile. You can begin by purchasing a pair of good binoculars and a field guide.

How To Find Birds

Although it is almost impossible not to see any birds on your ventures, you can increase the number of species with some advance planning. You need to visit as many different habitats as possible during a day of bird watching because most birds tend to confine their activity to one particular habitat.

It is best to begin at dawn. Your first stop should be the desert because they are most active in the early hours of the morning. From the desert you can go to the fields or thickets. Until mid morning most songbirds are busily searching for food and singing. From mid morning till late afternoon land birds are quiet, while the birds of the beaches, and estuaries and aquatic marine habitats are active all day.

The greatest variety of birds can be seen during the migration seasons. It is good to plan several field trips during the spring and fall.

Bird Houses

The saguaro, or giant cactus, is the oldest continuously operated apartment house in the world. There are five kinds of birds entirely dependent on its presence. These include the Mearn's Gilded Flicker, the Gila (he-la) Woodpecker, the Arizona Crested Flycatcher, the Saguaro or Mexican Screech Owl and the most interesting is the Elf Owl. Other birds which freely nest in or on the saguaro are the Western Red-tailed Hawk, Swainson Hawk, American Sparrow Hawk, Western Horned Owl, Ash-throated Flycatcher, purple Martin, House Finch and occasionally the morning Dove. The struggle for existence is intense and engrossing and the individualities of its residents as diverse as any found in the area. No observer can see it all, but it can stir the imagination forever. You can observe these habitants before you cross the border in the Organ Pipe Cactus National Monument.

Take time to enjoy this relaxing pastime, but please do not take or molest any birds, their nests, eggs, or young.

Local Habitats

After crossing the border at Lukeville, perhaps 20 meters north of the Sonoyta River bridge there is a dirt track leading east along the north bank of the river. Take this track east about 2 km to the dam. Along the way you pass through excellent desert scrub that harbors Crissal, Bendire's and Curve-billed Thrasher, Rufous-winged Sparrows, and other typical desert species. Below the dam there is a rather lush growth of riparian vegetation in which Orange-crowned, Black-throated Gray, and Yellow-rumped Warblers, Black Phoebe, Anna's Hummingbird and others dwell. If you happen to be around this patch of riparian vegetation during the spring or fall migration you may find many other species in abundance.

About 20 km below the border you will see typical desert birds including numerous Phaninopepla and Albert's Towhee. If you are lucky you can set your sights skyward and catch a passing Cooper's Hawk darting through the blue sky. North of the airport you may find a small group of Lawrence's Goldfinches foraging on some weeds.

In Old Port you will find the first of many Yellow-footed Gulls, several Western Grebes and Black Thurnstone. The rocks below the street on the Malecón are littered with Heerman's Gulls which are very common in Puerto Peñasco. You may spot a lonesome Elegant Tern flying by.

In the area around Las Conchas you will see many varieties of gulls, one of which is the Glaucous-winged Gull. Gulls are scavengers, using their strong hooked beaks to pick up nearly anything they can spot floating in the water.

On the road to Playa Encanto you may see the Sage Sparrow. Before reaching the beach take the road to the Estero where you will see Ring-billed Gulls in abundance; the Heerman's Gull is second in abundance. You may find a number of Red-breasted Merganser's in the Estero along with several Western Grebe. Shorebirds are quite numerous on the mud flats of the Estero including several noisy and conspicuous Long-billed Curlews. American Oystercatcher is scattered among the numerous peeps; and Black Ostercatcher are among the more common American variety. The best find of the day can be the immature Sabine's Gull sitting on a small mud in the flats. You may observe a Le Conte's Thrasher, an Ash-throated Flycatcher, an Allen's Hummingbird or two and a Sirfbird.

If you take the road to Cholla Bay and park in the large open area at the center just below Pelican Point, take a walk toward the coastline. You will find a large feeding flock of seabirds made up primarily of Brown Booby's. These exotic birds got their unflattering name from sailors who thought they were incredibly stupid to land on ships and allow themselves to be caught. Searching among this flock of birds you will spot the Blue-footed Booby as well as the Brown Pelican's. You may see a group of diving ducks called Greater Scaup, and some Surf Scoter's. Walk west along the rocks and look for a Western Gull or two. Out on the beach near JJ's Cantina you will see a huge area of mud flats when the tide is out. You may see more Curlews, several Whiumbrel, numerous Snowy and Wilson's Plover. In the distance look for American Avocet. On the east side of Pelican Point at the end of Sandy Beach you may not see many birds due to the limited rock which enables many species to perch and submerge.

Back on the highway toward Puerto Peñasco there seems to be a general dearth of birds in the settlement. Not much more than starlings, Great-tailed Grackle and Inca Doves.

Sonoran Desert

*Not to have known – as most men have not – either the
mountain or the desert is not to have known one's self.*
-Joseph Woodkrutch
The Desert Year

Early explorers recorded little of the true nature of the desert.
They were not greatly interested in the beauty of the landscape,
plants, birds and reptiles. Instead, they sought gold and dominion
over the land.

With hours of diligent observation you can find an amazing
number of plant and animal species. To enjoy a wide variety of
desert environment in a larger territory, you should spend two weeks
or even a month exploring. The best times of the year are in spring
or autumn when the weather is comfortably warm, the wildlife very
active, and cactus life at its best.

Fantastic scenic displays of Sonoran Desert vegetation and
panoramas of mountains and plains can be seen and explored in the
Organ-Pipe Cactus National Monument. You can observe firsthand
the organ-pipe cactus, cholla cactus, barrel cactus, cat's-claw,
mesquite, ironwood, and a multitude of showy flowers in season.
Cactus wrens may nest in the cholla's beside your trailer while white-
winged doves scurry across the ground.

Take Puerto Blanco Drive and follow historic trails which wind
throughout the national monument. See the desert springs and
many varieties of birds at the man-made oasis at a place called
Quitobaquito. For fantastic scenery, weird plants and unusual
animals the Sonoran Desert is unsurpassed by any other on the
North American continent.

The Spanish conquistadors were the first outsiders to contend with the deserts of the new world. The Sonoran and Chihuhuan regions were *altiplanos or desiertos*. The words were used interchangeably and carry the same connotation. The lands were dry, hot in summer, and cold in winter. Then came the "Yankees" and the Southwest became "desert" with a different meaning. Originally the English word had not been limited to a hot dry land, but applied to an empty "deserted" land. Yet when the Yankee newcomers took over from the Spanish, their eyes saw the word *desierto* on the maps and their minds translated it into terms of the Sahara – the sandy bareness of North Africa being the desert familiar to men of English heritage. "Wasteland" became a virtual synonym for "desert" and "appalling," "dreadful" and "lifeless" became the standard adjectives in spite of the fact that much of the North American desert is remarkable for both beauty and life.

Distinctive because of its variety of cacti and the numerous trees and other plants with small leaves or no leaves at all, the Sonoran Desert, or Arizona Desert, extends over the lower elevations of southern Arizona, northwest Mexico and much of Baja California. Puerto Peñasco is located in the middle of this desert.

Traveling from the United States across the border at Lukeville, you will observe a variety of living things and the dynamic nature of the desert becomes more meaningful. Observing the interrelationships between plants, animals, soil, weather and physiography will increase your appreciation of the complexity and intrinsic beauty of this arid land. Take the time to discover the desert's variety, its daily rhythm bringing hourly changes in color, temperature and voices of the day or night.

When one becomes familiar with the names of a few dozen plant species, how they keep company with other plants, and how they seem to prefer different soils and locations, the vegetation of the desert becomes interesting and unique.

Cactus

Tall cacti are the symbol of the Sonoran Desert. Two general types among them, those with a central trunk that branch well above the ground and those with many branches springing from a common base at ground level. Cactus was probably once related to the violets and begonias, evolving through the ages as the environment changed. More than 70 species of cactus have been listed for Arizona and many of these are found in the Sonoran Desert area.

Saguaro - These cacti are so abundant and beloved in Arizona that the saguaro blossom is the Arizona state flower. The massive, spiny green trunk can measure one to two feet in diameter, with two to ten or more stout upward curved branches and can reach a height of fifty feet or more. The biggest cactus at Saguaro National Monument was fifty-two feet tall, had fifty-two arms, an estimated weight of ten tons, and an age of perhaps 235 years.

Growth takes place at the tip of trunks and branches, the most water-saturated part of the plant. The growing period begins as soon as the summer rains arrive in mid-July and continues until they taper off a month or six weeks later – the wettest time of the desert year and also the hottest. The densest stands of saguaros often are on the hottest slopes, which face south and southwest catching the full force of the sun. Blooming from late April to June, as many as two or three hundred buds ringing the tips of main trunks and crowning branches. Temperature directly affects the flowering success which follows a pattern around the stem. The morning sun warms the east side of the cactus three or four degrees above the rest of the plant and gives buds there a head start. By late afternoon, the sun swings around and heats the stem's west side, but little time is left before sundown and the cooling of night. As a result, west-side buds may never open and those on the north may stay mere nubbins.

Gila woodpeckers and gilded flickers are perhaps the saguaro's best vigilante committee. They peck open a saguaro trunk to "drink" from the watery pulp using only one hole per year, pecking a new one each spring. These holes serve as a camouflaged nest, storing and keeping eggs cool.

Nest holes are so much in demand that beginning in April competition for them becomes keen. Rather than go in search of a mate and risk loosing his hole, he may use a special "advertising" song to lure a female into range. When a female responds and comes close, the hopeful bachelor will pop in and out of his prized hole, hoping to stimulate her urges to the same pitch as his. For some species the number of available nest cavities almost surely limits population more than the availability of food does. In various locations, springtime fights over holes cause a higher mortality than occurs from predators or for any other reason. With the young safe inside an adjacent cavity, the male can leave the major responsibility of defense and feeding to the female and devote a part of his attention to seeking a second mate and starting a second brood. Providing for their needs initially allows him simultaneous families, and thereby benefits the species.

Brown bats frequently roost within the saguaro holes in the summer, pack rats and cactus mice occasionally take over holes as much as twenty feet above the ground. They gnaw spiral corridors up to the nests, feeding on saguaro pulp as they go. They can also climb up outside, navigating the thorns and ribs without fashioning a special passageway.

The Tohono O'odham (Papago) Indians of the area have harvested the delicious fruit of the saguaro for centuries. Using long poles made from the ribs of the saguaro itself, the Indians knock the fruit from the cactus before Sonoran Desert animals have had a chance to get it all. The fruit – a three-inch, greenish, egg-shaped capsule splits open to reveal a bright-red, sweet pulp imbedded with innumerable tiny black seeds – is used by the Indians to prepare syrup, jam and ceremonial wine. Their ancient food-preserving techniques are often observed during the harvest season by fascinated onlookers in the workshops that are conducted, with the help of the O'odham, by the Arizona-Sonora Desert Museum located approximately fourteen miles west of Tucson, Arizona.

Cholla - Of all the jointed cacti, jumping cholla (pronounced *choy-uh*) seems to irritate people the most. They are considered the untouchables of the plant world. Legend has it that the armed joints "jump" out and attach themselves to a passerby. When the joints brush by the side of a pant leg they detach from the plant and instead of falling to the ground, roll up under your pant leg, making a pincushion of spines. This is a good thing so far as the plant is concerned. Cholla thus propagates itself since the hitchhiking joints root easily, drawing on stored moisture and nutrients until the new little spiny horrors are established. White to pink flowers streaked with lavender and large pear-shaped fruits which hang down in branched chains make this one of the most distinctive of cacti.

"Chainfruit cholla" is the size of a small tree that has dangling clusters of spiny joints and fruits. Since the joints loosen at the slightest touch it also is called "jumping cholla." Other cholla cacti grow stiffly branched, one of them looking something like deer's antlers and another like oddly jointed pencils. Teddy-bear cholla is covered with thorns that cover the joints and give a softly napped look, but the name is a hoax since its stab hurts the most of all.

Organ Pipe Cactus - Low winter temperatures and temperate conditions mark the Arizona organ pipes with curious pitched-in constrictions where tips have been frosted and stopped growing, then resume when hot weather returns. Organ pipes have thicker stems and fewer flutings the farther north they grow. Along the Arizona-Sonora border at Sonoyta, Mexico, these cacti actually look like a different species from those at Guaymas, 250 miles to the south, where winter temperatures hold about seven degrees warmer.

All columnar cacti develop thickened stems toward their northern range, regardless of the latitude where that northern extreme happens to fall. Increased volume in proportion to their surface slows the loss of heat to the atmosphere and prevents freezing. Stems from Sonoyta cacti typically have five ridges, and the cross section looks like fat five-pointed stars. Those from Guaymas may have as many as eleven ridges, and look like gears with sharply protruding teeth. Most species are valued for their delicious fruit. Cuttings are often planted closely in rows for hedges or fences.

Desert Trees And Shrubs

The trees of the cold deserts develop root systems that reach down to perennial water. Consequently they do not cast their leaves at the first sign of drought, nor do they store water in succulent stems as do the cacti. As you go southward in the desert, it is important to note the increasing variety of trees with drought-resisting and drought-enduring devices.

Most desert shrubs are long-lived. Their deep root systems which many species penetrate to the water table, enable them to persist through long droughts. Shrubs compete with one another. Established bushes become widely spaced, each with its own territory for moisture supply. Some compete with other plants by excreting toxic substances into the soil or by dropping leaves containing materials that inhibit germination and growth of other plant seedlings.

Century Plant - The century plant, which resembles some of the yuccas, produces a plume like flower stalk capable of growing as much as a foot or more a day. Members of this family have narrow knife or toothed shaped leaves that are clustered at the base of each plant. The stemless plant produces a branched yellow flower that spikes after ten to fifteen years and then dies leaving small plants growing at its base.

Fiber from these leaves is used for hemp. Some species contain sap that is fermented to produce a cheesy-smelling intoxicating drink. In southern Mexico, different species of the century plant furnish fiber, soup, fermented drink, and a distilled drink known as mescal.

Joshua Tree - The flower buds of Joshua trees were roasted and eaten by desert Indians and still furnish food for Mexican ranchers in Baja California. It is difficult to forget the starkness of the Joshua Tree, especially when the silhouette is viewed against an evening sunset. The trunk is thatched with stiff gray dead leaves. The burly distorted branches are giant pincushions of leaves, sharp as daggers with saw-toothed edges.

Blooming occurs in March or April. Cream-white flowers appearing in clusters eight to fourteen inches long at the tips of the branches. They sometimes reach forty feet into the air. The flowers of the Joshua tree, common to those of other yuccas, are linked in partnership with the female yucca moth, which lays her eggs and seem to pollinate the flowers deliberately. Without the pollination of the yucca moth, the Joshua tree could not reproduce.

Joshua trees and their fallen branches are sanctuaries for a menagerie of creatures ranging from the desert night lizard to flickers, woodpeckers, flycatchers, wood rats, mice, snakes, ants, and termites.

No one knows how long a Joshua tree lives, but a hundred years may be a conservative estimate. They have been present in the desert for ages and the leaves have been found in the fossilized dung of the extinct giant ground sloth. Although Joshua trees can be found in southern Arizona, the best place for seeing them is in the Joshua Tree National Monument, where many square miles of beautiful high desert country are preserved.

Ironwood Tree - The desert ironwood tree may date back some 700 to 800 years and be the longest living tree in the desert. The wood is second worldwide in density and weight. Shaving and sawing does not have any affect on its rough surface. In spite of its hardness, boring beetles can chew the wood and mistletoe invades its tissues. The indigo flowers produced by the ironwood in summer adds a subtle fragrance to the desert air. A red sap sometimes bleeds from the tree which attracts bees, hummingbirds and ants.

Ocotillo - Ocotillo always intrigues the first-time visitor to the desert. It is one of the most distinctive of shrubs and one of the thorniest. The short woody crown produces a cluster of spreading branches that grow to a height of twelve to twenty feet. The plant is leafless through much of the year. Spring or summer rains initiate a crop of green leaves which turn red as drought follows the rainy period. They may sprout and shed as many as six or eight crops of leaves per year. New leaves are grown quickly because ocotillo constantly keep moisture and nutrients available specifically for that purpose. Only two or three days after a rain every thorny brown stalk of a drought-blighted ocotillo will be upholstered with green-tender, succulent leaves, which are vulnerable to the next drought.

Scarlet or salmon-colored tubular flowers of the ocotillo are produced after the end of the winter rainy season. The flower clusters resemble red flames at the ends of the branches. They make the plants especially discernible when viewed against a dark background of volcanic soils and rocks. Ocotillo, however, is most abundant on rocky slopes and on compact soils, where sheet flooding does not wash out its spreading shallow root system.

Paloverde Tree - This small, shrubby tree is part of the pea family, *leguminosae,* native to Arizona and northern Mexico. It remains leafless most of the year. The green-barked paloverde stand along the desert washes like twiggy willows. The blue paloverde is the most striking of the species because of the smooth gray or blue green bark. It grows to thirty feet, has spiny twigs, two-stalked leaves with two to four pairs of leaflets on each stalk, small yellow flowers, and flat brownish pea pods.

Sagebrush - Sagebrushes are among the most abundant and widely distributed of desert shrubs. The name is derived from the odor of its leaves reminiscent of the herb, sage. With the absence of this shrub much of the desert fauna would cease to exist. Sagebrush, for example, is one of the important species in the diets of antelope and deer. It is life itself to the sage grouse, which eats the leaves, builds its nest in the bushy cover, and finds concealment for itself and its chicks when predators are around.

Fringed sagebrush grows in the deserts of Mexico and through most of the western United States. It is a half-shrub, a term used to describe perennial plants with woody bases from which stems arise. It is an intriguing plant because of its clustered and aromatic foliage, and usefulness as an indicator of livestock range condition. When grasses are thinned by heavy grazing, fringed sagebrush becomes more abundant. In turn when it is overgrazed, it assumes a mat form.

Big sagebrush is one of the larger shrubs, attaining a height of six to eight feet. Each leaf has three teeth at the apex. Bigelow sagebrush is characteristic of three-parted leaves, the black sagebrush is a three-tip shrub. Identification of individual species requires attention to such attributes as shape and color of leaves, presence of hairy coverings on the leaves, and characteristics of inflorescence.

Yucca - The connections between plant and animal world are many, perhaps none in the desert are more dramatic than that of the yucca family. The broad-leafed yuccas can be distinguished from similar plants by examining their flowers, inflorescence, and leaves. They have rosettes of narrow stiff sword shaped leaves, elongated, dagger-like, or bayonet-shaped, either at the base or top of the stem.

The best known Southwestern species are *glauca* which grow to about six feet and produce giant lilies that reach thirty to forty feet high bearing heavy spikes of creamy-white flowers. These bell-like blossoms form huge clusters. Fragrance of the flowers which open at night, attract the yucca moth, their only means of pollination. Moths later emerge when yucca flowers open. The female gathers pollen from one flower, rolls it into a ball, flies to another flower, lays four or five eggs, and inserts the pollen mass in the opening thus formed. The larva eat about one half the approximately two hundred seeds produced by the plant. The yucca can be fertilized by no other insect.

The leaves produce long fibers which were used by Indians in earlier times for weaving cloth, cordage, baskets and other domestic items.

A blooming ocotillo is one of the many showy plants you will see in the Sonoran Desert between Ajo, Arizona and Sonoyta, Mexico

Rocky Point
Street and Area Map

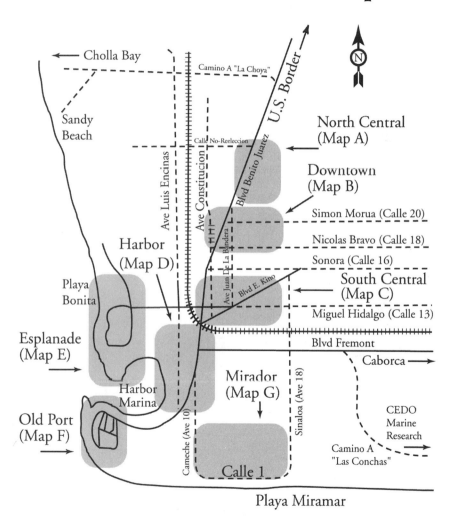

Cholla Bay

Camino A "La Choya"

U.S. Border

N

Sandy
Beach

Calle No-Reeleccion

Ave Luis Encinas

Ave Constitucion

Blvd Benito Juarez

North Central
(Map A)

Downtown
(Map B)

Simon Morua (Calle 20)

Nicolas Bravo (Calle 18)

Sonora (Calle 16)

Harbor
(Map D)

Ave Juan De La Bandera

Blvd E. Kino

South Central
(Map C)

Playa
Bonita

Miguel Hidalgo (Calle 13)

Esplanade
(Map E)

Blvd Fremont

Caborca

Harbor
Marina

Mirador
(Map G)

Sinaloa (Ave 18)

Old Port
(Map F)

Cameche (Ave 10)

CEDO
Marine
Research

Camino A
"Las Conchas"

Calle 1

Playa Miramar

Map A - North Central Rocky Point

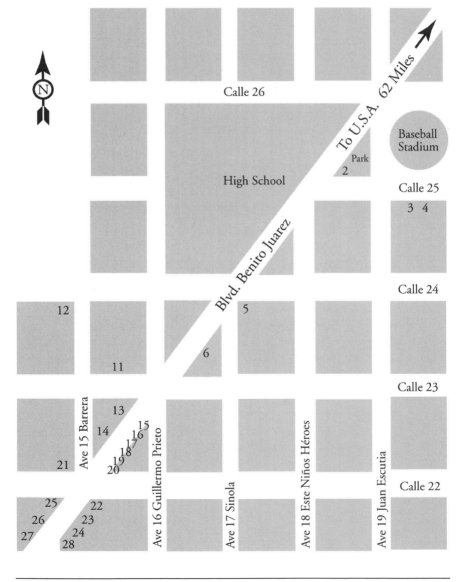

Calle 26

To U.S.A. 62 Miles

Baseball Stadium

Park 2

High School

Calle 25

3 4

Blvd. Benito Juarez

Calle 24

5

6

12

11

Calle 23

Ave 15 Barrera

13

14

15

16

17

18

19

20

21

Ave 16 Guillermo Prieto

Ave 17 Sinola

Ave 18 Este Niños Héroes

Ave 19 Juan Escutia

Calle 22

25

26

27

22

23

24

28

1. Agua Solar
2. Pepos II
3. Posada del León Hotel
4. Restaurant
5. Bus Depot
6. Pemex Gas/Auto Parts
7. Asadero Tacos
8. Mi Casita Hamburgers
9. Osel Paints
10. Joyeria Reyna Jewlers
11. Pinturas Yacabados
12. Video Genesis
13. Estafeta Express Mail Service
14. Kota's Express Mail Service
15. Money Exchange
16. Pathfinder Travel
17. Paint Store Luisa
18. Lupita Candy
19. California Produce
20. Tecate Beer
21. Del Estudiante Stationery
22. Video Store Max
23. Krirval Children's Clothing
24. Boulevard Uno Clothing
25. La Flor de Mochoacana
26. Fabric Merlins
27. Money Exchange
28. Atlas Auto Parts

Map B - Downtown Rocky Point

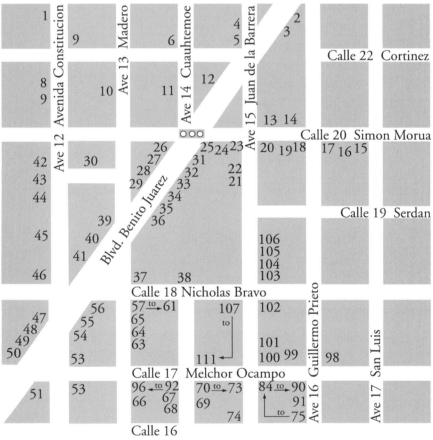

1.	La Huerta Store	56.	Tecate Agency
2.	Dr. Samie Rodriquez Gomez MD, Emergency	57.	Rocky Imports
3.	Hector Lizarrga	58.	Video Mudo
4.	Richie Auto Parts	59.	Barber Shop
5.	Abarrotes Market	60.	El Imparcial Newspaper
6.	Coca Cola Distributor	61.	Pan Bueno Bakery
7.	Laundromat	62.	Movie House
8.	Hotel Pariso del Deslerto, Restaurant & Bar	63.	Cortinas Seaside Windows
9.	Tienda	64.	Veel Hardware
10.	Paint Store	65.	Guiseppes Cafe
11.	Auto Parts	66.	Hotel Gil
12.	Bakery	67.	Music Store
13.	Centro De Salud Urbano Hospital	68.	Joya Jewlery
14.	Santa Fe Clinic	69.	Print Store Gary
15.	Farmicia Santa Fe	70.	Sports Store
16.	Medical Center	71.	Foto Studio 2000
17.	HSA Refrigeration	72.	Public Telephone
18.	Vet Clinic	73.	Sombreria Mr. Poncho
19.	Zigle Clinic	74.	Motel Carmelita
20.	Zygle Pharmacy	75.	Joyeria Max's Jewlery Repair
21.	Consulto rio Medical/Dental	76.	Dec Oraciones Imperales
22.	Locksmith	77.	Exclusive Ambar Children's
23.	Video Star	78.	El Futuro Newspaper Printing
24.	Brillante Jewlery	79.	Comercial Salmo's
25.	Portugal INS	80.	Paint Comex
26.	Pemex Gas	81.	Dulces Lupita Candy
27.	Arizona Auto Repair/Parts	82.	Dulces Paty Candy
28.	Strauss Records	83.	Impacto
29.	My Javy's Hamburgers	84.	Lewis Kimberly Jewlery
30.	Exclusive Brenda Clothing	85.	Fliama Botique
31.	Pinacate Hills Shoes	86.	Lunamendez Children's
32.	El Torito Meat Market	87.	Cleaning Supplies
33.	Casserv Money Exchange	88.	Cafe Combate Beanery
34.	Motiel Ceullar Telephone	89.	Asadero El Palomar
35.	Dr. Padilla, Dentist	90.	Peluqueria Yeyo Barber
36.	Tena Liquor	91.	Deguille Hair Salon
37.	Pemex Gas	92.	Discos Accessories
38.	Bonel Travel Agency	93.	Long Distance Telephone
39.	Don Antonio Pharmacy	94.	USA/Mexico Electronics
40.	La Bellota Market	95.	Loncheria Las Mesitas
41.	Immigration Office of Puerto Peñasco	96.	Liberia Nueva/Zapateria Child Shoes
42.	El Rey Clothing	98.	Buster Video
43.	La Perla Jewlery	99.	Farmicia Del Sol
44.	Michael's Imports	100.	Ls Sonorense
45.	El Pueblo Supermarket	101.	La Fabula Pizza
46.	Comex Ferreteria Mobil/Auto Parts	102.	Puerto Peñasco Municipal Hospital
47.	Loncheria	103.	Miscelanea Lopez Clothing
48.	Servi-Rents	104.	Muebleria Economica
49.	Ferplomar Hardware & Home Furnishings	105.	Ropa Novedades Clothing
50.	Key Shop	106.	Mubeleria Principal
51.	Corona Agency	107.	Telephone Offices
52.	Furnature Super	108.	Gutycor Perfume
53.	Costa Azul Bar	109.	Fruit Drinks & Ice Cream
54.	La Junta Bar	110.	Picos Telephone Service
55.	Dentist	111.	Lux Pharmacy

Map B - Downtown Rocky Point   255

Map C - South Central Rocky Point

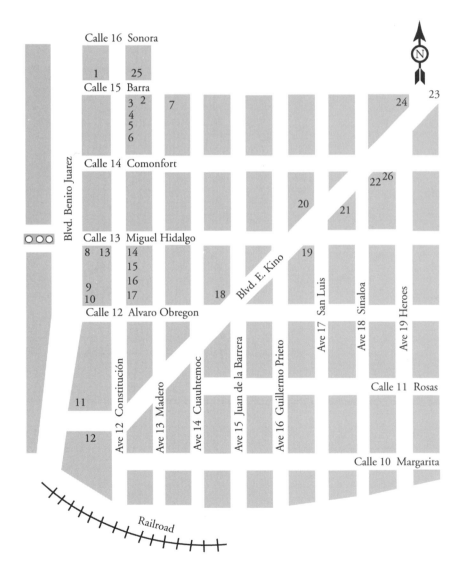

Calle 16 Sonora

1   25

Calle 15 Barra

3 2   7

4
5
6

Blvd. Benito Juarez

Calle 14 Comonfort

20   21   22 26

24   23

Calle 13 Miguel Hidalgo

8 13   14   19

15
16   Blvd. E. Kino
9   17   18

10

Calle 12 Alvaro Obregon

Ave 17 San Luis

Ave 18 Sinaloa

Ave 19 Heroes

11

Ave 12 Constitución

Ave 13 Madero

Ave 14 Cuauhtemoc

Ave 15 Juan de la Barrera

Ave 16 Guillermo Prieto

Calle 11 Rosas

12

Calle 10 Margarita

Railroad

1. Vendors
2. Rigors Beauty Shop
3. Victor Fruits & Vegetables
4. Video Vive
5. San Andrés Pharmacy
6. San Andrés Clinic
7. Hotel Villa Granada, Bar & Restaurant
8. Serfiñ Bank
9. Manny's Office
10. Rocky Point Times Office
11. Fruit Vendors
12. Rocky Tile
13. Car Wash
14. Bakery D'Irma
15. Lizola Electric & Hardware
16. Peñascos Hardware & Plumbing
17. Bebezucos Infants Clothing
18. P.H. Pharmacy
19. Dentist
20. Suprema Tackle
21. Playas Del Rey Restaurant
22. La Cura Restaurant
23. La Merced Market
24. Cristal Glass & Aluminum
25. Apostolic Church
26. Aztlan Restaurant

Map C - South Central Rocky Point   257

Map D - Harbor
Rocky Point

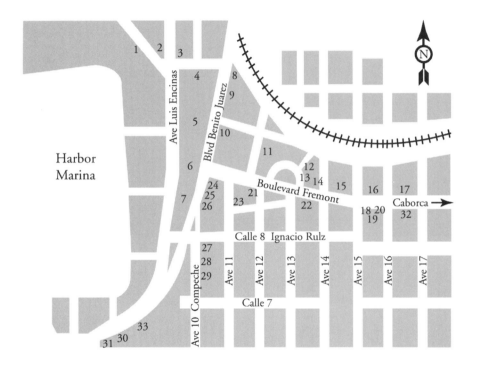

Harbor
Marina

1 2 3

Ave Luis Encinas

Blvd Benito Juarez

4 8

9

5 10

11

6 12

13 14 15 16 17

Caborca →

7 24
21 25
26 23 22

18 20
19 32

Calle 8 Ignacio Rulz

27
28
29

Ave 10 Compeche

Ave 11

Ave 12

Ave 13

Ave 14

Ave 15

Ave 16

Ave 17

Calle 7

33
31 30

Boulevard Fremont

1. Caterpillar
2. Taller Para Welding
3. Distribcliones Ara Paints
4. Navy Hospital
5. High School
6. Public Library
7. Aubitoriom
8. California Money Exchange
9. Jim Bur Center
    Auga Potable
    Sahari Childrens
    Satellite Systems
    Video Centro
    Super Market
    Holanda Drugs
    Luis & Co. Beachcombers
    La Artesiana Mexicana
10. Bancomer Bank
11. Chamber of Commerce
12. Telegraph Office
13. Post Office
14. Proaset Realty
15. Red Cross
16. Mr. Amigo Bar & Restaurant
17. Discotheque
18. Baja 1000 Automotive
19. La Ranita
20. Liquor Store Brisa
21. Fire Department
22. Notary
23. Car Wash
24. Police Station
25. City Hall
26. Banamex Bank
27. Tienda Michoacana
28. Farmicia Hegar
29. De. Juan R. Garcia, M.D.
30. Optica Pau
31. Dr. Hernandes, DDS
32. Immigration Services
33. Latitude 31

Map E - Esplanade Rocky Point

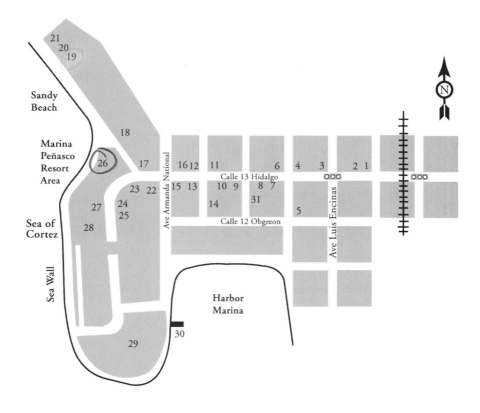

Sandy Beach

Marina Peñasco Resort Area

Sea of Cortez

Sea Wall

21
20
19

18

26

17

16 12 11

6 4 3 2 1

Calle 13 Hidalgo

Ave Armanda National

23 22

15 13

10 9 8 7

27

24

14

31

25

5

28

Calle 12 Obgreon

Ave Luis Encinas

Harbor Marina

29 30

1. Matedials Cananea
2. Dulceria y Nerveria Cri-Cri
3. Roca Marine
4. Tecate Playa-Hermosa Agency
5. Pescadores Bar
6. El Tio Juan Taqueria
7. Señorial Motel, Bar & Restaurant
8. Caliente Race Track
9. Hansel Ice Cream
10. El Callejon Bar
11. Motel Playa Azul
12. Villa Las Palmas Restaurant
13. Lisan Liquors
14. Bandidos Nite Club
15. Sand And Sea Rentals
16. Corona Sub Hermosa
17. Gamma's Restaurant
18. Peñasco Beach Club
19. Playa Bonita Hotel
20. Puesta del Sol Restaurant
21. Playa Bonita R.V. Park
22. Playa Hermosa Hotel
23. Cocodrilos Bar & Grill
24. Del Mar at Los Conchas
25. Commercial Shopping Area
26. Plaza Las Glorias Hotel Bar & Restaurant
27. Parking
28. Condominio Pinacate Villas & Condos
29. Naval Base
30. Boat Slips
31. Money Exchange
32. Brooks Real Estate

Map F - Old Port Rocky Point

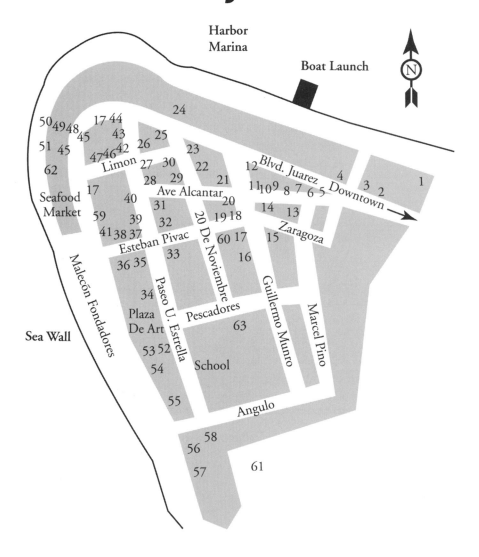

Harbor Marina

Boat Launch

N

24

50 4948 45 17 44
51 45 43
47 46 42 26 25
62 Limon 27 30 23
28 29 22 12 Blvd. Juarez
21 Downtown
17 Ave Alcantar 11 10 9 8 7 6 5 4 3 2 1
Seafood 40 31 20 14 13
Market 59 39 32 19 18
41 38 37 20 De Noviembre Zaragoza
Esteban Pivac 60 17 15
36 35 33 16

Sea Wall

34 Paseo U. Estrella
Plaza Pescadores
De Art 63
53 52
54 School

55

Angulo

58
56
57 61

Malecón Fondadores
Guillermo Munro
Marcel Pino

1. TruValue Hardware
2. Las Palmas Artesianias
3. Yolanda Silva Gyora Insurance
4. Sun N' Fun Rentals &
   Diveshop
5. Oceano Property Management
6. Cookie Cutters
7. Victoria Originals
8. Pompano's Market
9. El Delfin Anilgable Restaurant
10. Casa Guzman
11. El Espacio Bar & Restaurnat
12. Rock Shop
13. Notary Public #42
14. Curios Wendy
15. Liquor Store
16. Corjenio Bakery
17. Mexican Curios
18. Tienda
19. Go Fly A Kite
20. Old Port Deli & Restaurant
21. Pueblo Viejo
22. Casa Bonita Home Furnishings
23. Dr. Luis Vasquez, M.D.
24. Realty Network
25. Hotel Peñasco
26. Puerto Peñasco T-shirt Co.
27. Pemex Gas
28. Paloma Blanca Curios
29. Barber Shop
30. Danny's Restaurant
31. Better Edge Vertical Blinds
32. FM3 Office
33. Catholic Church
34. El Puerto De Oro Design
35. Bubbles and Things
36. Thrifty Ice Cream
37. Beach Company
38. Blue Marlin Restaurant
39. Mexican Curios
40. Bela Vista Suites
41. Lily's Restaurnat
42. El Tanichee
43. La Cita Restaurant
44. Sea Side Treasures & Beach
    Shop
45. Seafood Eateries
46. Cheikys Pizza
47. Roberto's Italian Broiler
48. Como Tu Clothing
49. Amigas Handicrafts
50. Rotweiler Bar
51. Mariscos Kenos Seafood
52. Culture House
53. La Paloma Curios
54. Botique
55. Costa Brava Hotel, Bar &
    Restaurant
56. Viña Del Mar Hotel & En
    Rocky Disco
57. Maria Bonita Restaurant
58. Tobacco Shop
59. Old Port Galleria
60. Pablos Casa De Amatista
61. La Cassa de Capitan
62. Señor Amigo
63. El Futuro Marketing

Map G - Mirador
Rocky Point

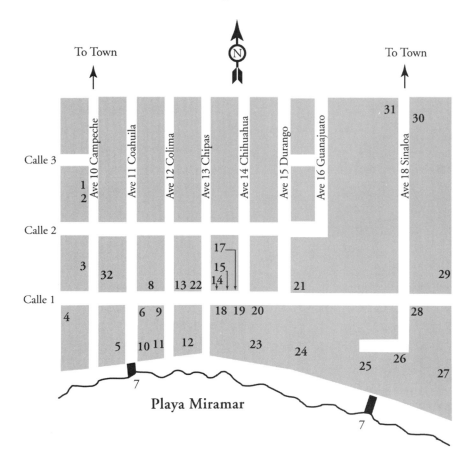

To Town

N

To Town

Calle 3

Ave 10 Campeche
Ave 11 Coahuila
Ave 12 Colima
Ave 13 Chipas
Ave 14 Chihuahua
Ave 15 Durango
Ave 16 Guanajuato
Ave 18 Sinaloa

31
30

1
2

Calle 2

3
32
8
13 22
17
15
14
21
29

Calle 1

4
6 9
18 19 20
28

5
10 11
12
23
24
26
27
25

7

Playa Miramar

7

1. Margaritavilla
2. Curio Shops
3. Fiesta de Cortez Hotel/Marichi's Bar/Restaurant
4. Mar Brisas Town Homes
5. Miramar R.V. Park
6. Restaurant Tropics
7. Small Boat Ramps
8. Sunrise R.V. Park
9. Espresso Express
10. Manny's Beach Club Rentals
11. Manny's Bar & Restaurant
12. Las Olas Condos
13. Happy Frog Seafood
14. Law Office
15. Don Julios
17. Pilar's Kitchen
18. Tienda
19. Rocky Garden Restaurant
20. Pizza
21. Senorial R.V. Park
22. Pink Cadillac Restaurant
23. El Mirador R.V. Park
24. Playa de Oro R.V. Park
25. Pitahaya Bar
26. Granada del Mar Hotel
27. Playa Elegente R.V. Park
28. San Rafael R.V. Park
29. Vista Oro Retirement Community
30. Ranis Ranis Disco
31. Best Western Playa Inn
32. La Palapa Condos

Cholla Bay, Rocky Point
Las Conchas & Encanto

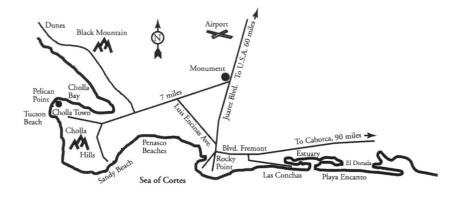

Sonoyta Street And Area Map

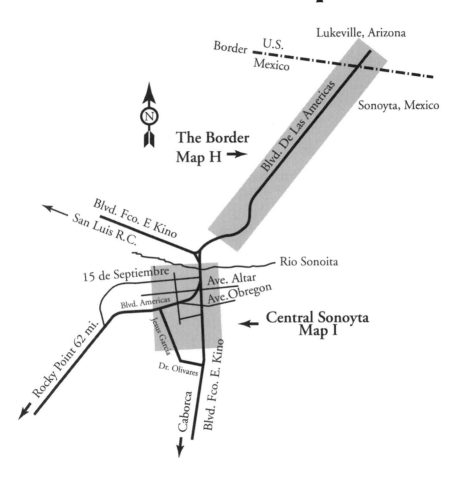

Lukeville, Arizona

Border — U.S.
Mexico

Sonoyta, Mexico

Blvd. De Las Americas

N

The Border
Map H →

Blvd. Fco. E Kino
San Luis R.C. →

Rio Sonoita

15 de Septiembre

Ave. Altar
Ave. Obregon

Blvd. Americas

Central Sonoyta
Map I →

Rocky Point (62 mi.)

Jesus Garcia

Dr. Olivares

Caborca

Blvd. Fco. E. Kino

Map H - The Border

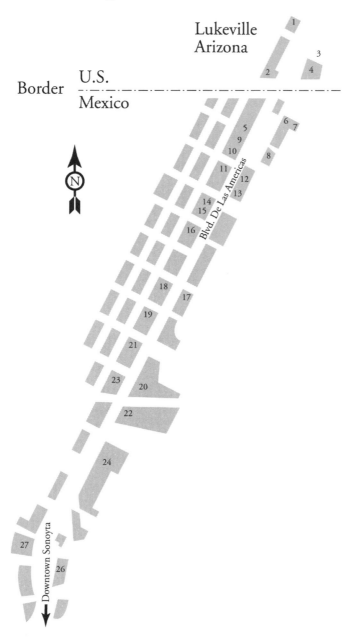

Lukeville
Arizona

Border U.S.
Mexico

1. Gringo Pass Chevron
2. Gringo Pass Shopping Center
3. Gringo Pass Motel/RV Park
4. U.S. Customs
5. Mexican Immigration
6. Avana Fronteriza
7. Bank
8. Fianzias
9. Mexican Insurance
10. Despacho Juridico - Public Phone
11. Copies - Mex Insurance
12. Liquor Store
13. Custom Broker
14. Secretaria de la Contratoria General de la Federeacion
15. Secretaria de Aricutuara y Recursos Hidraulicos
16. Abarrotes la Linea
17. Bakery
18. Dentista, Dr. G. Javier Valenzuela P.
19. Miscelanea Carmelita, Honda Store
20. Servico Los Pinos Lubricadode Autos
21. Insurgenies, Afianzador
22. Santa Cruz Title
23. Agencia Aduanal, licensed customs broker
24. Limpiaduria, Cleaners
25. Disco Angeles
26. Estetica Manjares, Beauty Shop

Map I - Central Sonoyta

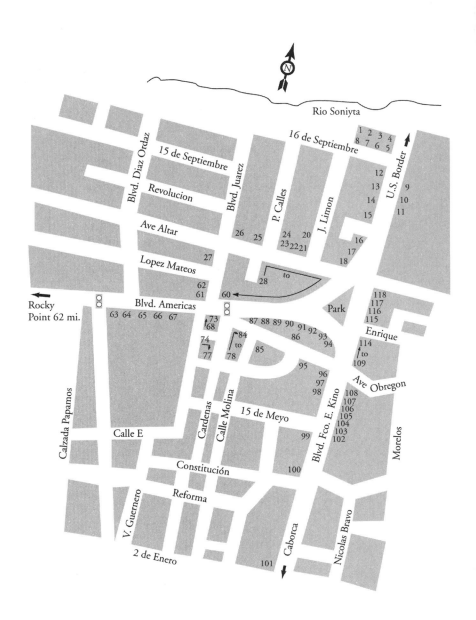

1.	Michoacan - Juice
2.	Hectors Tacos
3.	Money Exchange
4.	Libreria
5.	Botica San Luis
6.	Imprenta Papelera
7.	Dr. Roberto Cirujano - Dentist
8.	Video Exitos
9.	Carwash
10.	Pemex Gas
11.	Super Food Store/Rest Tierra Del Sol
12.	Excelsior Motel - Cafe
13.	Estafeta - Courier Service
14.	Cimarron Bar - Cafe
15.	Motel San Antonio
16.	Casa de Servicios - Money Exchange
17.	Bancomer
18.	Bar Cimmaron
19.	Casa de Regalos
20.	Video Venus
21.	Elias Clothing
22.	A.P.S.
23.	Beauty Shop de Maria
24.	Police Station - Post Office
25.	Las Palmitas - Children's
26.	Motores Sonoyta - Cars
27.	Church
28.	Tienda - Store
29.	Telnor - Phone Service
30.	Comercial el Papeleria
31.	Pan Bueno Bakery
32.	Pineda Refacciones Access
33.	Foto Studio Lizbeth
34.	La Bamba Juice
35.	Licores Tony
36.	Servicos Cambarios - Money Exchange
37.	Montoya Money Exchange
38.	Floreria Francis - Flowers
39.	Papeleria - Art/Office/Copies
40.	La Escondida - Baby to 15 years
41.	Tecata Angecia
42.	Corona Distributor
43.	Casa de Servicios - Money Exchange
44.	Medico Dr. Francisco Urbalejo - Dentista
45.	Woody Hats/Boots
46.	Novedades Elarabe - Clothing
47.	Dulceria Carrosel - Candy
48.	Novedade Chicano - Clothing
49.	Farmicia Celiz
50.	Dr. A. Altamiranco - Children
51.	Zapateria Paty
52.	Tacos
53.	Mercado Bonanza
54.	Joyeriala Perla
55.	Artesians Felix - Curios
56.	Shoe Store
57.	—
58.	Curios Eadies
59.	Regalos Paloma
60.	Detalles Francis
61.	Helados Ice Cream
62.	Barber
63.	Dulceria Consuelo - Candy
64.	Pastereria Pringipessa - Cakes/Pastry
65.	El Pinto Tenis - Boys Shoes
66.	Dulce Ria Nena - Candy
67.	Novedades Shalimar - Shoes
68.	Fruteria Guadalupana
69.	Elrinconcito - Gaucho Bar
70.	Billares Corona
71.	Farmicia Moderna - Public Phone
72.	Mini Super Sahara
73.	Sala Belleza Mayra - Beauty
74.	Biciclentas El Centro Accessories
75.	Clothing Shop
76.	Novedades Bambino
77.	Discoteca Cynthia
78.	Benito Juarez Town Square
79.	Animal Hospital
80.	Modes Vannes
81.	La Flor de Michoacan
82.	Tienda
83.	Barber Shop
84.	Taqueria Lupita - Tacos
85.	Clothing Store
86.	Tortilleria Sarabia
87.	Mercado Excelsior
88.	Riverias Fashions
89.	Tortillas de Harina
90.	Taquertia Las Palmas
91.	Vasquez Curios
92.	Restaurant Mr. Baynes
93.	Bar Alsur de la Frontiera - South of the Border
94.	Motel Sol Del Desierto
95.	Madera La Economica
96.	Mariscos Cafe
98.	Pollos Cano's
99.	Auto Electric Gonzales
100.	Sotos Bar
101.	Motel Nora
102.	Federal Police Station
103.	Sonoyta Hospital
104.	Riveras Pinturas - Paint
105.	Miscelanea Kino - Lottery/Copies
106.	Taco Stand
107.	Tienda
108.	Alma Department Store
109.	Lavamatic
110.	Centro Musical
111.	Barber Shop
112.	Las Cazuelas
113.	La Rosita Carniceria
114.	Banemex
115.	Restaurant Cecy
116.	Cassette Tape Store
117.	Refacciones Accessories El Paseo

Map I - Central Sonoyta   271

Spanish Lingo For The Savvy Gringo

ENGLISH	SPANISH	PRONUNCIATION
Yes	*Sí*	see
No	*No*	noh
Please	*Por Favor*	pohr fah-bohr
Thank you	*Gracias*	gra-theeahss
Hello	*Buenos días*	bway-noss dee-ahsss
Good-bye	*Adiós*	a-dyohss
How are you?	*¿Cómo está usted?*	koh-moh ess-ta oo-steth
Very well	*Muy Bien*	mwee byen
Excuse me	*Perdóneme*	pehrdoh-neh-may
Give me	*Déme*	day-may
How much is it?	*Cuánto?*	kwahn-toh
I don't understand	*No comprendo*	noh kom-prehn-dho
The check	*La cuenta*	la kwen-tah
Breakfast	*Desayuno*	deh-sai-yoo-noh
Lunch	*Comida*	co-mee-day
Dinner	*Cena*	thay-nah
I would like	*Quisiera*	kye-sier-ah
To eat	*comer*	ko-mayr
A room	*una habitación*	oo-nah ah-bee-tah-thyo-n
Where is?	*Dónde está?*	dohn-day ess-tah
the station	*la estación*	la ess-tah-thyohn
a hotel	*un hotel*	oon-oh-tel
the toilet	*el servicio*	el ser-vee-the-o
the bathroom	*el baño*	el bahn-yo
When?	*Cuándo?*	kwan-doh
I would like	*Quiero que*	key-air-oh keh
Yesterday	*Ayer*	ah-yayr
Today	*Hoy*	oy
Tomorrow	*Mañana*	mahn-yah-nah
To the right	*A la derecha*	ah lah day-ray-chuh
To the left	*A la izquierda*	ah lay eeth-kyayr- duh
Straight ahead	*Adelante*	ah-day-lahn-tay

Months of the year and days of the week

January - *enero*
February - *febrero*
March - *marzo*
April - *abril*
May - *mayo*
June - *junio*
July - *julio*
August - *agosto*
September - *septiembre*
October - *octubre*
November - *noviembre*
December - *diciembre*

Monday - *lunes*
Tuesday - *martes*
Wednesday - *miércoles*
Thursday - *jueues*
Friday - *viernes*
Saturday - *sábado*
Sunday - *domingo*

Numbers

1 *uno* (oo-noh)
2 *dos* (dose)
3 *tres* (trayss)
4 *cuatro* (kwah-troh)
5 *cinco* (theen-koh)
5 *seis* (sayss)
7 *siete* (syeh-tay)
8 *ocho* (oh-choh)
9 *nueve* (nway-bay)
10 *diez* (dhee-ehs)
11 *once* (ohn-thay)
12 *doce* (doh-thay)
13 *trece* (tray-thay)
14 *catorce* (kah-tor-thay)
15 *quince* (keen-thay)
16 *dieciséis* (dyeth-ee-sayss)
17 *diecisiete*
  (dhee-ehs-ee-see-eh-teh)

18 *dieciocho*
  (dyeth-ee-oh-choh)
19 *diecinueve*
  (dyeth-ee-nywaybay)
20 *veinte* (bayn-tay)
30 *treinta* (trayn-tah)
40 *cuarenta*
  (kwah-ren-tah)
50 *cincuenta*
  (theen-kween-tah)
60 *sesenta*
  (say-sen-tah)
70 *setenta*
  (say-ten-tah)
80 *ochenta*
  (oh-chen-tah)
90 *noventa*
  (noh-ben-tah)
100 *cíen* (thyen)

The Rocky Point Gringo Guide

Popular words

a little - *un poco*
a lot - *mucho*
all - *todo*
also - *también*
always - *siempre*
asprin - *la aspirina*
automobile - *un coche*
bad - *malo*
bargains - *gangas*
WELCOME - *BIENVENIDO*

excuse me - *perdóneme,*
   con permiso
family - *familia*
far - *lejos*
fine - *bueno*
for - *para*
from - *de*
girl - *la muchacha*
give me - *déme*
go in - *entrar*

just a minute - *un momento*
large - *grande*
leather - *cuero*
leave me alone! - *¡váyase!*
lets go! - *¡vamos!*
vacant, unoccupied - *libre*
madam - *señora*
man - *hombre*
Mr. - *señor*
Mrs. - *señora*

no entry - *paso prohibido*
price - *precio*
private - *privado*

breakfast - *el desayuno*
gentelmen - *caballeros*
closed - *cerrado*
child - *niño* (boy) *niña* (girl)
ladies - *damas*
dirty - *sucio*
dollar - *dólar*
school - *escuela*
exchange - *el cambio*
evening - *la noche*

go out - *salir*
free - *gratis*
gum - *el chicle*
hour - *hora*
made in - **hecho en...**
hello! - *¡hola!*
men - *hombres*
hot - *caliente*
I - *yo*
inside - *dentro*

much - *mucho*
do not touch - *no tocar*
nothing - *nada*
now - *ahora*
occupied, - in use *ocupado*
okay - *está bien*
open - *abierto*
over here - *acá*
over there - *allá*
outside - *fuera*

reserved - *reservado*
rest rooms - *baños*
toilets - *retretes*

prohibited - *prohibido*
no smoking - *prohibido fumar*
purse - *la bolsa*
question - *una pregunta*
quickly - *rápido, pronto*
quiet - *quieto*
rain - *la lluvia*

right away - *pronto*
exit *salida* -
English spoken - *se habla ingles*
she - *ella*
shower - *la ducha*
soap - *el jabón*
street - *calle*

table - *un mesa*
tell me *dígame*
they - *ellos*
this evening - *esta noche*
tip (gratuity) - *la propina*
too (also) - *también*
too much - *demasiado*
towel - *la toalla*
TV set - *el televisor*
you (singular polite) - *usted*

vanilla - *la vainilla*
sale - *venta*
wait! - *¡espere!*
what? - *¿cómo?*
who? - *¿quién*
why? - *¿por qué?*
with - *con*
woman - *la mujer*
yes - *sí*
your - *su*

Basic statements and questions

Hello. I would like a tourist guidebook of Rocky Point, please. *Buenos Días. Quisiera una guía turística de Rocky Point, por favor.* (bweh-nos dhee-has kee-syehr-ah oo-nah gee-ah too-ree-stee-kah deh Rocky Point, pohr fah-bohr)

How much does it cost? *¿Cuánto cuesta?* (kwahn-toh kweh-stah)

What time is it? *¿Qué hora es?* (kay oh-ra es)

Can you help me? *¿Puede ayudarme?* (pweh-dhay ah-yoo-dhar-meh)
Do you have something cheaper? *¿Tiene algo más barato?* (tyeh-neh al-go dhay mahs bah-rah-to)

You are very kind. Thank you very much. *Usted es muy amable. Muchas gracias.* (oos-teh-dh ehs mwee ah-mah-bleh. moo-chahs grah-syahs)

How much do I owe you? *¿Cuánto le debo?* (kwahn-to leh dh-eh-bo)

Do you accept credit cards? *¿Acepta Ud. tarjetas de crédito?* (ah-sep-tah oos-teh-dh tahr-heh-tahs dhay dreh-dhee-toh)

I'm going to pay in cash. *Voy a pagar al contado.* (boy- ah pah-gahr ahl kohn-tah-dho)

Can you recommend to me a restaurant? *¿Puede usted recomendarme un restaurante?* (pweh-dhay oos-teh-dh reh-ko-mehn-dhahr-meh oon rehs-tah-oo-rahn-teh)

Everything is satisfactory. The check, please. *Todo es satisfactorio. La cuenta, por favor.* (toh-dho ehs sah-tees-fahk-toh-ree-o. lah kwehn-tah, pohr fah-bohr.

Here is the money. *Aquí tiene usted el dinero.* (ah-kee tyeh-neh oos-teh-dh el dhee-neh-ro)

Is there a store here in this neighborhood? *¿Hay una tienda aquí en ésta vecinidad?* (ah-ee oo-nah tyehn-dha ah-kee en ehs-tah beh-seen-dh-ah-dh)

Tell me, please, where is the nearest restaurant? *¿Puede decirme, por favor, ¿dónde está el restaurante más cercano?* (dhee-gah-meh, pohr fah-bohr, dhohn-dhay ehs-tah rehs-tah-oo-rahn-teh mahs sehr-kah-no)

What is the direction to go to . . .? *¿Cuál es la dirección para ir a...?* (kwahl ehs lah dhee-rehk-syohn pah-rah eer ah . . .)

Can you tell me if it is far from here? *¿Puede decirme si está lejos de aquí?* (pweh-dhay dhay-seer-meh see ehs-tah leh-hos dhay ah-kee)

I would like to buy a few things. *Quisiera comprar algunos artículos.* (kee-syehr-ah kohn-prahr al-goo-nos ahr-tee-koo-los)

I don't like this. Do you have any others? *No me gusta. ¿Tiene otras?* (noh meh goos-tah. thehn-eh oh-trahs)

A table for me (for two persons), please. *Una mesa para mí (para dos personas), por favor.* (oo-nah meh-sha pah-rah mee (pah-rah dhos pehr-soh-nahs), pohr fah-bohr)

I would like to spend a few days at the beach. *Quisiera pasar algunos días en la playa.* (kee-syehr-ah pah-sahr ahl-goo-nos dhee-ahs ehn lah plah-ya)

Where can I change my clothes? *¿Dónde puedo cambiarme?* (dhohn-dhay pweh-dho kahm-bee-ahr-meh)

We're going to leave early tomorrow morning. *Vamos a partir temprano mañana por la mañana.* (bah-mos ah pahr-teer tehm-prah-no mah-ny-ah-nah pohr lah mah-ny-ah-nah)

Before what time is it required to vacate the room? *¿Antes de qué hora hay que desocupar la habitación?* (ahn-tehs dhay kay oh-rah ah-ee kay dhay-so-koo—ahr lah ah-bee-tah-syohn)

I would like to settle my account, please. *Quisiera arreglar mi cuenta ahora, por favor.* (kee-syehr-ah-reh-glahr mee kwehn-tah ah-oh-rah, pohr fah-bohr)

My stay in your hotel and in your country has been plesant. *Mi estancia en su hotel y en su país ha sido agradable.* (mee ehs-tahn-see-ah ehn soo o-tehl ee ehn soo pah-ees ah see-dho ah-grah-dhah-bleh)

Menu words

Sopas - Soups
sopa de fideos - noodle
sopa de Tomate - tomato

caldo de Pollo - chicken
sopa de verduras - vegetable
sopa clara - consomé

Ensalada - Salads
ensalada verde - green
lechuga - lettuce

ensalada mixta - mixed
ensalada de pepinos - cucumber

Carne - Meat
bistec - beefsteak
callos - tripe
cerdo - pork
chuleta - cutlet
cocido - stew
conejo - rabbit
cordero - lamb
costillas - ribs
gallina - fowl

hígado - liver
lengua - tongue
pato - duck
pavo - turkey
pollo - chicken
rosbif - roast beef
ternera - veal
tocino - bacon
res/vaca - beef

Cooking Terms
asado - roast
cocido - broiled
empanizado - breaded
frito - fried

muy fritu - well done
poco fritu - rare
tostado - toast

Pescado - Fish
almejas - clams
anchoas - anchovies
anguilas - eels
arenque - herring
atún - tuna
bacalao - cod
calamares - squid
cangrejo - crab
caracoles - snails

cigalas - small lobster
camarrones - shrimp
gambas - prawns
langosta - lobster
lenguado - sole
mejillones - mussels
ostiones - oysters
pulpo - octopus
vieiras - scallops

Huevos - Eggs
huevos escaltados - poached
huevos por agua - soft
huevos duros - hard-boiled

tortilla - omlet
huevos fritos - fried eggs
huevos revueltos - scrambled

Legumbres - Vegetables
arroz - rice
cebolla - onion
col - cabbage
colifior - cauliflower
esparragos - asparagus
espinacas - spinach
guisantes - peas

judías verdes - string beans
papas - potato
pepino - cucumber
remolachas - beets
setas - mushrooms
tomate - tomato
zanahorias - carrot

Frutas - *Fruits*
albaricoque - apricot
aguacate - avacado
cerezas - cherries
ciruela - plum
dátil - date
frambuesa - raspberry
fresa - strawberry
granada - pomegranate
higo - fig

limón - lemon
manzana - apple
melocotón - peach
naranja - orange
pera - pear
piña - pineapple
plátano - banana
toronja - grapefruit
uvas - grapes

Postres - *Desserts*
buñuelos - fritters
compota - stewed fruit
flan - caramel custard
fruta - fruit

galletas - tea cakes
helado - ice cream
pasteles - pastries
torta - cake

Bebidas - *Beverages*
agua - water
agua mineral - mineral water
café - coffee
cerveza - beer
ginebra - gin
jerez - sherry
jugo de naranjas - orange juice
jugo de tomate - tomato juice

leche - milk
sangría - red wine, fruit juice
sidra - cider
sifón - soda
té - tea
vino blanco - white wine
vino tinto - red wine

Condimentos - Condiments
ajo - garlic
azucar - sugar
hielo - ice
mantequilla - butter

mostaza - mustard
pan - bread
pimienta - pepper
queso - cheese

Restaurante - *Restaurant*
menú - menu
plato - plate
antojito, botana - snack
tenedor - fork
cuchara - spoon
cuchillo - knife

taza - cup
vaso - glass
servilleta - napkin
palillo - toothpick
la cuenta - the bill

Hotels and Condos

agua caliente - hot water
aire acondicionado - air cond.
alberca, piscina - swimming pool
baño - bath, bathroom
bar - bar
cama - bed
cama extra - extra bed
cama matrimonial - double bed
hamaca - hammock
amueblada - furnished
cuarto - room
sala - living room
estufa - stove
casa - house
por la semana - by the week

catre - cot
cobija - blanket
comedor - dining room
cuarto doble - room, double
gerente, dueño - manager
llave - key
regadera - shower
ruido - noise
ventilador, abanico - fan
electricidad - electricity
recámara - bedroom
cocina - kitchen
criada - maid
rentar - rent
se vende - for sale

Auto Parts

air filter - *filtro de aire*
alternator - *alternador*
auto parts - *refacionaria*
axle - *eje*
battery - *acumulador, batería*
battery cable - *cable de acumulador*
brakes - *frenos*
brake drum - *tambor*
brake fluid - *líquido de frenos*
gas tank - *tanque de gasolina*

cable - *cable*
camshaft - *arbol de levas*
carburetor - *carburador*
clutch - *clutch*
clutch petal - *pedal de clutch*
coil - *bobina*
condenser - *condensador*
crank shaft - *cigüeñal*
cylinder - *cilindro*
distributor - *distribuidor*
distributor cap - *tapa de distribuidor*

electrical system - *sistema eléctrico*
frame - *chasís*
fan - *ventilador*
fly wheel - *de motor volante*

head gasket - *empaque de la cabeza*
headlights - *faros*
horn - *klaxón, bocina*
hose - *mangera*

fuel pump - *bomba de gasolina*
fuse - *fusible*
gas cap - *tapón de gasolina*
gas line - *tubo de gasp;oma*
gasket - *empaque, junta*
gear - *engrane*
generator - *generador*

manifold - *múltiple*
exhaust - *múltiple de escape*
intake- *múltiple de admisión*
master cylinder - *cilindro mastro de frenos*
motor - *motor, máquina*
mechanic - *mecánico, maestro*
muffler - *mofle*
oil - *aceite*
oil filter - *filtro de aceite*
oil pump - *bomba de aceite*
rings - *anillos*

compression - *anillo de compresión*
oil - *anillo de aceite*
rotor - *rotor*
seal - *retén*
shaft - *flecha*
shock absorber - *amortiguador*
solenoid - *solenoide*
spark plug - *bujía*

tow truck - *grúa*
transmission - *transmisión*
exhaust - *escape*
intake - *admisión*
wire - *alambre*

hose clamp - *abrazadera*
ignition switch - *switch*
jack - *gato*
king pin - *perno*
lever - *palanca*
main bearing - *metales de bancada*

pickup truck - *camioneta*
piston - *pistón*
points - *platinos*
push rod - *levador*
pressure plate - *plato de presión*
pulley - *poleta etractor*
radiator - *radiador*
radiator cap - *tapón de radiador*
re-cap tire - *recubierta*
relay - *relé*
spark plug wire - *cable de bujía*

starter - *marcha*
steering wheel - *volante*
tail pipe - *tubo de escape*
thermostat - *termostato*
tie rod - *barrilla de dirección*
tighten - *apretar*
tire - *llanta*
tire balance - *balanceo*
tire tubless - *llanta sin cámara*

valve cover - *tapa de punterías*
van - *combi*
wheel - *rueda*
windshield - *parabrisas*
wrist pin - *perno*

Tools

allen wrench - *cruceta*
bag - *bolsa*
bolt - *tornillo*
bucket - *cubeta*
can opener - *abrelatas*
chisel - *cincel*
crescent wrench - *perico*
drill & bits - *taladro y brocas*
extension socket - *extensión*
file - *lima*
nail - *clavo*
nut - *tuerca*
phillips screwdriver - *desarmador de cruz*
pipe wrench - *llave stillson*
pliers - *pinzas*
rope - *soga*
sandpaper - *papel de lija*
sissors - *tijeras*
screwdriver - *desarmador*

flashlight - *lámpara de mano*
flashlight batteries - *pilas*
glue - *pegamento*
grease - *grasa*
grill, cooking - *parrilla*
hammer - *martillo*
hardware store - *ferretería*
hose - *manguera*
key - *llave*
sewing needle - *aguja*
screwdriver - *desarmador*
shovel - *pala*
string, twine - *cuerda*
tape - *cinta de aislar*
thread - *hilo*
tools - *herramientas*
washer - *rondana*
wire - *alambre*
wrench - *llave*
zipper - *cierre, zipper*

Fishing and Diving

bait - *carnada*
diving mask - *visor*
equipment - *equipo de bucear*
fishing rod - *caña*
hook - *anzuelo*
lure - *curricán*
sinker - *el plomo*

snorkle - *snorkle*
speargun - *arpón, pistola*
spearhead - *punta*
spear shaft - *flecha*
swim fins - *aletas*
to dive - *bucear*
to fish - *pescar*

Health

antibiotic - *antibiótico*
aspirin - *aspirina*
burn - *quemadura*
bandage - *venda*

headache - *dolor de cabeza*
medicine- *medicina*
pain - *dolor*
pill - *pastilla*

capsule - *cápsula*
cramp - *calambre*
cold, flu - *gripe*
cotton - *algodón*
cough - *tos*
diarrhea - *diarrea*
shot, injection - *inyección*

sick - *enfermo*
stomach ache - *dolor de estómago*
sunburn - *quemadura del sol*
toothache - *dolor de muelas*
toothpaste - *crema dental*

Telephone and Bank

a call - *una llamada*
change - *cambio, feria*
collect - *cobrar*
credit card - *tarjeta de crédito*
long distance - *larga distancia*
viajero
signature - *firma*

money - *dinero, lana*
number - *número*
operator - *operador*
teller window - *caja*

Bibliography

American Medical Association *Handbook of First Aid and Emergency Care.* New York: Random House, 1990.

Books, John *Fit For Life First Aid.* New York: Gallery Books, 1987.

Burke, Michael *Hippocrene Companion Guide to Mexico.* New York: Hippocrene Books, 1992.

Conrad, Jean Baptiste *Mexico, What To Know Before You Go.* The Learning Tree Publishing Co., 1981.

Crutchfield, James A. *It Happened In Arizona.* Helena, Montana: Falcon Press Publishing Co., Inc., 1994.

Curtis, Lindsay R. M.D. *How To Save A Life Using CPR, Cardiopulmonary Resuscitation.* Tuscon, Arizona: HP Books, 1981.

Davis, Barbara L. *Birds of the Southwest, Volume 1, Guide to Birds of the Desert and Grasslands.* Tucson: Treasure Chest Publications, Inc.: 1986.

De Mente, Boye. *Insider's Guide to Rocky Point, Nogales, Guaymas, Mazatlan. La Paz.* Phoenix, Arizona: Phoenix Books/Publishers: 1975.

Dodge, Ida Flood. *Our Arizona.* New York: Charles Scribner's Sons: 1929.

Faulk, Odie B. *Destiny Road: The Gila Trail and the Opening of the Southwest.* New York: Oxford University Press, 1973.

Franz, Carl *The People's Guide To Mexico.* Santa Fe, New Mexico: John Muir Publications: 1992.

Gaetjens, Charles J. *The People & The Legends of Ajo, Arizona.* Ajo, Arizona: 1993.

Helms, Christopher L. *Sonoran Desert, The Story Behind The Scenery.* Seoul, Korea: Dong-A Printing and Publishing, 1991.

Hornaday, William T. *Camp-Fires On Desert And Lava.* Tucson, Arizona: The University of Arizona Press, 1908.

Hill, Myles E, & Goff, John S. *Arizona Past and Present.* Cave Creek, Arizona: Black Mountain Press: 1970.

Hine, Robert V. *Bartlett's West: Drawing The Mexican Boundary.* New Haven and London: Yale University Press, 1968.

Howels, John *RV Travel In Mexico.* Gateway Books, 1989.

Howels, John & Merwin, Don *Choose Mexico.* Gateway Books, 1994.

Kitteredge, Mary *Emergency Medicine.* New York and Philadelphia: Chelsea House Publishers, 1991.

Martin, Douglas DeVeny *An Arizona Chronology.* Tucson, Arizona: University of Arizona Press: 1963.

Miller, Joseph *Arizona Cavalcade The Turbulent Times.* New York: Hastings House Publishing: 1962.

Miller, Joseph *The Arizona Story.* New York: Hastings House Publishing: 1952.

Mosher, Charles MD. *Emergency First Aid.* New York: Beekman House, 1978.

Roca, Paul M. *Paths Of The Padres Through Sonora.* Tucson, Arizona: Arizona Pioneer's Historical Society: 1967.

Smith, Gusse Thomas *Birds of the Southwestern Desert.* Pico Rivera: Gem Guides Book Company: 1986.

Terres, John K. *The Audubon Society Encyclopedia of North American Birds.* New York: Wings Books: 1995.

Udvardy, Miklos D. & Farrand, John Jr. *National Audubon Society Field Guide to North American Birds.* New York: Alfred Al. Knopf Publishing: 1994.

Underhill, Ruth Ph.D. *The Papago And Pima Indians of Arizona.* Palmer Lake, Colorado: Filter Press, 1979.

Wheelock, Walt *Beaches of Sonora.* Glendale, Arizona: La Siesta Press: 1972.

Whetten, Nathan L. *Rural Mexico.* Illinois: The University of Chicago Press, 1948.

Index

P

Pacifico, 104
Palm Sunday, 223
Palo Verde, 204, 248
Papago, 206, 208, 210, 244
Parking, 59
Passport, 18, 19, 25
Pemex, 59, 135, 136, 228
Personal checks, 24
Pesos, 35
Pest control, 143, 168
Pests, 22
Photography, 24, 143, 168
Pimeria Alta, 211
Pinacate Mountains, 191, 192, 201, 202, 204, 205, 206
Pinacateños Indians, 202, 203
Piñatas, 176
Plumbing, 143, 168
Police, 111, 115
Portuguese Man-of-War, 124
Post Office, 111, 144, 168
Printing, 146
Prohibited articles, 25, 26
Property Management, 144, 168
Prostitution, 102, 103
Puffers, 124, 235, 236

Q

Queso, 87
Quinceañera, 225

R

Radio Room, 112, 182
Radio Station, 146
Railroads, 111
Rainfall, 32
Rattlesnakes, 192
Real estate, 151, 156, 157, 158

Recreational vehicles, 23, 65
Red Snapper, 186
Ren, Charlie, 213, 214
Red Cross, 111, 115
Religion, 222, 219
Reservation agencies, 72, 73
Ron Rico Rum, 104

S

Sailfish, 186
Salmonella, 121
Sagebrush, 248
Saguaro, 204, 238, 243
Sandals, 176, 177
San Luis, 17
Sarape, 173
Scorpion, 124, 235
Scorpion, 124, 235
Scuba diving, 187
Sea of Cortéz, 181, 184, 215, 229, 234, 235, 237
Shrimp, 15
Sierra Pinta Mine, 191, 192
Snake bites, 125
Snorkeling, 187
Sonoyta, 17, 43, 49, 50, 57, 208, 210, 216
Sonoran Desert, 31, 210, 241, 242
Souvenirs, 25, 169
Spaniards, 192, 203, 208, 209
Spotted Sea Bass, 186
Sport fishing, 179, 180
Staphylococcus, 121
Stationery, 146, 171
Stingray, 127, 234
Stone, John, 213, 214
Straw, 177
Sunburn, 33, 127
Superior, 104

About The Author

During her 24 years in the airline industry and 16 years as a flight attendant with Frontier Airlines, Mary Weil has traveled to more than 27 countries and 45 tropical islands.

Her true passion is traveling, laced with adventure, searching out stretches of white sand beach under clear blue skies. Mary heard stories about fresh seafood, margaritas, and a shallow clear ocean in Mexico after moving to Arizona from Colorado. These stories prompted a weekend in Puerto Peñasco. Following the rumors of sun and sand, Mary "discovered" the most beautiful beaches this side of the Mississippi river. Over the next four years, Weil found herself making many trips to this unpretentious little town.

Mary discovered that Puerto Peñasco was more than just a small fishing village catering to college students celebrating the freedom of spring break.

From her desire to share with others the best way to see and enjoy the peace, beauty, and warm hospitality of out southern neighbor, *The Rocky Point Grigo Guide* was born.

Mary is a successful Travel Writer and a Travel Consultant to friends, associates and business owners. Her travel articles have been published throughout the United States and Mexico.

ORDER FORM

For extra copies of the *Rocky Point Gringo Guide* fill out the form below:

Please send me # copies _____ x $ 14.95 = _____

State tax # copies _____ x $ 1.03 = _____

Postage and handling (4th class) # copies _____ x $ 3.00 = _____

Total = _____

_____

Name _____

Address _____ Apt. _____

City or town _____ Zip code _____

Books will be mailed when your check is received. If ordering from Mexico please allow approximately three weeks for delivery.

PAYMENT: • Check   • Money Order

Please, make check payable to: **Frontier Travel Adventures**
                        Mail to: 925 W. Baseline Road, Box 105-H1
                                Tempe, Arizona 85283-1100

Thank you for your order.